The Myth of Ham in Nineteenth-Century American Christianity

Black Religion / Womanist Thought / Social Justice
Series Editor Linda E. Thomas
Published by Palgrave

The Myth of Ham in Nineteenth-Century American Christianity

Race, Heathens, and the People of God

Sylvester A. Johnson

ISBN 978-1-349-99961-3   ISBN 978-1-4039-7869-1 (eBook)
DOI 10.1007/978-1-4039-7869-1

THE MYTH OF HAM IN NINETEENTH-CENTURY AMERICAN CHRISTIANITY
© Sylvester Johnson

Reprint of the original edition 2004

First published in 2004 by
PALGRAVE MACMILLAN™
175 Fifth Avenue, New York, N.Y. 10010 and
Houndmills, Basingstoke, Hampshire, England RG21 6XS
Companies and representatives throughout the world.

PALGRAVE MACMILLAN is the global academic imprint of the Palgrave Macmillan division of St. Martin's Press, LLC and of Palgrave Macmillan Ltd. Macmillan® is a registered trademark in the United States, United Kingdom and other countries. Palgrave is a registered trademark in the European Union and other countries.

ISBN 978-1-4039-6562-2

Library of Congress Cataloging-in-Publication Data
Johnson, Sylvester A., 1972–
    The myth of Ham in nineteenth-century American Christianity :
race, heathens, and the people of God / Sylvester A. Johnson.
        p. cm.
    Includes bibliographical references and index.
    ISBN 978-1-4039-6562-2
    1. Ham (Biblical figure) 2. African Americans—Religion. 3. United
States—Church History—19th century. I. Title.
BS 580.H27J64 2004
277.3'081'08996073—dc22   2004040096

A catalogue record for this book is available from the British Library.

Design by Newgen Imaging Systems (P) Ltd., Chennai, India.

First edition: December 2004
10 9 8 7 6 5 4 3 2 1

Contents

Series Editors' Preface

Sylvester A. Johnson's book presents the first major scholarly investigation into how the myth of Ham figures as a substantive aspect in the history of the critique of black religion. Usually one equates Hamitic studies with the white supremacist moves of white Christians during U.S. slavery and today's occasional weird biblicists who carry on this tradition against African Americans. The curse of Ham derives from the Christian book of Genesis, chapter nine. Here a drunken Noah awakes from slumber and discovers a cardinal sin of his youngest son, Ham. The younger has viewed the naked, intoxicated elder. The writers of Genesis have Noah cry out a curse on not Ham, but on the descendants of Canaan, Ham's son (and Noah's own grandson). Their perpetual condemnation translates into the status of slaves for the offspring of Noah's other two sons. Thus, white supremacist Christians have interpreted Africans and black Americans as the children of Ham and they, therefore, should have been slaves and must continue to be subordinates to Christian white power. Given this primary usage of Hamitic mythology, Sylvester A. Johnson queries the Hamitic narrative from the perspective of black people. In a word, what meanings surface when Ham's children (in this case, African Americans) are, in fact, the chosen (and not the cursed) people of God?

The Myth of Ham in Nineteenth-Century American Christianity takes on this query during the height of white Christian demonization of black people, the period of the nineteenth century. At stake fundamentally, argues Johnson, was the inextricable knot-like relation between sustaining the anti-Negro Ham fantasy and the fashioning of white (Christian) identity. And this conscious theological move included white Christians from all regions of the nation (i.e., west, east, north, and south). Thus the Bible becomes an integral tool for crafting and congealing a sense of white religious American citizenship at the expense of Ham's reputed dark-skinned children. What Johnson does, however, is not a simple and less intellectually interesting move of debating how black people fought against and discarded the claim as Ham's descendants. Quite the contrary, *The Myth of Ham* delves deeply into black religion to ascertain how black Christians embraced both the notion of being Ham's offspring and simultaneously the notion of being God's people. The crackling, creative tension between appropriating the dominant discourse's deployment of the negativity of the curse of Ham, on the one hand, and, on the other, the concurrent self-description as people of God leads to a novel resolution of these surface contradictions faced by African Americans. Fundamentally, in this appropriation is the full human status of blacks. If the latter were not children of Ham, then they languished in the limbo of heathenism or bestiality because only through genealogical ties to Ham, the descendant of the original human creation, could black folk assert their human beingness. Marked as the ultimate other and as illegitimate persons, African Americans, in Johnson's pioneering book, confront head-on Hamitic rhetoric and its concomitant denotations of divine favor and disfavor. Is it possible to build an inclusive American people in the midst of debates over privileged argumentation against an America as the inclusive people of God? In his response, Johnson clears the path for a rejuvenated understanding of race, religion, nation, and citizenship.

The Myth of Ham in Nineteenth-Century American Christianity is a theological, historical, and sociological approach to race and, thereby, is emblematic of the Black religion/Womanist thought/ Social justice Series. And it fits directly within the Series' mission: to publish both authored and edited manuscripts that have depth, breadth, and theoretical edge and that address both academic and nonspecialist audiences. The Series will produce works engaging any dimension of black religion or womanist thought as they pertain to social justice. Womanist thought is a new approach in the study of African American women's perspectives. The Series will include a variety of African American religious expressions. By this we mean traditions such as Protestant and Catholic Christianity, Islam, Judaism, Humanism, African diasporic practices, religion and gender, religion and black gays/lesbians, ecological justice issues, African American religiosity and its relation to African religions, new black religious movements (e.g., Daddy Grace, Father Divine, or the Nation of Islam), or religious dimensions in African American "secular" experiences (such as the spiritual aspects of aesthetic efforts like the Harlem

Renaissance and literary giants such as James Baldwin, or the religious fervor of the Black Consciousness movement, or the religion of compassion in the black women's club movement).

Dwight N. Hopkins, University of Chicago Divinity School
Linda E. Thomas, Lutheran School of Theology at Chicago 2004

Preface

Every author has a story to tell, a story that lies behind the work itself. Giving some glimpse of mine helps to clarify the analytical concerns of this book. This study emerged through my reflections during graduate school upon American religious attitudes, trends in scholarship, and my own experience of difference within American culture. I literally cannot remember any part of my childhood when I was not somehow involved with Christianity. At age nine, I was "born again." By my mid-teens, I found myself preparing to deliver my first sermon and was ordained a few years later. Members of my family were overwhelmingly affirming. And the encouragement—respect, even—of friends and acquaintances was always there. I never doubted that they took pride in my religious commitments.

My theological development underwent a steady progression toward a very evangelical, dogmatic framework. By the time I entered college, I was ready to convert the entire world to the Christian faith. I settled for missionary work in Arkansas, however, during the summer after my sophomore year. I returned to college inspired to supplement my degree training in chemistry with a minor concentration in religion. I wanted to bank up my theological knowledge so that I could attend divinity school and, later, start my own church. I chose to start with an introductory course to the Hebrew Scriptures. That was to be a pivotal decision.

For the first time, I was exposed to the academic study of religion. I was able to consider the history and development of Jewish and Christian traditions in light of their social, subjective, and existential implications. Under the gentle but critical tutelage of Ronald Liburd and Stephen Angell, professors of religion at Florida A&M University, I was sensitized to the sociality of religious experience and to methods of historical criticism.

I began to consider ideas and to contemplate conflicts that I had harbored about my theology but had not allowed myself to pursue. I recall feeling that, for the first time in my life, I had begun simply to *think*, without boundaries or inhibitions. This was accompanied, moreover, by a traumatic change in my worldview. I had earlier been so sure of Christian claims. Now, I began to realize that I did not want to be a Christian. At the same time, my interest in studying religion increased.

My friends and colleagues who were Christians had little patience for this metanoia and tried to convince me I was making a terrible mistake. Also, I was quickly made to understand that I would no longer be preaching at the church where I was an associate minister. In retrospect, I know they were no more hostile toward me than I would have been toward others earlier. At the time, however, I was taken aback by the rejection. I lost almost every friendship I had because I was no longer a Christian. I was regarded as an unmitigated faith disaster.

I had never before experienced such intimate rejection. I had always encountered tremendous respect from most people who knew me. Now, however, I existed in their minds essentially as an error that needed to be corrected. Even my own family, although they still considered me part of the family, began to regard me as an embarrassing secret.

I was entirely unprepared for the experience. How could all the people who had known me and with whom I had previously shared love and acceptance suddenly come to treat me as an illegitimate thing? For the first time in my life, I felt ugly. But I knew the answer to this. I knew it because I had done the same thing to and had believed the same thing about others. It mattered not how sincere they were or who they were; if they were not Christian, they lacked the most important, overriding quality. They had rejected God, and I would never affirm that rejection. I would never accept them. Now, the shoe was on the other foot, so to speak, and I knew that I would have to change the way I lived.

I had to learn to live as an alien—as an illegitimate thing—in a world strangely familiar yet not mine. Because Christianity is so deeply embedded in the knowledge-culture of most Americans, regardless of race or class, I knew that I would meet with this form of rejection for the rest of my life. I attempted to interact with the few non-Christians I knew but was shocked to find that most of them, although they were not practicing Christians, still accepted the ideas of Christianity and were appalled because I did not.

Graduate school was a wonderful change. I was able to converse with persons who had studied the traditions of Christianity and who were intellectually serious about it. My professors were not a few times taken aback by my unorthodox, often crassly styled suggestions. But they gladly offered me critical feedback and assured me that, more than anything else, they wanted me to cultivate my intellectual acuity and sound scholarship. I plied my most keen analysis to fathom the complex developments of Christian ideas because I wanted to understand the world that those ideas had produced. I realized that my experience of radical alterity outside of Christianity was neither unusual nor a privatistic experience nor a happenstance. It was directly produced by a history of ideas about history itself. It was the inevitable outcome of centuries spent clarifying and elaborating on the meaning of being people of God.

Among my African American colleagues in graduate school, I felt a strange tension or ambivalence regarding racial "belonging." One the one hand, I was treated amiably and was well respected. On the other hand, it was very clear to me that Christianity was regarded as normative. And those who were not Christians (such as I) were something ominously other than normal. For African Americans particularly, Christianity has become the fundamental mode of "remembering" black history. Being a Christian, for most, is not only religious rectitude; it is also part of "being black." This tension led to me to devote serious attention to the history behind rigidly associating black identity with Christian identity.

I began to consider this attempt to describe blacks' history as a religious conundrum. My ideas about this developed slowly but steadily. Was not the entire history of defining Christian identity burdened with the task of explaining "Israel" vis-à-vis those who were not the people of God? And had Christianity itself not arisen with anxiety over locating identity in reference to the people of God? I then began to wonder what had compelled African Americans to cling so tightly to Christian identity as a way of articulating their history when in fact most black Americans were not Christianized until the late-nineteenth century. Could it be that this process of representing identity somehow connected with the most fundamental dynamics of Christians' attempts throughout history to grapple with the meanings of being people of God? Was the contemporary African American interest in finding "blacks" in the Bible, for example, merely an attempt to correct the racist portrayals of everything divine or sacred as white? Or was there in addition something about the "history" of African Americans at stake? It was at this point that the Hamitic idea seemed to offer some explanation, proffering a way to reconstruct the scene of a perennial crime, so to speak. In the symbolic world of American Christians, Ham was supposed to be the ancestor of the Negro race, a people understood to be Christian only as of late. And yet, Ham was a heathen par excellence.[1] *What did it mean, then, for the children of Ham to be the people of God?* With this question began the study before the reader.

Chapter one introduces the meaning and scope of nineteenth-century ideas about Ham by demonstrating that the primary concern of the Hamitic idea was not slavery apologetics, as is widely presumed, but racial origins. The second chapter situates the ideological milieu of Hamitic rhetoric by tracing the history of the Hamitic idea in early traditions of Judaism, Christianity, Islam, and more elaborately in American Christianity. I point to the American idiosyncrasies of the Hamitic idea that racialized the Hamitic subject and that associated God with a racially divine people.

Chapter three interprets what was at stake in African Americans' ambivalent appeals to a pre-Christian and ancient past. The fourth chapter builds on this development in order to parse the meanings of racial and religious illegitimacy that inhered so powerfully in black Christian missions and race uplift strategies. I assess how black Americans viewed continental Africans and Negroes of the American South who were not Christians.

Chapter five considers the problems posed by the idea of an original people of God and engages the major thrusts of black theology in order to proffer a rejoinder to the conundrum of divine identity and its principle of alterity as such have come to shape modern American religion.

Acknowledgments

It is a humbling task to contemplate the many wonderful people who have made this book possible because simple words of acknowledgment are paltry tokens that can never truly express the depth of my gratitude. James H. Cone has been the bedrock of my most formative intellectual development. Dr. Cone advised me as both a master and a doctoral student. It seems so long ago that I first walked into his office at Union Theological Seminary to inquire about studying with him. He had the resolve to believe in my intellectual abilities and potential when I myself was not so sure. As an advisor, Cone provided honest feedback in a timely manner. And I have him to thank for refusing to let me produce less than my best. Cone also introduced me to the blues as a compelling genre for understanding a cultural expression of human worth and longing and for just *listening*. In many subtle, complex ways, he has inspired me to be a better human being and to speak out for justice. And I am forever thankful for his guidance and our friendship.

Christopher Morse and Michael Harris were also on my dissertation committee. Morse taught me to appreciate and to take seriously a myriad of theological perspectives that I naïvely and wrongly assumed had nothing to do with my interests. I can still recall the seminar I took with him on Karl Barth's *Church Dogmatics*; he has been a brilliant teacher and will remain a lasting influence. His invaluable feedback on the dissertation was meticulous and engaging. Harris opened my eyes to the complex nature of imagining history. That seminar in "Problems" (of history) still rings clear in my mind as I contemplate the relationship between theology and history. Harris urged me to sit with the deeper, historical, methodological implications of this topic. His intellectual impact on me is greater than he may ever realize.

There are several others who have been especially instrumental in my formation. Vincent Wimbush opened my eyes to a phenomenological approach to understanding texts and textuality. The seminars and conversations I had with him radically resituated my understanding of complex social problems. He has been an inspiring, teaching, and kindred spirit when I most needed it. Judith Weisenfeld, who taught at Barnard College, has also been a significant force. Her seminar on African American religion and her brilliant analysis of religious performance and difference have provided critical guideposts for me to contemplate problems of alterity in black religion. She graciously, willingly listened to me as I struggled to develop an approach to tackling religious topics. She has never hesitated to give honest feedback and prudent advice. Union has been gifted with some of the most eminent faculty in the world. At some point, I crossed paths with all of them during my graduate studies there. They are all part of what makes Union such a special place to develop intellectually.

My relations with then-student colleagues have been a vital resource as well. Clarence Hardy and Gabriella Lettini were conversation partners who breathed life into my efforts to move from compulsion to thought to articulate analysis. They have continued to remain intellectual partners who proffer diverse, substantive rejoinders to common concerns. And historian David Jackson, my colleague at Florida A&M University, has been an invaluable asset. His feedback and intellectual generosity have saved me from errors and have enriched my reflection on a number of issues.

My wife Heather Nicholson, who is truly my partner in life, read many copies of the early manuscript when we were in New York. She has continued to be a conversation partner. There are no words to express the joy of my having found so many gifts—love, intellectual companionship, unfailing support—in one person. And my dear daughter Ayanna is a wonderful presence of joy who keeps the laughter at the surface of my life.

This page intentionally left blank

1

The People(-ing) of God

Introduction

To be American is to be the people of God. This idea has animated the studies of Israelitic themes in American religion. From being the American "city on a hill" to the decidedly white supremacist notions of Manifest Destiny to black antislavery themes of Exodus toward freedom, the social forms of participation in American religious identity have been overwhelmingly contingent upon self-understanding tied to the Israelitic narrative of being people of God—God's Israel.[1] This does not, of course, mean that every single American throughout history has subscribed to the identity. The point, rather, is that the Israelitic myth, as a cultural narrative, has sustained in the West a dominant form of "narrative knowledge."[2] It has encoded and transmitted foundational ideas about reality and identity. Israelitic appropriations, in this manner, have exerted the most enduring narrative influence upon the American religious imagination.[3]

Writers such as Regina Schwartz, Martin Marty, Gayraud Wilmore, Sydney Mead, Eddie Glaude, Michael Walzer, Albert Raboteau, and Conrad Cherry have interpreted Israelitic self-understanding to be a major force in American thought. The idea of being God's "Israel" has been so pervasive and recurring that Glaude and Walzer have described it as a fundamental lens for interpreting American experience.[4] Among any number of social groups in America—whether ethnic, denominational, or racial—one finds a consistent pattern of recourse to this Israelitic grand narrative for articulating religious, racial, or even national identities. And whether or not one agrees with the implications of such recourse, it is nevertheless clear that participation in Israelitic self-understanding has overwhelmingly informed social experience and identity in the United States of America.

Studies of the American "Israel," in general, have related the topic of Israelitic self-understanding to white American religious groups.[5] More recently, however, historians have studied its relevance for black Americans.[6] Albert Raboteau, particularly, concludes that appropriations of Israelitic identity have been a major influence on black American Christianity. And he introduces a discussion of an "African American Israel" by positing that there was more than one "Israel" in America due to America's legacy of slavery and racism.[7]

Race and slavery, indeed, overwhelmingly conditioned the forms of American Christianity, and intellectual responses to this history are very attentive to the fact. Such becomes evident when one considers that the theme of Exodus, as a source for resisting slavery, is the category of choice for discussing the influence of biblical narrative upon African American Christianity, although some such as Delores Williams have strongly cautioned against the limitations of this theme.[8] Black theologians especially have drawn upon the fact that black Christians believed the story of the Exodus to be directly relevant for their own time and circumstances.[9] Eddie Glaude emphasizes this same point when he argues that chosenness and whiteness worked symbiotically to define race and nation in opposition to Negroes as the "radical other." He asserts that black Christians appropriated chosenness through antiracist participation and thereby "became the nation of Israel, the chosen people of God."[10]

American studies scholar Wilson Jeremiah Moses has also produced significant material on chosenness and messianism in African American Christianity. His *Black Messiahs and Uncle Toms* examines the jeremiads in black Christianity that appealed to a sense of divine justice, American destiny (Christian destiny) and covenant responsibility.[11] Through a patently Millerian schema, Moses makes significant departure from Glaude and Raboteau when he argues that such themes in black Christianity best demonstrate conformity to white American traditions. The works of David Howard-Pitney, Jon Butler, and Nathan Hatch have paralleled Moses' proposals regarding the relationships between Christian identity, American identity, and biblical themes.[12]

Writers in historical, theological, and biblical scholarship have critically examined the perplexities of black Americans' encounter with the symbolic world of Christianity and self-understanding as people of God. The works of Charles H. Long, Theophus Smith, Judith Weisenfeld, Regina Schwartz, Vincent Wimbush, Randall Bailey, Anthony Pinn, and Forrest G. Wood are representative.[13]

Native American theologians have produced pointed responses to the problems of Israelitic identity *qua* people of God in the North American context—for example, Vine Deloria, Robert Warrior, and George Tinker. Warrior and Deloria especially have shown that Native Americans have occupied the figurative role of "Canaanite" peoples— that is, people who are indigenous to the land that settlers seized for themselves as people of God, while representing the identities of indigenous people as villainous heathens, worthy of genocide.[14]

The relationship between religion and legitimacy has become clearer from studies that have investigated nineteenth-century themes of race uplift, especially through social reform and club movements— Elizabeth Davis, Evelyn Brooks Higginbotham, Beverly Washington Jones, Anne Meis Knupfer, and Dorothy Salem. Knupfer indicates, for instance, that Christian womanhood became a problematic ideal because concerns for "virtue" or moral womanhood were racialized (antiblack) and often confounded the intersection of gender, race, and religious identity.[15] This gendered aspect of religious legitimacy is also present in the work of Kelly Brown Douglas. She lucidly examines the myriad ways blacks were perceived as sexual deviants and points to the artificial need for blacks to represent the race as morally and physically "normal." Douglas' discussion makes evident that black existence was rendered abnormal and that gender-inflected illegitimacy was inscribed onto the very bodies of black men and women.[16]

The bulk of scholarship on Hamitic identity in American religion occurs in studies of proslavery ideologies or in histories of white American religion or, more frequently, histories of "Southern" culture or "Southern" religion.[17] Rarely is Hamitic identity—or the "myth of Ham," as it is more commonly referred to—related to the narrative forms of identity in either white American Christianity or African American Christian thought. Peterson, for example, describes the myth of Ham as essentially a white Southern worldview, and he devotes merely two or three lines to discussing what Hamitic identity meant to blacks. Stephen Haynes, more recently, has recognized that African Americans were key interlocutors in Hamitic discourse. With the exception of Robert Hood, no major study has undertaken an examination of Hamitic identity as a substantive component in the history of black religion.[18]

All of these writers have contributed to unraveling the myriad ways black Americans appropriated narrations of divine peoplehood— being an "American Israel" of God. Consistently unexamined, however, is the underside of this Israelitic identity—the Hamitic legacy of black

Americans. Because the fundamental "fact" of racial origins rendered blacks the descendants of Ham—Ham was the ultimate representative of the heathen—one must inquire into the effects that Hamitic identity produced among black Christians. To consider the influence of Israelitic narrative upon religious self-understanding is to query how African American Christians understood themselves within the context of racial and religious symbolism.

It is one thing to regard Hamitic identity rhetorics as convenient strategies existing mainly to prop up proslavery polemics. It is quite another to situate Hamitic identity as part of a worldview comprising popular and scholarly ideas of racial origins and sustaining the religious self-understanding of multiple social groups in America. This latter emphasis is underrepresented in current scholarship. Yet, such an approach becomes necessary for understanding the significance that Hamitic identity and Christian symbols held for African American Christianity specifically and American religion broadly.

In light of such, this study examines a familiar theme in nineteenth-century American religion—rhetorics of Hamitic identity, more commonly rendered the "myth of Ham"—in order to interpret the idea of being people of God. The myth identifies the Negro as a descendant of Ham, who was a son of the biblical figure Noah. In the biblical legend (Genesis 9:18–28), Noah curses the posterity of Ham and specifically indicates that they will be slaves to other peoples. American slavery apologists made frequent recourse to this story in order to justify the institution. And most studies of the myth are concerned with this aspect of Hamitic rhetorics—as slavery apologia—to the point of representing the myth as endemic to Southern proslavery interlocutors.[19]

One should recognize an important irony about classifying the Hamitic idea as essentially Southern. It is true, for instance, that Northerners frequently opposed chattel slavery and were among the most ardent publicists against the institution. An honest treatment of whiteness in the North, however, should lay to rest any ideas that the North was not racist. American slavery was exactly that—*American*, existing in the North, South, West, and East. One can, for instance, make sense of the dismantling of Reconstruction and the myriad of crises that victimized ex-slaves and their descendants only when recognizing that both Southern and Northern whites understood the Negro as a racial "other" and cooperated to suppress the civil and human rights of Negroes. Even when white Northerners condemned Southern whites' views on slavery, these Northern whites still identified with whites of the South because they shared a common racial identity.[20]

The Negro, on the other hand, whether slave or free, was . . . well . . . a *Negro*—relegated to being one of "those people." George Fredrickson makes this point, in a fashion similar to that of Stephen Jay Gould, when he notes that Abraham Lincoln, who is lauded for ending slavery by decree, nevertheless believed that Negroes were inferior to the white race and desired that they remain separate from whites.[21] It should become evident, in other words, that American racial reality designated Negroes as (questionably) human beings of a different *kind*. The experience of white identity, which is the originary basis for racism, was in now way exclusive to the South. One should avoid, for this reason, the exaggerated attempts to inscribe a radical distinction between Southern and Northern racial world-views. The deeper issue behind racism and racialism, in other words, was not slavery but identity and existence—what kind of creatures were they? It is, as Lewis Gordon describes, the old issue of the human totem pole: Negroes were at the bottom because they least signified being human, in the eyes of white Americans.[22]

What does this have to with the Hamitic idea in America? In a word, everything. Although most studies regard the Hamitic idea as a Southern phenomenon, I am emphasizing that virtually all Americans, across racial groups and regions, regarded the Negro as a descendant of Ham; American Negroes themselves, especially, referred to this "fact." Hamitic identity, as *sensus communis*, was primarily about originary concerns, not slavery apologia, a point that I will demonstrate at length in this introductory chapter.[23]

Another factor should inform a reading of this study. Nineteenth-century ideas about Christian identity and race were conditioned by certain demographic circumstances of earlier colonial settlement. The various peoples who had arrived in colonial America usually brought with them a pre-existing familiarity with Christianity and the story of God's Israel.[24] Such, however, was not the case for blacks who arrived on the same shores. Rather, it was through the American experience that many of them, over time and across generations, were to become acquainted with Christianity and would adopt that identity for themselves.

This process of Christianization for black Americans peaked in the wake of Emancipation, as black churches gained greater institutional visibility and ascendancy. And unlike the descendants of European settlers in the New World, black Christians who came to understand themselves as non-heathens—that is, they had become people of God—recognized simultaneously that they were descendants of the primal personal embodiment of the heathen *qua* non-Christian—Ham, the progenitor of the Cushites and Canaanites. The racial anxieties of Ham's children in America derived, as Wilson Moses aptly suggests, from their desire to be "children of Pharaoh as well as children of Israel."[25]

Finally, it is important to situate the focus of this study and the correlative aims it presumes by emphasizing the intersection of race discourse and religious self-understanding in American religion. This study examines the American episode of the Hamitic idea— nineteenth-century Hamitic rhetorics—in order to study a specific instance of a more general idea—being people of God. To be Hamitic was to be descendent from those who historically were not people of God, according to the biblical "record." Ham, for instance, was the ancestor of Canaanite people and is repeatedly represented in Christian and Judaic thought in antithesis to those-who-know-and-are-affiliated-with the one true God.

The ultimate point of this study, thus, is not to produce a historical interpretation of African American Christianity per se, although this study is necessarily concerned with the history and historiography of black Christianity as part and parcel of American religion.[26] I examine Hamitic rhetoric, rather, in order to interpret the idea of being people of God through the *underside* of its signification—namely folk whose locus before the task of envisioning an American Christian identity requires them to "explain" their previous racialized, heathen identity and somehow to make departure from it. In this way, I mean to interpret what in Christian theology is formally designated "ecclesiology."

Ecclesiology is most frequently regarded to concern what it means to be, "the Church." This study inquires into a particular aspect of the ecclesial idea, namely divine identity—the Church as the people of God. The Church as the people of God has been a frequent point of concern in ecclesiology, whether by conciliar debate (e.g., the Schleitham Confession of 1527), narrative construction (Justin Martyr's second-century *Dialogue*), or political injunction (the Donatist controversies of the fourth and fifth centuries). The consistent source of narrative knowledge about being people of God is the grand narrative of Israelite election and participation in historical relation to the Israelite deity—what I have herein referred to as the Israelitic myth.

Having said this, however, I would clarify that what is examined here is not churches per se but the meanings of divine identity as this idea has been concretely manifested through sociality—that is, as the people-of-God idea has been expressed through or has influenced the historical, the symbolic, the intersubjective, and the like. The instance of nineteenth-century Hamitic-identity claims offers compelling commentary about the complexity of divine affiliation and the affirmation, empowerment, and imperilment that inevitably attend divine identity. On the one hand there is a narration—a telling of history, an account of what happened—that is propagated with the intention of inviting all to become people of God. On the other hand, there is the searing mark or signification of illegitimacy inscribed onto those who are not people of God or who have only "recently" arrived. What does this signification suggest? What do the *signs* mean? This study emerges in response to the question.

The Hamitic Crisis in Nineteenth-Century Rhetorics

The idea that there were three basic races—though divisible into subcategories—dominated nineteenth-century beliefs about race. Unique to the American experience, furthermore, was the fact that these three races had come together—the "yellow," the "white," and the "Negro/Black"—to constitute a single nation. This three-race formulation is represented repeatedly in ethnological rhetoric of the era.[27]

Also pervasive in nineteenth-century rhetorics of Hamitic identity is an urgent concern for identifying and justifying the racial and religious *locus* of American Negroes. On the one hand, to claim Hamitic descent was to demonstrate, through ethnology, the significant role of Negroes in ancient history. The reader will quickly observe, for instance, that black Americans in the latter 1800s consistently based discussion of the Negro's history on biblical and archaeological data regarding Egypt and Ethiopia. Both of these, as ancient kingdoms, were well reputed for their cultural and technological achievements. The majority of white scholars then denied that these were indigenous "black" civilizations.[28]

It was such a denial that provoked sharp rebuff from Benjamin Tanner, a leading bishop of the African Methodist Episcopal denomination. Tanner was one of the more prolific writers on this topic, and in 1898, he published a pamphlet entitled *The Descent of the Negro* after the (white) Methodist Episcopal Church asserted in its religious education materials that "it is not certain whether or not the Negro race descended from Ham."[29] Tanner cites the Methodist Church's Sunday School literature.

> Ham: His name means "heat," and perhaps refers to the climate of the land of his posterity. The earliest empires of history, those of Babylonia and Egypt, were both Hamitic, as were the Canaanites, Phoenicians, and Carthaginians. The descendants of Ham built the pyramids and the Tower of Babel and were the earliest navigators and traders. It is not certain whether or not the Negro race descended from Ham.[30]

Tanner proceeds to discuss the implications of such a claim. First of all, if the Negro race were not descended from Ham, then the Negro would be "Pre-Adamite."[31] This would mean that the Negro was not a member of the human family (i.e., descended from the sons of Noah) but was perhaps a beast of some sort. Tanner defends the authority of the Bible, which is certainly the basis of the entire discussion on Ham in the Methodist materials. He then proceeds to argue for the crux of the Hamitic claim—to be Negro is necessarily to be a descendant of Ham. He points to the obvious connection between American Negroes and their land of origin, asserting that "the dullest blockhead of the most out-of-the-way country school knows that the father of the black fellow whom he is all the time meeting, came from Africa. . . ." In dissent against the claims of the Methodist Episcopal literature, Tanner insists,

> Our argument is that Ham is the father of all Africa, and the Negro being of Africa, is necessarily of Ham.
>   The Negro is a man. He is of Adam. He is of Noah. The Negro is a brother, and will be until science can demonstrate the Bible to be no more than a fable—that Moses made mistakes, and the divine Son of God, with men hitherto supposed to be inspired, endorsed them.[32]

The obvious reasons for such emphasis were the elaborate (but then-widely believed) claims that whites had been responsible for any and all forms of "civilization" throughout human history and that blacks had no history worth speaking of. There was, therefore, a strong motivation for embracing Hamitic identity. This affiliation secured a claim to history and culture featuring blacks not as slaves but as independent nations maintaining their own societies and affairs with little or no regard for whites.

Overshadowing the claim to historical presence, however, is the anthropological factor—the Negro *qua* human. This always lay at the heart of the fight concerning significations of the Negro or blackness: whether the Negro was human or some other type of creature. The belief expressed in Acts 17:26 that God had made "of one blood all nations" was oft repeated. One should not, moreover, read Tanner's emphasis on biblical authority as merely an unheeding Biblicism or fanaticism. As I will argue, the stakes of Hamitic discourse and divine identity were motivated by deep anxieties over legitimacy and identity. It was through recourse to the biblical record that whites, blacks, and Native American Christians accessed—or conjured,[33] one might say—their ancient histories. As Tanner opined, the Bible was the best authority

> upon the matters about which we write . . . not because it is the best attested of any, but the best because it is the only authority the race possesses upon the questions under discussion. It alone throws light upon man's creation and the early dawn of the races. Herein the literature of the Hebrew transcends in value the literature of all others.[34]

On the other hand, both the biblical record and popular consensus in the 1800s regarded the "children of Ham" as heathens who, having enjoyed a distant, bygone era of cultural endowment, had suffered demise because they had refused to worship the one true God. This idea spawned a torturous schism within the psyche of American Negro Christians because they were compelled both to affirm or uphold the African past, on the one hand, as a "golden" age of greatness and, on the other hand, to redeem Africa from its benighted state through preaching the gospel of Jesus Christ.

One finds harsh descriptions of pre-Christian Negro life in the works of both black and white ideologues. Because the American experience was inextricably wed to the process of Christianization—that is, blacks encountered Christianity primarily because they had been forcefully displaced and enslaved—there emerged an inevitable "what if?" What if the Negro race had not received the Christian gospel? What if Africa's children had remained ignorant of the truth and had continued in pagan or heathen ignorance?

Two other writers, George W. Williams and Rufus Perry, will serve to exemplify the Hamitic crisis endemic to the era. George Williams was a minister by training and occupation. He developed a deep concern for the historical representations of Negroes that denied the race any meaningful historical existence. He eventually decided to investigate the African past for himself and devoted seven years to studying primary and secondary sources. Williams culminated this period of erudition by authoring the first major history of black Americans.

He begins by identifying his intent to counter the "absurd charge that the Negro does not belong to the human family." He recounts the narrative of Noahic generation in order to discuss the fact that the Negro is not a beast but is descended from Ham—a fact that was "admitted by the most consistent enemies of the blacks."[35] For it was not merely that the Bible, through its genealogical narratives, was viewed as a source for understanding racial difference. The Bible was *the* single most reliable and *only* ancient source of ancient genealogies.

Rufus Perry was a black American scholar contemporaneous with Williams and wrote about ten years after Williams' *History* was published. Perry also sought to counter dominant arguments that emptied Negro identity of human, historical, and cultural significance. He recapitulates the preeminent understanding of racial origins,

> The primary divisions of men made by nature's color-line are three,— the white, the black and the yellow,—having for their respective ancestral heads, Japheth[,] Ham and Shem, the three sons of ancient Noah.[36]

The biblical account of Noahic descent, in other words, was primarily understood to account for Negro origins, and Ham was the progenitor of the Negro race. The idea of a curse and the association between Ham and slavery were not the most important themes. It is paramount to understand this in order to appreciate fully the rupture that Christian identity induced among African American Christians. The "myth of Ham" was only secondarily viewed (by *some*) as justification for slavery in the American South. First and foremost, the Noahic account answered the originary concerns of not only ethnologists and religionists but also any other general publics who posed the pressing question: From whence came the Negro? Almost no one seriously rejected the "fact" that the Negro was produced through Hamitic descent. That Hamitic ancestry was understood primarily to explain Negro origins is evident, in part, when considering that the curse of Ham *qua* justification for slavery was continually *debated* throughout America—the meaning and validity of the curse were constant points of contention.[37] It was far more exceptional, on the other hand, for anyone to question the "fact" that Ham was the progenitor of Negroes.

What emerges then, given such a worldview, is a conundrum of symbols and narratives that conditioned the task of imagining an American identity. In light of the Israelitic themes in American social experience, one might view American identity formation as a virtual pageant in which peoples in United States of America saw themselves as descendants of those who crossed over to America, left the boats, stepped onto the stage of the American experience, took up their divine identity scripts, and performed "Israel." For descendants of European settlers, the transition was one into a New World open to settlement, acquisition, economic opportunity, and gainful exploration. All occurred under the auspices of a provident, gracious God who had already determined that they should inherit a bounteous land in order to build a Christian society that would be a "city on a hill."[38]

There were no contradictory terrors in this script for Europeans as racial selves because they were already a Christian *people*. And although European Americans knew that their Jute and Saxon ancestors had been "pagan" barbarians at one time, this "memory" performed no confounding role before the task of imagining an American self. When they gazed back upon the land from which their forebears had come, they envisioned not a land of ravaging heathens whose humanity was questionable, but a *Christian* motherland from whose nest they had ventured in order to form a more perfect society.[39]

Black Americans, however, did not fare so well in this American pageant. Their performance was beleaguered by the burden of acting out a double script, lining the roles of both the people of God and the children of Ham—heathens. Ham represented, in the American religious imagination, the Canaanite negation of knowing the true God. It is for this very reason, George Williams suggests, that God had ordered their genocide via Joshua. This defining aspect of Canaanite existence, moreover, as quintessentially heathen, was the symbolism that divine identity produced. The divine identity governed by the Christian myth construed that there was, first of all, such a thing as "the heathen" and, second, that heathenism was despicable to God and to the people of God. Because the heathen did not worship the one true God, Ham's descendants were, in the words of George Williams, the very "enemies" of God, "in all that that term implies."[40]

It becomes evident, therefore, that participation in the American pageant of identity required of black Christians a rupture from something left behind. For, unlike Euro-Americans, black Christians who gazed back upon the land of their origin—the Dark Continent—beheld an abode of heathens whose existence was delimited by a lack of civilization and culture. These Africans were depraved, furthermore, because they had forsaken God. And it was through the American experience that they came to know this God and were thus able to escape treacherous existence in spiritual darkness. Having left behind a legacy of heathenism, American Negro Christians could live in the light of the gospel because, just as surely as white Christians, they too were people of God. They had become God's Israel.

In light of such narrative knowledge, it becomes evident that black Americans who participated in Christian self-understanding had to overcome a particular racialized challenge—I term it the contradiction of being heathen—in order to appropriate Christian identity. Most succinctly, because black Americans encountered Christianity as a racial group, they had to explain the "problem" of not having been people of God prior to the American experience. The situation is one of a non-biblical, heathen people encountering or negotiating the symbolic, narrative world of Christianity. The context imposes a peculiar liminality; in this situation, a problematic folk comes to occupy an ontological fissure or disjuncture between (legitimate) divine identity and racialized, heathen existence. There persists a nagging uncertainty or irresolute, anxious regard for the condition of the race because of this complex past. This anxiety constitutes an existential crisis of Hamitic identity. And this crisis of existence is the heuristic focus of the present study.

Race and Narrative in the American Canaan

Race discourse concerned narrations that associated God with a *people*. Some people were people of God. Others were not; they were heathens. The heathen as a social construct, furthermore, was symbolically associated with Native Americans and Negroes. And this confluence of the religious and the racial definitively shaped American religious experience. It authored the riddle of race and religion that would continue to beleaguer American Christianity in that century and the next. Ultimately, it confounded attempts to image/perceive the humanity of the Negro, and it bred incredible mythologies of ontological whiteness. The confluence of race and biblical narrative, in other words, is rightly viewed as an anthropological concern because it chiefly regards the question of which people are treated as human beings and which are not.[41]

American religious themes were founded upon the biblical story, and explanations of race identities were a subset of that worldview. The Bible in the post-/Reconstruction era was, after all, just that—*the* Bible—not a collection of disparate ancient texts but a singular document comprising one continuous narrative. The thriving higher criticism in Germany at the time had barely begun to make ripples in nineteenth-century American scholarship, and popular notions of scripture were usually disturbed only enough to generate strident apologetics. The Bible, furthermore, was not merely a book. It was the lens for understanding the world and the looking glass for glimpsing social (i.e., collective) selves. This is why both black and white authors cited biblical narratives and genealogies to explicate (the fictions of) their racial histories. And they did so without the slightest hint of irony or qualm.

The story (of Israel) was the conceptual module used to *make sense* of history, of events. If one wanted, for instance, to find out the role or condition of one's race in ancient times, one looked to the biblical record. Paramount to this story was the reality of the God who destines the unfolding of world history through electing a people—a race—to inherit "the land," to purge heathenism from that land, and to propagate knowledge of the one deity in a covenant relationship with that God.[42]

The Negro has been the American riddle of the sphinx, the perennial "how come?" of racial curiosity. Although the origins of whiteness (as identity) pose a more beneficial object of critical reflection, the historical reality is that whites have projected racial curiosity upon non-whites. And the most exoticized of these has been the Negro. Robert Hood, in his *Begrimed and Black*, provided a cogent treatment of symbolic constructions associated with black peoples. Describing the disparaging patterns of white American race theories, Hood suggested that discursive productions of race were driven by a deep-seated revulsion for symbolic blackness that, although quintessentially American, predated the American experience. Hood traced across cultures and centuries a history of racial and semiotic antiblackness. His concern, he identified, was the tendency of some cultures to associate darkness and dark bodies with ontological evil, human depravity, and existential abasement.[43]

At the forefront of such an intellectual query is Gay Byron's groundbreaking work of ethno-political rhetorics about blacks and symbolic blackness in early Christianity. The study is destined to become a standard reference because she develops a sophisticated taxonomy of rhetorical strategies that signified upon blacks and blackness. Byron clarifies the ambivalence that attended early Christian ideas about evil and darkness, Ethiopians/Egyptians and vices, legitimacy and identity. And she demonstrates the architecture of such discourse functioned as an ideological strategy that cohered toward the task of world-making, of constructing community.[44]

Regina Schwartz, in her study of violence and religious identity formation, identifies biblical worldviews as foundational to these developments. Schwartz examines the way difference of peoplehood and of religion is defined and how such is contingent upon religious sense or logic. Her argument advances that the story of Israel and its narrative assumptions—as biblical traditions—have immensely influenced Western society. The result has produced ideational patterns of alterity—that is, distinctive ways of defining "us" and "them" through religious, racial, and cultural modes.[45]

Hood's diachronic, cross-cultural study of semiotic blackness, Byron's culture-critical reading of ethno-political rhetorics, and Schwartz's examination of monotheism and identity violence together model an evocative interrogative posture essential to understanding the Hamitic idea. On the one hand, there is the complex othering or alterity (Schwartz's emphasis) that attends the biblical idea of divine identity—"us and them."[46] Here lie the seeds for constructing the heathen, for encoding in misanthropic terms the existence of those who are not people of God. The "us and them" dichotomy is not coincidental, but essential to divine identity.

On the other hand, there exist racial identities in the American context that are hierarchical and antiblack; they are preeminently modern, as Audrey Smedley emphasizes. One cannot locate explicit examples of modern racism in antiquity. Modern ideas about race arose amidst the contexts of the Enlightenment, the Reformation and, most importantly, colonization.[47] Yet, it seems that Smedley's overall compelling thesis must be qualified because Robert Hood demonstrates that hostility toward symbolic blackness, which is an essential if not foundational ingredient of modern racism, is a semiotic complex that predates modernity and is attested in antiquity. Blackness has existed as a metaphysical, symbolic concept. And it has been associated with certain folk, dark peoples, particularly Africans.[48]

Throughout post-Columbus American history, these racial identities have been explained through the language and symbols of biblical narrative. And they communicate judgments about existential legitimacy and moral qualities. The most critical meanings, in the religious sphere, define blackness beyond the pale of divinity and locate black folks outside of the history of those who are people of God.

American Israels

The American racial and religious imagination has been contingent upon a narrative lens—seeing the "world" through the story of God's "Israel." One would be hard-pressed to explicate the realities of race in America in the absence of biblical ideas. The idea of being God's "Israel"—that is, God's people vis-à-vis other peoples, with concomitant "responsibilities" and/or provisions—has been central to American religion, and it hinges on the myth of chosenness. European settlers who first arrived on North American shores brought with them the Israelitic myth. This narrative lens, most simply put, explained the nation or folk as the chosen people of God destined to inherit a "new" land and to be a moral and religious exemplum for the rest of the world. Sydney Mead and Martin Marty have been among the most influential writers on this topic. Marty's *Righteous Empire* examines this idea as the "Anglo-Protestant" ethos, an apt phrase that captures both denominational and racial nuances of this aspect of American religion.[49]

Another school of thought is represented by Conrad Cherry and Robert Bellah. Bellah, in 1967, published a very provocative essay on civil religion in America that spawned substantive debate over the meaning of American religion and its relevance for interpreting the nation's history. Bellah's thesis strongly affirms the idea of covenant as the basis for American religion. Bellah argued that the most pristine form of this covenant belief lay in a contract with God whereby American colonists believed that God had granted favor upon them—they were to inherit the "new" land of the Americas. This favor was contingent, however, upon the condition that the people honor God with moral uprightness, obedience, and consideration for those to whom they were to be an example.[50]

This principle suffered demise, according to Bellah, and became corrupted as the nation became more secular. Bellah's work has been somewhat of a call for the nation to regain the proper attitude of reverence and uprightness in lieu of what he perceives to be the decadence of secularity. Critical to Bellah's hermeneutics is his valuation of national unity, homogeneity, and consistency. The nation, at its best, makes a united effort to embrace and fulfill the covenant relationship with God.[51]

Cherry's collection of essays and speeches, in line with Bellah's ideas, represents the American Israel concept, the putative demise of which he chronicles. He suggests, for example, that the Massachusetts Bay Colony Governor John Winthrop embodied the ideal understanding of being a chosen people when he warned the colonists that divine favor should not become an opportunity for pride and undue ambition. Rather, they were to demonstrate their gratitude by upholding the highest principles of truth and respect for God, one another, and other nations. Cherry is well aware that chosenness became conflated with white aspirations of imperialism and conquest; he clearly regards such, however, as abuses of the Israelitic idea.[52]

Although Cherry departs somewhat from Bellah, both emphasize the original integrity of the Israelitic idea and interpret its history subsequent to the Revolutionary War as a gradual departure from the pristine meaning of chosenness. While Cherry uses the "non-racial" framework of Robert Bellah in order to develop his interpretation of the American Israel, other writers such as Albert Raboteau and Eddie Glaude have since argued for an analysis of the Israelitic idea in American religion that takes seriously the representations of race.[53]

Raboteau concurs with Cherry and Bellah when he emphasizes an original integrity or essential probity about Israelitic identity in America. He too discusses the first colonial statesman John Winthrop and points to the covenant aspect of chosenness—there were certain conditions attending the status of being favored by God because such election was for an ultimate purpose.

But Raboteau makes a significant departure when he suggests that there were two Israels in America. African American churches, he reasons, cannot be reduced to colored versions of white denominations but must be regarded as independent formations. African American Christians' understanding of identity, faith, and the Christian gospel did not merely mimic white religion but, rather, introduced an original interpretive dimension because the faith of black Christians was forged by a desperate struggle for recognized human status and freedom. Until 1865, most of these blacks experienced the American Promised Land as a virtual "Egypt"—that is, a land of slavery—rather than one of long-awaited freedom and liberation. It is this irony that forms the basis of Raboteau's thesis, an irony that is largely ignored by Bellah and Cherry.

The most recent major study of this subject is Eddie Glaude's *Exodus!* Glaude's is a very theoretically developed analysis of religion, race, and nation in the formation of African American Christianity. Most compelling is his argument that chosenness became the basis "for interpreting the time and space of America." He sets out to demonstrate that African American Christianity, contingent upon a pragmatic freedom struggle, radicalized an American appropriation of chosenness that had sunk to the level of equating whiteness with chosenness. Rather than touting racial chauvinism, he suggests, African American Christians reconnected Israelitic identification with its biblical emphasis on God's advocacy for historically victimized peoples.[54] He chronicles the development of racial attitudes and constructions of otherness that marginalized blacks and obscured their humanity. Even before the nineteenth century, Glaude asserts, "freedom was understood over and against the unfreedom of black slaves; divine election was read along racial lines; and America was fast becoming a white man's nation!"[55]

Glaude contributes a sobering reminder that the story of Israel is a product of imagining the nation, of defining peoplehood. And he shows that American ideas of chosenness were formed in tandem with American racial beliefs. Race, then, necessarily becomes a contingency for any examination of an American Israel.[56]

This process of defining collective identity is not merely an American episode, he recognizes, but attends the very idea of being chosen of God. On this point, he acknowledges that "the Exodus story lends itself to chauvinistic and territorialist readings." But its relation to black Christianity "mandated ongoing struggle, for the promise was temporally uncertain." In this sense, Glaude shares with Raboteau, Cherry, and Bellah an abiding optimism about the roots of the Israelitic myth. Glaude, however, is aware that white American appropriations emphasized conquest and racism; he chronicles these racialized appropriations with commanding depth and evenhanded scrutiny. Ultimately, he provides a compelling case that prevailing rhetorics of peoplehood cannot be severed from the concept of being people of God. This is one enduring meaning of being "Israel." But also, in direct critique of Eugene Genovese, he contends that the story of Israel provided African Americans with the language of nation, solidarity, and faith that was essential to their freedom struggle. Not only were black Christian appropriations frequently materially interested instead of otherworldly (contra Genovese), but also such appropriations redeemed the Israelitic theme from its misinterpretation by white Christians.[57]

In light of Raboteau's and Glaude's revisionist readings, the more ominous leanings of the Israelitic myth might seem somewhat redeemed. Their interpretations of the theme and their attention to its racialized import in America are certainly corrective to the trend in scholarship that ignores or trivializes the myriad ways race differentiated American performances of being "Israel."

There is, nevertheless, another dimension that neither Glaude nor Raboteau addresses that was hinted at in a much earlier essay by Charles Long in 1974. In "Invisible People and Visible Religion," Long pointed to the critical works that examined the Israelitic theme in American religion, specifically in the wake of Bellah's essay. The most significant expressions of American religion rendered invisible or demonic the historical religions of blacks and Native Americans.

American religion, Long suggests, comprises such traditions of "conquest and suppression" that one must query the relationship between the problems of racial exclusion and Christianity, even as such have been experienced by historically non-Christian peoples who have appropriated the religion for themselves.[58]

In contrast to Raboteau and Glaude, who identify all of the problems of race, exclusion and domination or conquest as foreign to the religion of Christianity, Long has suggested that such problems are neither intrusions nor abuses but, rather, are inherent to Christianity and should be understood with greater complexity instead of categorizing them as alien to the faith. The immediate study takes seriously Long's analysis and pays heed to the caveats he has foregrounded.

Race and the Israelitic Myth

The uses of Hamitic identity serve as a heuristic in order to interpret the idea of being people of God. This study will proceed by way of suggesting (1) that the Hamitic idea primarily concerned originary anxieties and racial (il)legitimacy, (2) that divine identity "peoples" God by associating God with a people/race, and (3) that this "peopleing" of God is fundamentally a racial idea contingent upon an alterity principle that encodes "others" as illegitimate and thereby produces problems of existence. Hamitic discourse is a product of the recurring and, I believe, justified (though unjustly necessary) attempts to advance and to defend the idea that "the black"—the dark "body"—is human. What is being proffered here *ultimately* concerns not merely an African American situation or even historical Christianity per se. The inquiry and rejoinder *qua* thesis involve, rather, human anxieties, arguably universal, that pertain to existential legitimacy and that are contingent upon acts of narration and ultimate identification.

This study employs the hermeneutical assumption[59] that such liminality affords an opportunity to understand something about Christian identity *qua* being people of God that is otherwise not so readily observed—its racialized overtones.[60] This racial contingency is one of *peoplehood*. The reality of race finds its life in the phenomenology of belonging to or being a member of a people, a group. It is patent today that race is a fiction. It is just as apparent that there has been no decline in racialism. Despite a proliferation of studies that demonstrate greater genetic variation within racial groups than among them, and notwithstanding that many scientists in the twenty-first century no longer consider race to be a scientific category, race as a social force continues undisturbed.[61]

Why? There are several reasons. Primary is the fact that race was first a folk schema or popular worldview before it became the object of scientific valorization. And as a popular worldview, race was grounded in the idea of belonging to one folk or people vis-à-vis another. This social meaning of race has persisted over time and has remained the fundamental manifestation of race in its experience or phenomenology. In other words, although theories of race have been primarily taxonomic—that is, ostensibly concerned with categorizing—the meaning of race has been contingent upon *belonging to* a folk or people.

When nineteenth-century Harvard University Professor Lewis Agassiz, for instance, touted the supremacy of Nordic and Teutonic peoples as white, Agassiz believed that he was *part of* or a member of the race being discussed. Even modern scientists who deny that race is a scientific category today experience this identity of belonging to one racial group or another. This is why race is such a compelling fiction. From another direction, the one-drop rule phenomenon in America indicates that being white has meant not being colored, not being one of "those people." *The point is that the phenomenology of race chiefly concerns peoplehood.*

The reader will likely take exception to my use of race for interpreting the idea of divine identity. Such a pairing of concepts would make most experts cringe. But my motivations for doing so will become clearer as the rhetorical productions of racial and religious identity in Hamitic claims are examined. The American "moment" of the Hamitic idea is especially compelling for the very reason that the peoplehoods of race and religious identity were so conspicuously conjoined.[62]

This conundrum of Hamitic legacy poses a heuristic question for studies of African American Christianity's emergence specifically and American Christianity more broadly. Black Americans occupied a position that compelled them to hold in tension two opposing narrative identities: identity as people of God—an American Israel—and identity as heathens—children of Ham. What, then, did it mean for black American Christians to share in a self-understanding as people of God while also "remembering" an evil past and experiencing an evil identity as Ham's descendants? Did this dual locus of identity bear any significance? Did it influence, in some significant way, the emergence of black Christianity? Did it condition, in important terms, American religion?

Two major considerations must be addressed in order to explicate this subject. First is the confluence of race and biblical narrative in nineteenth-century American history. Second is the meaning of being an American Israel—the American Israel was plural and comprised contradictions for various folk. For American Negroes, it signaled or demanded a certain newness, becoming a "new people" of sorts.

The confluence of race and narrative chiefly concerns the idea that the "white, yellow, and black" peoples of the earth were the three basic racial groups of human beings that corresponded to the three sons of Noah. These characters, as narrated in the book of Genesis, repopulate the earth in the wake of a catastrophic flood. Theoretical constructions of race were largely based upon this biblical explanation. Understanding this fusion between race identity and biblical narration is essential to appreciating what was at stake in nineteenth-century claims over Hamitic descent.

American theories of race during the nineteenth century, in addition, relied heavily upon burgeoning European race scholarship. Structural anthropology, as a discipline, underwent its most formative development during this century. Science historian Stephen Jay Gould, in his *Mismeasure of Man*, recounted the history of attempts to explain the existence of Negroes, Native Americans, Asians, and other non-white peoples of the world during this period. The domain assumption of race theorists, Gould demonstrated, rendered the social identity of whites as normative. European and white American scientists assumed that the physiognomy of whites was normal and constituted the original condition of human beings. The "problem" of racial variation was, essentially, the occurrence of deviance from white phenotypic expressions. How did human beings become non-white (abnormal)?[63] This was the heuristic paradigm of race theory.

Biblical narrative, furthermore, was foundational to the domain assumptions of both religious and scientific ideologues of race. A strict religious–scientific dichotomy, in fact, eventually breaks down because such is inadequate for understanding nineteenth-century views of race; frequently, *both* scientists and Christian religionists who sought to explain race variation relied upon biblical narrative, despite the fact that they usually disagreed over details of biblical authority. Both religionists and scientists presumed, for example, that the races descended from Noah's three sons. Racial histories were consistently founded on biblical ideas.[64]

Audrey Smedley has rendered a compelling account of the history of race as an idea. She traces this history as a strictly modern occurrence, from the sixteenth century to the present. Race theories underwent tremendous change, attributing racial differences first to environmental agents and later to biological, innate factors. Smedley, for this reason, has argued that race ideas are characterized by this fragile, shifting proclivity. She advances that not only have definitions of whiteness changed—Italians and European Jews, for example, were formerly viewed as nonwhites—but also definitions of race itself have been very unstable.[65]

Smedley does, however, identify several consistent aspects of American race ideas. First of all, white theorists consistently assumed a hierarchy of races. Race was not a condition of variety with equality but a gradation of humanities, and the Negro was consistently at the bottom of the anthropological totem pole. Negro theorists and their Euro-American allies, on the other hand, usually fought to counter such claims on the basis of anthropological equality—human beings might be substantially different but were equally human.

Race theories were also consistently tied to racialized social histories—that is, the idea of racial accomplishments; Europeans and Euro-Americans read back into all of human history the newly created social identity of whiteness and thereby claimed the Greeks and Romans as heroes of the race.[66] Most importantly, based on biblical narrative, they claimed Japheth as their Noahic ancestor. And they consistently argued that all human beings were originally white—Adam and Eve and all other pre-Noahic peoples. The assumption, here again, is the world of biblical narrative. In like fashion, black American theorists also read Negro racial identity back into history in order to buttress arguments for the humanity of the Negro.[67]

Nineteenth-century American race discourse, whether religious or scientific, was persistently *theological*.[68] Race ideas bore immediate implications for claims about the deity and about human access to divine knowledge and divine identity. And the most enduring renditions of these claims identified the white race as first peoples who had first knowledge of the one true God. This one true God was none other than the deity revealed through the Hebrew religion taken over by the Christian myth. What was at stake *theologically*, therefore, was not a mere association between white identity and the Christian religion. At stake was nothing less than the race-ing of divinity, the people-ing of God.

Narrating the People of God: Heathen Existence and the Phenomenology of Christian Identity

What are the ideas, the points of narrative knowledge, that the Israelitic myth communicates, and how do such become relevant for

American religion? It is paramount to provide a rejoinder to this question because it underlies the point of the study. The thesis of this study suggests that the narration of divine identity, the Israelitic myth, encodes noetic keys to "apprehending" divine identity in contrast to "others" who are not divinely identified. That American religion is contingent upon biblical ideas is patent. The works of Martin Marty, Sydney Ahlstrom, Gayraud Wilmore, and Albert Raboteau have made this abundantly clear.

But what of the myth specifically? There is, after all, no unified storyline in the myriad of texts constituting what has come to be called "the Bible." To speak of "the Bible," in this sense, is at best naïve and at worst disingenuous. "The Bible," rather, is a collection of texts of different eras, genres, and authors. These texts derive from different theological traditions and often present conflicting accounts, etiologies, and ideologies.[69]

There is, however, a shared context and logic so fundamental and paradigmatic as to constitute a *metanarrative*—something akin to what historian Robert Berkhofer terms a "Great Story"[70]—without which nothing makes sense. This metanarrative is the story of the Israelite deity who elects or chooses a *Volk*, a people, commands their exclusive worship and loyalty, and provides them a land of their own—land taken from the unfortunate victims of the deity's genocidal hatred. In relation to the peoplehood, to the land, and to cultic purity—that is, maintaining rectitude and exclusive, faithful loyalty to the deity—arise a plethora of narrations that reflect upon a pristine past, a problematic present, and a promised future.

Regina Schwartz, in slightly different language, makes a related point when she identifies the chief occupation of the Bible to be "imagining and forging collective identity."[71] This task of identity maintenance, she explains, is what the various texts have in common. For this reason, the Bible as a product and symbol is indispensable to understanding the categories of nation, people, race, and ethnicity in Western modernity.

Edward Said, Homi Bhabha, Joyce Appleby, and Regina Schwartz have also discussed the role that narration plays in forming or sustaining national identities. To tell the story of the nation, Bhabha suggests, is to invent the nation. Bhabha posits that the act of narration is essential to social identity because it creates a shared history and social memory. Said, in a similar vein, examines literature produced since the inception of European colonization in order to assess patterns of visibility and suppression in narrative representation. Not everyone, he concludes, occupies a common locus of power or peril in narratives: some ascend to success; others suffer demise.[72] Joyce Appleby, Lynn Hunt, and Margaret Jacob have applied Benedict Anderson's analysis of "imagined communities" to describe inventions of national identity in U.S. American historiography and construal of the American self. Drawing upon consensus-building ideas produced such a history and identity scheme that narratized national self-understanding as Christian fulfillment; this was deeply wed to Anglo-Saxon ideas of election.[73]

Schwartz, however, has most directly linked acts of narration to Israelitic appropriations in modern nationalisms. Like Said and Bhabha, she grounds the role of narrative in forming national identities and in creating kinship. Her treatment is especially relevant for a study of Hamitic rhetoric in American religion because she gives great attention to the alterity concomitant to viewing the nation as people of God. This aspect of identify formation is so crucial, Schwartz maintains, that violence must be understood in part as a product of identify formation. In this sense, "violence is not only what we do to the Other. It is prior to that. Violence is the very construction of the Other."[74] And this construction as the core of alterity becomes critical for discussing the Hamitic idea. This alterity, Schwartz argues, is produced because identity as people of God depends upon a necessary other— the heathen, those who are not people of God.[75]

Moreover, one should not view this metanarrative as exclusive to the Hebrew Scriptures because it is only through this Israelitic narrative and its ideological context that stories of Jesus and Jesusine religion make sense in the Christian myth. Writers have frequently characterized the New Testament as inclusive vis-à-vis the Old Testament. But when one comprehends the codes of narrative knowledge that the Christian myth transmits, one understands that New Testament texts only reinforce the assumption that some folk are people and others are not; it is only through becoming one with the people of God, their deity, and their narrations that any Others may enter the body of folk affirmed by and affiliated with divinity. In fact, one might argue that the Christian tradition presents a more difficult problem because it assumes a more explicitly universal scope and has acted upon that scope of sight through zealous missionary strategies.

It is in the above sense that divine identity, in the biblical ideal, takes shape and has meaning. Divine identity is self-understanding derived from a relationship with the deity, a relationship that is differential because not all people share it. Those who are people of

God have a specific understanding of themselves vis-à-vis those who are not.

In order to grasp the meanings at stake for the subjects generating such desperate articulations in the nineteenth century, one must realize that modern American notions of race and American religious ideas were tethered one to the other by the cord of legitimacy. *Black American Christians encountered Christianity as the Negro (Hamitic) race of non-Christian folk.* One cannot overemphasize this. This meant that, as a racial group, Negroes were illegitimate existents and constantly sought to change this condition as progressively and completely as possible. Such was not the case for their Euro-American counterparts. Although pristinely Mediterranean, Christian identity to some degree was made to signify Western whiteness itself.[76]

Europeans had undergone this same process of being alienated from their historical religions and cultures by expansionist Christianity. But this occurred during and prior to the Middle Ages, certainly before the development of modern racial identities; that is, there were no "white" heathens because white identity did not exist at that time. By the time of the Reformation, European nation states assumed and heralded the reign of Christendom; the contentions were denominational and factional.

In the wake of the Trans-Atlantic Slave Trade and the holocaust of slavery, however, the public meaning of "Negro" and "Africa" were finely wedded to "backward," "uncivilized," and "heathen." It was generally assumed throughout Christendom, by the nineteenth century, that Africa stood in need of redemption; the means of that redemption may have been debated, but never the need. Africa and its peoples were illegitimate. Something was gravely amiss with them, and no less than civilization and the Christian gospel were the essential ingredients for amelioration.

From this, it becomes clear that Christian identity was certainly one sign of legitimacy vis-à-vis remaining heathen. This was the religious aspect. I have pointed to a second sphere of this problem, however—that of race. By the time of Emancipation, white supremacy had become elevated to the status of common sense. When one studies the discourse of blacks who defended the humanity of the Negro in light of their context, one can only be in awe. Consider that practically every part of Africa was under the heel of a violent system of European economic dominance. White intellectuals had generated a plethora of scholarship to support ideas of white supremacy that were previously argued without much "evidence."

In 1844, Samuel Morton had published *Crania Aegyptiaca*, which was filled with craniometric analysis of East African skulls that, after some scientific number-crunching, "proved" that Negroes were only slaves in ancient Egypt and had not been responsible for any cultural achievements.[77] In 1854, George R. Gliddon and Josiah Nott published their (in)famous *Types of Mankind*, in which they categorized the races of the world; the Negro, of course, was on the bottom rung and was only questionably human.[78] The French Count Arturo de Gobineau, by 1855, was renowned for his two-volume work on the inequality of human races, a crushing disparagement of the Negro race and boisterous exaltation of whites as the supreme race of people.[79]

In 1857, Chief Justice Roger Taney of the U.S. Supreme Court ruled that the Negro possessed no rights that whites were bound to recognize or respect (*Dred Scott v. Sandford*). This ruling, only superficially about the rights of fugitive slaves, effectively disqualified the Negro race from U.S. citizenship.[80] Even the Civil War itself, which was in many ways a moral boost to advocates of Negro freedom and Negro rights, became an opportunity for white supremacist strategies. The U.S. Sanitary Commission and the Provost Marshall-General's Bureau began anthropometric studies of white and Negro recruits in order to gather and eventually to publish data bolstering claims of white superiority; this was the first time such a volume of data had been gathered in the United States.[81]

Perhaps John Van Evrie is most representative of this historical "moment." His *White Supremacy and Negro Subordination* (1868) immediately commanded national attention with its "proofs" that not only were European civilizations superior to all others but also that all architectural feats and cultural achievements worth speaking of were European. In Asia, Africa, and even the Americas, any markers of "civilization" and technical skill, according to Van Evrie, had been developed by whites and not the peoples of color putatively autochthonous to those areas.[82]

The point is that white supremacy was not merely a slogan or worrisome claim. It was a manifest, documented "fact." Given such a milieu, by what reason or motivation could or would American Negroes counter the claim? How could they dare to speak out on behalf of their humanity and to articulate even a modicum of Negro significance in the ancient or contemporary world? That they did attempt at all is impressive. That they produced significant, persuasive material that successfully countered white supremacist claims is even more noteworthy.

What is central to the issue, fundamentally, is that nineteenth-century blacks believed in the human and historical worth of the Hamitic race, of the Negro. In the wake of Van Evrie's stultifying publication, Edward Wilmot Blyden could write in 1869 that the Negro race was ancient and reputable in historical greatness because they were children of Ham.[83]

2

Divine Identity and the Hamitic Idea in Historical Perspective

Introduction

American Christian ideas about (black) Africans as Hamitic were not recent inventions but had their origin in a long, complex tradition of Judaic, Christian, Islamic, and otherwise biblical thought. This history comprised descriptions of Ham as a great ancestor of early nations, as a moral failure who blighted a portion of humanity because of his sin against Noah, and as one to be distinguished genealogically and morally from the other posterity of Noah. As we shall see, he was regularly (though not exclusively) associated with the African nations of Ethiopia and Egypt. The various narrative productions of early Judaic, Christian, and Islamic traditions about Ham were critical ingredients in an eventual, consummate formula of religious and cultural antiblackness in American Christianity.[1]

Ham in Early Judaism, Christianity, and Islam

Traditions about Ham and Ham's descendants certainly were not racist (in the strictly modern sense) in their earliest, biblical forms. They tended, rather, to concern claims to land and peoplehood. A common pattern in biblical tradition was narrating claims about people who were understood as progenitors of tribes or nations in order to deploy meanings about those tribes or nations. The story of Jacob and Esau (Genesis 25:19–26), for example, served to explain why Ephraim (etymologically linked to Esau) was antagonized by Israel, the alternative name given to Jacob. Jacob and Esau were said to have been the progenitors of the respective nations, Israel and Ephraim. Because these characters never existed as historical persons, scholars have described them as eponymous ancestors—fictitious "progenitors" after whom a nation or people is said to be named. This practice of narration is anachronistic, of course, imaginative reading into an early past the identities and issues of a later period.

This is the most appropriate context in which to understand biblical narrations of Ham. The English *Ham* translates the Hebrew חם which is transliterated "Chām." The word appears seventeen times in the Hebrew Bible, usually referring to the mythical character of Noah's son (in Genesis and 1 Chronicles) and designating Egypt as the land of Ham—*eretz Chām*—in the Psalms.[2] Ham is frequently described as the ancestor or progenitor of the African nations Ethiopia (referred to as "Cush" in the Hebrew Bible) and Egypt. But Phut and the Canaanite nations—the Hittites and Jebusites, for instance—are also listed as his progeny (Genesis 10:6–20).[3] The name Ham has been commonly associated with "hot" or "heat" or "dark," due to the similar appearance of the words in Hebrew. But it seems best to regard the original meaning of *Ham* as a mystery lost to modern scrutiny.[4]

Ham's symbolic importance in the tradition of Hebrew legends is most immediately recognized through his position vis-à-vis his brothers Japheth and Shem. All were sons of Noah, through whom the earth was repopulated after a great flood destroyed the rest of humankind (Genesis 7–9); only Noah's family remained. Both Japheth and Shem are blessed by Noah, and their posterity, as Noah's character "predicts" in Genesis chapter 9, was to enjoy an auspicious future. But Ham accidentally sees his father naked (Genesis 9:22), and this evokes a curse from Noah. The narrative, for this reason, has been most frequently called "the curse of Ham."

It is clear, however, that Ham per se is not cursed in the biblical story. The recipient of the curse, rather, is Ham's son Canaan, another eponymous figure—that is, the "father" of the Canaanites. This legend of Noah's curse against Canaan is an etiology—a narrative attempt to explain conditions endemic to the milieu of the writer(s). The curse against Canaan was one of enslavement—the slave of slaves or lowest of slaves. Narrating a curse of Canaan signifies on the historical Canaanites.

These Canaanites were "a northwest Semitic people" who had long inhabited ancient Palestine. Ephraim Isaac recognizes, for instance, that they were "in a general racial-ethnic sense" related to the Israelites and Phoenicians. It is only fair, in fact, to recognize that Hebrews *were* ethnically and culturally Canaanites.[5] It is unclear whether the social setting behind the narrative was one in which Canaanites were enslaved by Israelites; the Israelite legends (e.g., in the book of Joshua) describing genocide and enslavement of Canaanites are imaginative, contradictory, and ahistorical. The more likely historical context for the legend of Noah's curse is the prominence of the Canaanites known as Phoenicians, who were far superior to the Israelites in social and economic power. They are targeted for derision in this legend of Noah's curse through ethnic disparagement rooted in the wishful thinking of the weak against the powerful. It is patent that the narrative produces a body of meanings that deride Canaanites by associating them with moral wantonness or evil and concomitant enslavement. They are recipients of disfavor with demeaning consequences.[6]

In addition to this ancestral or eponymic assignment, the Ham of biblical narrative tradition is consistently excluded from Israel and is differentiated from the other gentile nations as especially evil. It was patent in Israelitic thought, for instance, that only Yahweh's Israel possessed knowledge of the true or rightful deity and was in a jealously guarded covenant relationship with this deity. But with the emergence of *Judean* religion—that is, in the wake of Babylonian conquest and exile during the sixth century—other nations came to be regarded as eligible for participating in knowing and worshiping this deity. In other words, representations of Yahweh became less explicitly tribal and more universalist. Despite this development, however, the figure of the Hamitic in Jewish tradition remained an exception in the sense that Hamites were children of perdition because of Ham's sin.[7]

This abominable sin of Ham became a common refrain during the Common Era and frequently attended any mention of him. By the time of rabbinic Judaism, rabbis considered the name *Ham* to derive from the Hebrew root for "heat" and "blackened." One third-century transmission of a legend explaining Ham's blackness occurs in the work of Rabbi Hiyya, who related that God blackened Ham to punish him for breaking a ban against having sex while in the ark during the flood.[8] Some early rabbinic interpretations associated darkened/blackened skin to all of Ham's descendents as a form of punishment. David Goldenberg concludes that, by the ninth to eleventh centuries, however, this curse of blackness was regularly tied to Cush, one of Ham's sons, instead of all of Ham's descendents.[9]

The most intensive representations of Ham, however, were developing not within rabbinic Judaism but within early Christianity, as evident from patristic writings. Stephen Haynes has noted the function of anti-Hamitic ideology in the work of Augustine, Lactantius, Clement of Alexandria, and others. According to Augustine (d. 430 C.E.), Ham was "the symbol of the man in isolation, the clanless, lawless, hearthless man who, like heathen ethnics, did not know God." Lactantius, in a similar fashion, identified Hamites as the primal embodiment of wantonness and evil by designating the Canaanite descendants of Ham as the first nation to be ignorant of (Israel's) God; Egyptians, likewise, were the inventors of idolatry through worship of stellar bodies and statues. Of further interest is Clement of Alexandria's (d. 215 C.E.) denunciation of Ham for inventing magic and superstition. Haynes rightly concludes that early Christian writers roundly inscribed Ham as the prototypical man of evil, an "archsinner" whose descendants were preeminently heathens.[10]

Associations between the Hamitic and heat or darkness were part of an extensive Greco-Roman semantic world that inscribed evil figuratively. For example, Augustine understood Hamites allegorically in his *City of God* to represent the heretics who profaned the Christian faith.

> The name Ham means "hot" (*calidus*); and Noah's middle son, separating himself, as it were, from both the others, and keeping his position between them, is included neither in the first fruits of Israel nor in the full harvest of the gentiles, and he can only stand for the hot breed of heretics (*haereticorum genus calidum*). They are hot, because they are on fire not with the spirit of wisdom (*sapientiae*), but with the spirit of impatience (*inpatientiae*).[11]

Subsequent trends in medieval Christian, Muslim, and Jewish traditions would represent Ham more exclusively as the progenitor of Africans or dark-skinned peoples. Perhaps the greatest determinant for these subsequent developments was the burgeoning slave trade administered by Arab Muslims. Some of the most notorious manipulations of Hamitic symbolism before the American proslavery appropriation occurred during the Arab slave trade in Africa. The Muslim empire emerged rapidly and by the ninth century had begun to depend upon importing slaves from Africa and Europe. It was during this time that Africans became the victims of extreme ethnocentrism and colorism by Arab Muslims.

The eighth-century Muslim Wahb Ibn Munabbih wrote that Ham was originally white but that, because of Noah's curse, God changed Ham's skin color to black. This blackened Ham, according to Munabbih, was the progenitor of the blacks, whom he characterized

as eating fish and having teeth as sharp as needles. Munabbih listed
the descendants of these black Hamites as the Nubians, Zanj, Copts,
Ethiopians, and the like.[12] He was primarily concerned with explaining the origin of dark skin color. A similar explanation of Africans
occurs in the work of Ka'b Al-Ahbar, who lived during the seventh
century.[13]

For this reason, although the Qur'ân itself is devoid of antiblack
ideology, and despite the fact that many blacks converted to Islam and
became influential religionists, officials and Islamic intellectuals, disparaging invectives abound and greatly influenced Arab Muslims' attitudes toward the skin, hair, lips, and other caricatured features of
black Africans. In addition, these descendants of Ham were (again)
sexualized in deviant, excessive terms.[14]

The most conspicuous themes in these later traditions are Ham's
designation as the progenitor of dark-skinned, Negroid, or black peoples and Ham's moral alienation or demise due to his sin, most frequently articulated in tandem with Noah's curse. The continuity borne
with early Judaic and ancient Israelitic invectives, however, is located
in the style of alterity—difference as evil—that inhered to Hamitic
rhetorics. Ham and Ham's descendants, whether Ethiopian or
Egyptian or Phoenician, had always been evil. They were discursively
located in extreme antithesis to the people of God.

The Hamitic Idea in America

The early roots of Hamitic ideas are essential for understanding the
rhetorics generated in the nineteenth century. Most immediately relevant to this study, however, is the American cultivation of ideas about
Ham as both a symbolic and personal figure. Most conspicuous is the
fact that the African slave trade and slavery in the Americas constitute
the critical context without which the most significant Hamitic
rhetorics or ideas cannot be parsed. It was, after all, the holocaust of
slavery that forced significant numbers of Africans into the United
States. Without this trafficking and enslavement of millions of
Africans, there would be no discussion of Ham's children in America.

What is less patent, on the other hand, is a point I have suggested in
the introduction: Hamitic rhetorics and ideas *ultimately* regarded not
the problem of slavery but that of *existence*. First and foremost,
insofar as Americans were concerned, Ham was the ancestor of the
Negro race. Discussing the Hamitic presumed as problem the Negro's
existence and origin and the contradiction of being Negro in America.

In fact, by the nineteenth century, the Noahic account of origins was a standard explanation for the genesis of the three major races—the white, the yellow, and the black races. In 1856, less than a decade before American slavery was ended by decree, an anonymous essay in the *Southern Literary Messenger* observed that America's distinctiveness lay in the fact that "for the first time, the white man, the black man, and the red man stood face to face, and gazed upon each other in the New World."[15]

One begins to comprehend the essentials of the American spin on the Hamitic idea when examining the convergence of race and religious narrative. American developments of the Hamitic theme purported (1) that Ham's posterity enjoyed significant cultural and technological sophistication in the ancient world; (2) that Ham was morally blighted because of his sin against Noah, which produced consequences in American Negroes, his posterity; and (3) that the race of Hamites, as heathens, had not been among the people of God—their entry among this people is concurrent with the American experience. One can surmise some major aspects of these developments through a study of Hamitic ideas concerning Negro origins on the one hand and Negro slavery on the other.

The meaning of race and Hamitic ancestry was a national, and not merely Southern, concern. Although developments in scientific theories of origin were beginning to displace conventions of biblical recourse by the 1850s, Hamitic rhetorics continued to abound and would for quite some time thereafter. A few representatives indicate the ubiquity of Hamitic narrative logic: theologians such as Philip Schaff, a professor of theology at Union Theological Seminary in the North; Edward Wilmot Blyden, perhaps the most brilliant nineteenth-century scholar of Christianity, classical history, and Islam; Joseph Hayne, a South Carolina A.M.E. pastor; Samuel Harris, a professor of systematic theology at Yale Divinity School; Benjamin Tanner, a bishop in the A.M.E. Church; Thomas Stringfellow, a Baptist clergy of Virginia; and even scientists such as Samuel Cartwright, who practiced medicine in Louisiana. All urgently sought to persuade the nation of the Negro race's role and proper status based upon biblical narrations of Ham. These individuals and their colleagues proliferated rhetorics that definitively effected the semiotic "Americanization of Ham" during the latter half of the nineteenth century.

If one were in want of most simply classifying these debates into two polarized camps, a patent black–white bifurcation might suffice. Indeed, black interlocutors consistently plied Hamitic rhetorics to the end of advancing the status of American Negroes, while whites, with some important exceptions, interpreted the Hamitic idea in order to demean Negroes. But simplifications afford economy at the cost of subtlety. And one important subtlety that emerged was the complex of Negroes' attitudes/ambivalence toward the mythic person of Ham, and ancient Hamites. (The implications of this ambivalence will be further developed in the next chapter.)

In 1867, an ethnologist by the name of Buckner Payne published his second edition of *The Negro, A Descendant of Ham?* under the pen name "Ariel." Ariel set out to prove that Negroes were neither descendants of Ham nor human beings—they were beasts. The responses to Ariel's book indicate the temperament of many white intellectuals whose pronouncements on the origin and status of the Negro race burned with both a religious passion and social, philosophical pragmatism. It was certainly to the advantage of white Americans to prevent blacks from attaining significant advances in civil and human rights. The most effective means of preventing this was to sustain a public definition of whiteness contingent upon Negro inferiority. This inferiority was not superficial but ontological, cultural, and biological. As Audrey Smedley has emphasized, the idea of race has never been about difference among equals; it is pristinely hierarchical.[16] And it has encoded multiple dimensions of existence. White intellectuals and religionists encoded Negro identity and existence in extremist, disparaging terms.

Yet, one should be careful to avoid denying the authentic function of Hamitic rhetorics as part of a worldview. Racist interlocutors of the Hamitic idea were not winking an eye while mouthing "incredible" claims out of pragmatic motivations. To be white in the late nineteenth century was to be a descendant of Japheth, an Anglo-Saxon, a superior race vis-à-vis the inferior Negroes, *as a matter of course*. To think otherwise was to hold a minoritarian view, and to arrive at a different viewpoint required exceptional circumstances. Even the most celebrated and sophisticated opponents of slavery and injustice towards Negroes, such as William Lloyd Garrison and Abraham Lincoln, assumed the "fact" that Negroes were an inferior race unfit for equality.

Ariel's work is significant for this very reason because he built his entire argument in opposition to widely held ideas about Ham. His rhetorical strategies elucidated not only the major viewpoints he opposed but also the terms of debate. It is immediately apparent, for instance, that ethnological origins, the blackness of Ham, and the advanced cultural and architectural feats of ancient Egypt were central issues in Hamitic discourse. Ariel introduced his pamphlet by stating that it was not about slavery but instead concerned "ethnological and Biblical" arguments. Race was contingent upon ideas of origin and humanity, ultimate categories that Ariel recognized to be more fundamental than the issue of slavery. The most common language for discussing such was derived from biblical narrative. Ariel lamented the fact that Ham was widely presumed to be the primal Negro. And there is no hint of exaggeration when he suggested that all "learned men of the past and present age, the clergy and others" assumed Ham's status as the primal Negro. For this reason, he built a searing, bulleted argument that began by denying the Hamitic descent of Negroes.

Ariel's views of Hamitic descent distinguished him from almost every other interlocutor and ran counter to deeply entrenched ideas about Ham's racial or ethnic identity. He emphatically asserted that Ham and his descendants "were at [the time of the flood], and after the flood, and continue to be, *to this day*, of the white race," a race whose features he repeatedly summarizes as including "long, straight hair, high foreheads, high noses and thin lips."[17]

To support his claim, Ariel recapitulated the narratives of settlement and the generations of Canaan and Mizraim, two sons of Ham, since like produces like (10–12). He claimed that "millions" of exhumed mummies from Egypt (Mizraim), including one that he himself had handled, had straight hair and high foreheads. Ariel, in fact, suggested that God had actually instituted embalming among the Egyptians by revealing to them secrets of the art, in order to prove to nineteenth-century skeptics that Egyptians, as Hamites, were white and not of the black or Negro race (16–18).

Ariel countered the idea that the naming and cursing of Ham turned Ham into a Negro. He pointed out that Noah's curse was against Canaan, not Ham, and that other curses in the Bible never produced Negroid features, so why would this one? And he added, "The meaning of Ham's name in Hebrew is not primarily 'black' but 'sunburnt' " (8).

Next, he proceeded to show that Ham could not possibly have been a Negro as a member of Noah's family. He indicated, "Noah was perfect in his genealogy," "correcting" the KJV translation of "generations." This he took to mean that Noah was of white, unmixed descent. Since Ariel and his contemporaries unanimously held that the first human beings were white, Negroes could not possibly have come from Adam and Eve. Everyone in the world, he believed, was and had always been white except Negroes, who never descended from Adam and Eve.

Ariel's racial schema, however, differed in one important respect from those of his contemporaries. As he states, "It will be admitted by all, and contradicted by none, that we now have existing on earth, two races of men, the *white* and the *black*" (5). In contrast to the theories of Arturo de Gobineau, for example, Ariel explicitly stated, "The Jews belong to the white race" (9, 13, 15). Although he argued from a position of a two-race schema, most individuals of the nineteenth century believed there were three major races and located European Jews in a third red/yellow race category. But even the majority of these agreed that the Negro was radically different from the other two races.

Ariel continued by proffering that "God had long before determined, that the Japhetic race should govern the world." As for the Negro, on the other hand, "his history is as blank as that of the horse or the beaver."[18] Ariel, on this point, not only problematized the origin of the Negro but also touched upon a popular idea that Negroes had no history worth speaking of. Ariel, like John Van Evrie and others, espoused the view that every cultural, architectural, or technological feat of importance in all of human history was the accomplishment of whites.

Ariel, however, linked this to his belief that the God-given souls of whites inspired them with "a sense of immortality"; their lasting architectural endeavors evidenced this longing for immortality. Not so for the Negro, whose "building is only for the day" (44). Unlike whites, the Negro possessed no soul. The Negro, in fact, was an animal, the noblest beast of creation, but a beast, nevertheless. This was the heart of his argument. Because Negroes, like all other animals, must have been on the ark, and because Noah's all-white family were the only human beings on the ark, then the Negro *must* have been created along with the other beasts in the Garden of Eden. This point was the premium among Ariel's frequently noted "logic of facts."[19]

One peculiarity critical to Ariel's argument was his axiom that Adam named Negroes "man" (without the definite article) and that God, anticipating how Adam would name Negroes, used "man" vis-à-vis "the man" to distinguish Negroes (the beasts) and Adam (and Adam's progeny), respectively. From this point, he identified the worst sin of humanity, that for which God "destroyed every living thing on earth, save what was in the ark . . . the crime of miscegenating of *Adam's race with the negroes* [sic]." Just as the righteousness of the patriarchs, amidst their revelry and drunkenness, was their "perfect genealogy"[20] (i.e., race purity), so also the mission of the white race must be to keep pure their genealogy from the taint of (animal) Negro blood. Otherwise God would destroy the world again.

In further argument against the human status of Negroes, Ariel referenced the Pentateuch (Leviticus 21:18) to argue that Yahweh prohibited all persons with a "flat nose" from approaching the altar. This, Ariel expounded, proved that Negroes, characterized as having a flat nose, were not even allowed to worship God.[21]

Although Ariel's pamphlet comprised frequently pedantic logic, specious claims, and problematic renderings of scripture, many implications of his thesis were quite mainstream—Negroes were immensely different from the white race and were inherently and incorrigibly inferior. It is significant that both blacks and whites disagreed with Ariel on other points, however. Even his most racist contemporaries usually were not willing to concede that Negroes were other than Ham's descendants. To do so would undermine the idea of monogenesis—the belief that all human beings were commonly descended from a single pair of humans, namely Adam and Eve. Ariel's thesis demanded two separate creations. Besides, the idea that Ham was the primal Negro was too deeply imbedded in American racial thought to be undone by a single pamphlet of over-assuming argumentation. Ariel's critics did, however, agree with him that the Negro was inferior to the white race and posed a threat to white racial and cultural purity.

There is one other theme of major importance that becomes evident from Ariel's pamphlet. He devoted his concluding pages to a virtual genealogy of slaveholders, dating from biblical times to his own era, whom God had used to accomplish divine fiat. The list featured prominent figures from Abraham to George Washington—even Jesus is included because he was a member of "a white slaveholding nation." Ariel reasoned, "As a matter of history . . . God *always* selects *slaveholders*, or from a *slaveholding* nation, the medium through which he confers his blessings on mankind."[22]

Those who wished to counter arguments for Negro equality could rightly reference acts of divine terror or ill will upon the heathens and slaves as represented in the Bible. The book was an ambivalent one, at best, and blacks and their white allies just as frequently made recourse to such for their own agendas. But even the sharpest advocates of Negro rights could not conclusively disprove racist hermeneutics because the Bible itself was so problem-laden.

The fact that biblical narratives did indicate Yahweh's disfavor upon the Canaanites—Yahweh commanded both their enslavement and genocide, for instance—meant that American Negroes met incredible enigmas of narrative knowledge, which heightened anxiety over Christian identity and its underside—the specter of the heathen.

Whereas Ariel referred to aspects of Hamitic discourse in the wake of slavery's abolishment (i.e., post–Civil War), some of the most rigorous apologetics for Hamitic/Negro inferiority were antebellum. Slavery, of course, occasioned intensifying efforts on the part of whites to interpret the "curse of Ham" (or the curse of Canaan, to be precise) in order to justify slavery as the will of God. The eighteenth century, compared to the nineteenth, witnessed relatively few theological efforts to sustain this view. With the growth of the abolitionist movement in the 1800s, however, proponents of slavery felt tremendous pressure to defend slavery and to redeem its status as a justifiable institution under threat. Numerous slavery apologists rose to meet the challenge of the abolitionist movement. And the most conspicuous religious "truth" relevant to this controversy was the so-called curse of Ham.

There are two major reasons why this biblical narrative was so effective. First, it was common "knowledge" that Ham was the "original Negro" or Negro progenitor. Second, the story was *biblical*. And multiple American publics regarded the Bible as a divinely revealed source of unquestionable truth. One will note, for example, that virtually no one questioned the idea that Noah had actually cursed Ham's posterity. Perhaps the most radical interpretation was posed by the Negro historian George Williams, who went so far as to divorce this curse from the sanction of God; yet, Williams did this to avoid having to counter the prerogatives of the deity who can do no wrong.

The curse, nevertheless, was "real." And even Williams conceded that God indeed punished the Canaanites as enemies of the deity because they were heathens and not the people of God. The American debate ensued over whether or not the curse applied to Negroes in slavery in the United States. Under this view, Negroes were in America in order to fulfill a divine plan to cultivate the (white) American Israel by performing the manual labor necessary for the nation's progress and success.

One of the most influential figures in the North was Philip Schaff (1819–93), a theologian of the Reformed tradition. Schaff served as Professor of Church History and Biblical Literature at the Seminary of the Reformed Church in Mercersburg, Pennsylvania (eventually to become Lancaster Theological Seminary), from 1844 until 1865.[23] He and other faculty such as John Williamson Nevin and Friederich Augustus Rauch were most responsible for the "Mercersburg

Theology" prominent during the era.[24] Schaff later taught at the Union Theological Seminary in New York City, where he served as Professor of Church History. He influenced American Christians to focus on Christianity's historic traditions while emphasizing the challenges of ecumenism for the faith.

Although Schaff emigrated from Switzerland to the United States, he was well attuned to the issues and circumstances that defined the American temperament. And as a public intellectual, he frequently addressed such in his sermons and writings. When the United States teetered on the verge of a civil war over slavery, Schaff spoke out on the issue in order to set forth a biblical perspective on race and slavery in America. Due to repeated requests, Schaff published one of his most pertinent sermons on the issue, *Slavery and the Bible*, in 1861. The tract, popularly received among laity and endorsed by his colleagues, is an important index of public sentiment; it also demonstrates the rhetorical strategies that characterized Hamitic rhetorics among white interlocutors.[25]

Schaff attempted to interpret biblical references to slavery by narrating a virtual genealogy of slavery through the Christian canon. He mainly argued that Christianity and the Bible were neither proslavery nor antislavery but rose above such simplistic categories by introducing spiritual freedom and moral transformation through the gospel of Jesus Christ. Because Christianity is eternal and spiritual—not temporal—it leaves the social and legal matters of slavery to society and instead rids society of evils and reforms it so that slavery might do best what it should—civilize the inferior, heathen African race.

Schaff situated his discussion by examining the Noahic curse and Hamitic peoples. His logic is especially instructive because it shows how contemporary American Negroes were linked both to Noah's curse and to Ham. Schaff first quoted Genesis 9:25–57, which narrates the curse upon Canaan and the blessing upon Shem and Japheth; he identified Noah as a "preacher of righteousness," a "far-seeing inspired prophet to the new world after the flood." Noah, Schaff then explained,

> pronounces a curse thrice repeated upon one of his grandsons, and a blessing upon two of his sons, yet with regard not so much to their individual as their representative character, and looking to the future posterity of the three patriarchs of the human family.[26]

This emphasis resounded a major theme in American Hamitic rhetorics, the idea that there are three major races of human beings and that these three have their respective origins in Shem, Ham, and Japheth. Just as popular ideas of race at the time assigned particular dispositions to each race, so also did Schaff identify the representative characteristics of each racial progenitor.

> Ham, the father of Canaan, represents the idolatrous and servile races; Shem, the Israelites who worshipped Jehovah, the only true and living God; Japheth, those gentiles, who by their contact with Shem were brought to a knowledge of the true religion.[27]

It is evident here that the impetus to narrate is always contemporary, as is the signification or symbolism borne by narrative itself. Schaff had already suggested to his audience that Noah was mostly concerned not with these ancient individuals but with their "future posterity"—Jews, white Americans, and Negroes. "Idolatrous" and "servile" respectively signified the heathenism and slavery repeatedly encoded upon the bodies and identities of American Negroes. To this end, Schaff's sermon both drew from and contributed to popular ideas of Negroes that whites entertained. In other words, this form of representation relied on a racialization of the heathen subject.

He then recapitulated the history of the curse's fulfillment. First, Israelites conquered the Canaanites and enslaved them. Subsequent fulfillment occurred with "the successive dominions of the Persians, Greeks, and Romans, all descendants of Japheth, over the Phenicians [sic] and Carthaginians" (Ham's posterity). Then Japheth spiritually conquered Shem when Japheth's descendants converted to Christianity, whose true consummate revelation the Jews (Shem) rejected.[28]

There is, of course, the problem of the curse itself, because Ham was not the recipient of the curse; only one of his sons, Canaan, received the curse. American Negroes, furthermore, were linked to Ham by Ham's son Cush, not by Canaan. Many whites smoothed or glossed over this technicality. But Schaff tackled it head-on. Schaff first indicated, "The curse and the blessing of Noah extend still further and justify a wider historical application" than that of the ancient world. Although Noah directed his curse "of involuntary servitude" specifically toward Canaan, Schaff informed his audience that the curse had affected "nearly the whole of the posterity of Ham, or those unfortunate African races" who have suffered beneath "the rule of the Romans, the Saracens, the Turks, and even those Christian nations who engaged in the iniquity of the African slave trade."

Whether we connect it with this ancient prophecy or not, it is simply a fact which no one can deny, that the Negro to this day is a servant of servants in our own midst. Japheth, on the other hand, the progenitor of half the human race, who possesses a part of Asia and the whole of Europe, is still extending his posterity and territory in the westward course of empire, and holds Ham in bondage far away from his original home and final destination.[29]

Schaff conceded that only Canaan was the object of the curse. But it was sufficient to indicate what was already patent to Americans accustomed to experiencing the world through common meanings: Millions of Africans in America were the literal chattel of the white race—Japheth's posterity. It was already clear that Negroes—the "African race," were Ham's posterity. Through this rhetorical maneuver, then, Schaff confirmed what his audience already assumed. The children of Ham in America were living examples of Noah's curse upon Canaan. The semiotic association was sealed. Notice how Schaff conflated time and space through reading modern racial identities into the narrative. "Japheth . . . holds Ham in bondage" in America.

Schaff's audience knew this bondage of the Hamites was happening as he spoke. And the nation was about to go to war because of it. As he would later remind his audience, despite the fact that the slave *trade* was a great "iniquity," slavery itself was beneficent and absolutely necessary. As "a training school for the universal religion of the Gospel," slavery itself was controlled by God and would work to benefit Ham's posterity in America. It had, in fact, already raised the Negro "from the lowest state of heathenism and barbarism to some degree of Christian civilization." And, if allowed to run its course, it would effect Ham's children's "final deliverance from the ancient curse of bondage."[30]

On this point, Schaff, quoting Psalm 68:31, extolled the time when "Ethiopia shall stretch out her hands unto God." This text was commonly referenced by American clergy and laity alike who understood it as a prediction that the "Ethiopic race,"—that is, the Hamites or Negroes—would convert to Christianity and spread the Christian gospel throughout the continent of Africa.[31]

Patent throughout his discussion was Schaff's conviction that Negroes (the "African race") were inferior to whites and that "God alone . . . will settle the Negro question."[32] Despite his optimism for avoiding human intervention into the slavery question, however, the first shots of the Civil War were fired only a few months after Schaff published his tract.

Clearly, the Hamitic idea was not a provincial Southernism; it was germane to discourses on Negroes and slavery throughout America and the world. Schaff illustrates this succinctly. Yet, it is helpful to understand the subtleties of Northern views of the Hamitic race vis-à-vis those of Southerners.

Samuel Cartwright and Thornton Stringfellow were among two of the more prominent Southern personalities who contributed to white national discourse on "the Negro problem." Cartwright was a Louisiana physician who frequently treated Negro patients. As one of the state's most prominent doctors, Cartwright was selected to present his research on Negroes to the Louisiana State Medical Convention sometime during the 1850s. Thomas Stringfellow, on the other hand, was a Baptist minister of Virginia. Although they came from different backgrounds—scientific and religious, respectively—their views of race were largely concurrent.

Cartwright published several essays detailing the medical peculiarities of the Negro race. He referenced his first-hand observations of Negroes, in addition to studies in anatomy and craniometry; his writing essentially encoded Negro inferiority through the categories of medical knowledge. His "Slavery in the Light of Ethnology," published in 1860, clarified his previously published "findings" and conclusions on the Negro race. For instance, he wrote, "[Negroes'] digestive powers, like children, are strong, and their secretions and excretions copious, excepting the urine, which is rather scant." Or, again, "the Melanic [Negro] race have a much stronger propensity to indulge in the intemperate use of ardent spirits than white people."[33]

Cartwright similarly explained that Negroes, whose lung capacity was at least "20 percent less" than whites', consumed less oxygen and were thus less active and less productive. This contention constituted throughout the essay a sustained example of Negro inferiority. To judge blacks by the same standards as whites in a physical examination, for instance, "would indicate . . . a morbid condition where none existed" because it was the natural condition of blacks to exhibit a lower state of mental and physical fortitude.[34]

Whites, to whom Cartwright referred as "the master race," were more intelligent (their brains received a greater level of oxygen) and characteristically exhibited a greater "strength and activity of the muscular system," "a vivid imagination," and an "indomitable will and love of freedom."[35] On this basis, Cartwright proffered that slavery, far from being detrimental for blacks, was both auspicious and necessary. Citing the Pentateuch as the most authentic portion of scripture, Cartwright emphasized the injunction in Leviticus (25:44–46) that "the heathen" should supply the slave population for Israel.[36] The ethical motivation behind this command was revealed in the fact that "the Canaanitish [sic] race" possessed "a hebetude [sic] of mind and body . . . thus making a mercy and a blessing to Negroes to have persons in authority set over them, to provide for and take care of them."[37]

The American "descendants of Canaan," Cartwright assures his readers, flourished under the Southern conditions of slavery. And it was at the risk of effecting the ill demise of blacks that abolitionist whites argued for black freedom; the American "Canaanite" (Negro) was unable to sustain the exigencies of a free state. This was the genius of American slavery. In contrast to the classical slavery of the Roman Empire, from which manumission required only a legal pronouncement, the enslavement of Negroes was based upon the principle of inferiority; it was preeminently *racial*, and no legal declaration could effect a change in the Negroes' racial inferiority.[38]

Cartwright strongly believed that race—that is, innate, incorrigible difference in biological and mental constitution—was *the irreducible fact* of human existence. As a monogenist, he was careful to distinguish himself from polygenetic explanations of Negro origins. He described the Negro as a "prognathous species"[39] of humankind and wove a fantastic synthesis between scientific analysis and biblical narrative symbolism in order to discuss the Negro race in this fashion. But Cartwright immediately clarified that he did not "call in question the black man's humanity or the unity of the human races as a *genus*." To do so would undermine the basis of monogenesis. Rather, among the three races of humankind—the Negro, the oval-headed Caucasian, and the pyramidal-headed Asian—the Negro race most radically differed from the other two.

> The typical Negroes of adult age . . . are proved to belong to a different species from the man of Europe or Asia, because the head and face are anatomically constructed more after the fashion of . . . the brute creation [beasts] than the Caucasian and Mongolian species of mankind.[40]

Cartwright wrote that both "young monkeys and young negroes," while starting out with round faces, become prognathous with maturity. And although he conceded that "young monkeys and young Negroes are superior to white children of the same age," he demonstrated that ultimately the Negro race, with less cranial capacity and a deficient system of oxygenation, proved nothing more than the mental and physical inferior of both the "Anglo-Saxon" and "Mongolian" races.[41]

The prognathous American Negroes, Cartwright revealed, are variously named throughout history "as Canaanites, Cushites, Ethiopians, black men or negroes."[42] They were descendants of Ham. The ethnological peculiarities of the Hamitic race, furthermore, were recapitulated in the biblical account of racial origins. Just as the Negro walks with bent knees (like the apes), so also

> the verb, from which [the Negroes'] name is derived, points out this flexed position of the knees, and . . . clearly expresses the servile type of his mind. Ham, the father of Canaan, when translated into plain English, reads that a black man was the father of the slave or knee-bending species of mankind.[43]

The black color of the Hamitic race, Cartwright postulated, is not merely superficial but extends "down to the bones themselves." If Canaan's mother was a pure Cushite, he continued, she might have been as black inside as outside. He articulated a popular American idea of the origin of Negroes' skin color (contra Ariel), when he suggested that this blackness, like the mark of Cain, was an intervention from God to prevent Negroes "from being slain."[44]

He admonished those who, in the name of advocating Negro uplift, mistakenly believed the human genus to comprise only one species, for "the Bible . . . clearly indicates" there were three. Cartwright, like Schaff, argued that not only was slavery the natural condition of the Hamitic race but slavery was also *essential* to civilizing the Negro.[45] Those who said otherwise were guilty of not knowing the scriptures, which clearly set forth the proper status of that peculiar species, Ham's children in America.

Thornton Stringfellow resented the fact that abolitionists appealed to scripture in order to attack the institution of slavery. Stringfellow believed that such appeals either reflected an ignorance of scripture or were simply disingenuous. It was clear to him that God had decreed slavery. By providing humanity with the biblical record, God had sufficiently revealed the divine moral character so that Americans were without excuse for not knowing the appropriate status of the "Canaanites" or "Africans" among them. Stringfellow, like Phillip Schaff, was quick to recognize that slavery was germane to the social territory of the ancient world and was an assumed reality in biblical tradition. In fact, one needed only to read the history of God's auspicious dealings with Abraham, a slaveholder, and with the Israelites, a slaveholding nation, in order to surmise that slavery was anything but contrary to the divine scheme of things. God effected the divine plan through individual slaveholders and slaveholding nations.

In one of Stringfellow's influential essays, "Slavery in the Light of Divine Revelation," he discussed the Old Testament writings governing property ownership. Slaves, of course, were frequently indicated in property lists. Stringfellow, furthermore, emphasized the hereditary nature of biblical slavery in order to clarify its similarity to American slavery.[46]

Of further significance was the fact that Jesus did not usher in a new ethics with regard to slavery, according to Stringfellow. He maintained that Jesus had administered specific teachings for the early church to govern slavery. These teachings were evident not from the gospels but from New Testament letters such as Pauline texts and the books of Peter and Timothy. It was here that the apostles criticized those who interpreted Christian freedom to imply manumission. Most importantly, Stringfellow identified abolitionists of his era with those persons who opposed Pauline Christianity, which embraced the status quo and never sought to abolish slavery. For this reason, Stringfellow explained, Paul had explicitly written to Corinth that all should remain in whatever condition they were found upon hearing the gospel. That is why, concerning these abolitionists, Stringfellow could write that

> If Abraham were on earth, [the abolitionists] could not let him, consistently, occupy their pulpits, to tell of the things God has prepared for them that love him. Job himself would be unfit for their communion. Joseph would be placed on a level with pirates. Not a single church planted by the apostles would make a fit home for our abolition brethren, (for [all the churches] had masters and slaves).[47]

Stringfellow addressed another theme important for the "millions of children of Ham's descendants among" Americans, in a fashion similar to that of Schaff and Cartwright. Just as Israelite slavery improved the life of the heathens in ancient times by placing them in proximity to the knowledge of God, so also did American slavery effectively expose heathen Africans to the gospel. "In their bondage here on earth," multitudes of the Hamitic race had been made "freemen of the Lord Jesus Christ." This exposure, he opined, would "lead Ethiopia very soon to stretch out her hands to God."[48]

Common among the rhetorical flourishes of Schaff, Cartwright, and Stringfellow was their assumption that Noahic generation explained definitively the presence of the races. All related the Noahic curse to the situation of American slavery. But more fundamental was the fact of Japhetic, Shemitic, and Hamitic ancestry. The biblical forms and figures *made it possible* to interpret nineteenth-century experiences of race so that identities and history were intelligible and consistent with other social data. These nineteenth-century race texts reveal, in essence, the *performance* of ancient identities by modern selves. To participate in the world of American Christian symbols was to "locate" racial selves in the world of biblical narratives.

The People(ing) of God, American Whiteness, and Racial Heathenism

Ethnology, for this reason, constituted a field of knowledge populated with the elevated identities of legitimate folk and the demeaned identities of problematic people, whose dark bodies and ominous characters were illegitimate. Some things about them were fundamentally wrong. Hamitic themes in America, furthermore, sustained ontological suggestions about their referents. In other words, Hamitic rhetorics definitively characterized the "nature" of the Negro race by elaborating upon biblical knowledge and thereby encoding black existence in menacing terms that clung to the Hamitic (Negro) race despite the fact that black Christians identified as people of God. To be of the Hamitic race was to be incorrigibly stained with illegitimacy; it was to transgress the norms of rectitude by the mere fact of one's existence.

Lewis S. Gordon, a philosopher of existence, has extensively theorized antiblack racial representation as existential violence. Gordon eloquently identifies the meanings borne by the terms applied to peoples of African descent when he explains that "since black means sin, malevolence, inferiority, low, or bottom, the African element signals the road to such a marker of hell."[49] The issue is acutely tied to the conditions of coloniality and antiblackness. And at the heart of this signification is the tenet that "the black" is not human. It was precisely these significations that black Christians responded to by exercising their own recourse to the Hamitic idea.

To represent the Negro or the Hamitic subject as illegitimate went hand-in-hand with defining and elevating white American identity. And biblical figuralism was no less integral to this task than representing the Hamitic. One would be remiss to regard the Bible as *merely* a text or as *only* a source for making "sense" of history, of the times. Americans did not rely upon the Bible for only moral guidance and instruction in religious truths. The Bible represented this and more because *Americans performed the identities of the folk narrated in the biblical "record."* They understood themselves to be the peoples of whom they read. When they read the Bible or, more frequently, told, heard, or recalled Bible stories, they were participating in narrations about themselves, as they imagined it. These social selves, moreover, were preeminently *racial* selves. This point is essential to understanding the symbolic world of American Christianity.

Narrating Whiteness as Divinity

Seldom has white American identity been explored as a theological or religious manifestation. But the history of white American (racial) identity is one that crisscrosses the terrain of *religious* identity. The connection between religious and racial themes in Hamitic discourse compels one to investigate white racial identity and religious identity in order to understand how they are related.

Martin Marty's *Righteous Empire* is a classic study of American chosenness.[50] Marty is especially attentive to the racialized overtones of this theme and employs the term "Anglo Protestantism" to designate the racialized belief in destiny and chosenness that dominated American Christianity. More recent is *Exodus!* by Eddie Glaude.

Glaude has developed a compelling analysis of white identity and the religious rhetoric of chosenness from which the governing ideas of the American nation derived. Glaude examines the idea of chosenness operant during the colonial era and up to the mid-nineteenth century. What distinguished America from England "and all nations," he concludes, "was not language or ethnicity but the idea of chosenness."[51] Despite the popular Enlightenment concept of "the people," the complex of legal, social, political, and economic practices "constituted a parallel image of the nation, one that was (and is) thoroughly racialized." Indeed, Glaude concludes, the eventual turn of events clearly indicated that "white males were the chosen people."[52]

Glaude further suggests that race, specifically white identity, became the "fictive ethnicity"—a term he borrows from Etienne Balibar's model of nationalism—that was necessary for imagining a common peoplehood. The communal sensibilities associated with a religious community were effectively transferred to the state, per Balibar's model. But Glaude departs from Balibar's religion–state dichotomy because religious symbolism, at least in the United States, did not recede into the background. Rather, biblical figuralism—being God's Israel—remained an important operative that sustained white identity as supremacist, as chosen.[53]

Thomas Virgil Peterson, in his study of Southern religion, discusses American ideas about Ham as *myths* operating to sustain a comprehensive Southern worldview of slavery and racial hierarchy. Peterson devotes little attention to black Americans' appropriations of Hamitic identity, although he does recognize that many participated in Hamitic identity claims. And he risks mishandling an analysis of Hamitic rhetorics, American racism, and American whiteness when he treats them as particularly Southern phenomena. They were not Southern; they were American.

His study, nevertheless, provides a very developed, compelling assessment that demonstrates how biblical rhetorics converged with racial identities in the American South as a result of whites appropriating ancient or biblical identities. Most contributive is his conclusion that these appropriations were integral to the total lives of white Southerners—thus his use of the term "worldview" as a comprehensive schema for understanding reality.[54]

One cannot rightly separate the meanings of American race identities from the symbolic world of the Bible. It is one thing, in other words, to regard Hamitic rhetorics and appropriations of biblical narratives as religious fundamentalism essentially (e.g., Forrest Wood). It is quite another to designate such as the maintenance of identity. The latter neither excludes nor denies that fundamentalism attended the discourse. But when one recognizes the task of identity-maintenance as the fundamental function of these rhetorics, one begins to apprehend the ironic similarities and differences among various interlocutors.

European Americans imagined and sustained the social identity of whiteness through biblical appeals by signifying racial identity and configuring history in religious or theological terms. Most compelling, Peterson advises, were white Southerners' appeals to the myth of Ham for articulating the proper status of white citizens vis-à-vis Negroes. The arguments of Stringfellow and Cartwright, as discussed above, exemplify the modes of interpreting biblical identities and applying them to white Americans. Just as Cartwright argued for the separation of the races on the basis of Yahweh's peculiar dealings with Israel and the Shemitic and Japhetic races, so also did other Southerners draw upon the significations of peoplehood in the biblical world of knowledge in order to elaborate upon their own peoplehood over and against that of the Negro race.

The other aspect, understanding history in religious terms, meant that the very process of representing the history of the nation—telling what happened—was wed to religious identification. Succinctly, being white meant being destined by God to inherit the American Canaan and to exert dominion as a superior race. Reginald Horsman and Charles Reagan Wilson's studies of American religion are helpful on this score. Horsman's *Race and Manifest Destiny* is a sound study of the development of Anglo-Saxon identity in America.[55] Fundamental to the myth of Anglo-Saxon identity/supremacy was the shared belief that the European races embodied both the supreme form of government (republicanism) and religious, spiritual knowledge (Christianity).

Anglo-Saxon identity was predicated upon the belief that the Germanic tribes invading Rome in the fifth century practiced the highest forms of government, artistic cultivation, and civil liberty. Most importantly, during the Reformation, these Germanic tribes were associated with the Protestant Christian ethos and were narratively depicted as the true saints who endured persecution at the hand of the "Romanizers." John Foxe's *Book of the Martyrs* (*Acts and Monuments*) was the preeminent narrative recapitulation of this history. English Protestants, in this context, developed an especially sharp penchant for imagining themselves as the chosen people of God.[56]

Under the influence of rapidly emerging scientific racialism, European and American intellectuals began to merge the ideals of Anglo-Saxon racial supremacy and Christian supremacy. Horsman identifies the mid-nineteenth century as a critical point in Anglo-Saxon identity rhetorics. White Americans, he suggests, "had long believed they were a chosen people, but by the mid-nineteenth century they also believed that they were a chosen people with an impeccable ancestry."[57] American ideas of being a Christian nation, in Horsman's assessment, declined progressively from this point.

It would seem, however, that the Christian myth of election and divine identity was already problem-ridden because it necessarily constructed an illegitimate other. The "other" as Native American or as Negro was frequently victimized by historical forces of identity conquest and physical domination. In the early 1700s, Jonathan Edwards could interpret America as a Canaan of spiritual darkness, of heathenism. Just as God had placed Israel amidst the scattered Canaanite nations so that Israel might be a light unto the latter, so also would European Americans be a Christian light to the native heathens of the New World.

Edwards imagined, as did most of his white contemporaries, that Native Americans were worshiping the Satan known in Christian tradition. Their heathenism was, in effect, the very demonstration of Satan's evil empire, established as far away as possible from Palestine to prevent Native Americans from hearing the Christian gospel. Even more unfortunate than Native Americans, in Edwards' view, was the Negro race, who maintained a level of existence barely, if at all, above that of animals. So distant were they from the knowledge of God that their entry into Christendom would signal the coming of Christ and his consummate victory over spiritual darkness.[58]

Although Edwards spoke of the Christianization of Negroes and Indians in positive terms, he was also very clear that divine peoplehood was the most important stake. The Christian Church was at war against heathenism, and the suffering Christ of whom Edwards spoke so passionately quickly became the conquering Christ whose prerogative was to destroy the domain of heathenism. His understanding of this domination was preeminently racialized.

The point here is that Edwards' ideas of Christian supremacy and non-Christian alterity were characteristic, not anomalous, among white American religionists and necessarily devalued nonwhites for the simple reason that Europeans' encounter with nonwhites occurred through colonization. In this colonial context, the Christian folk were Europeans. Nonwhites who were Christians were the exceptions who proved the rule. The conversion of nonwhites spurred further interest in missionary conquests, yet the very scope of white Christian missionary plans depended upon a peopling of God that associated Christian existence with European identity.

It should become evident, then, that peoplehood was performed through both religious appeals and racial appeals (whether explained biologically or environmentally). In religious terms, both black and white publicists wanted to identify with the deity who rescued Noah; to affiliate with this deity was to affiliate with *das Volk*. This is the people[ing] of God. Second, white American interlocutors—whether Northern or Southern, whether scientists or clergy, whether well tempered liberals or "fundamentalist extremists"—all made consistent, unerring recourse to white identity. Third, white identity, by the nineteenth century, had become inextricably bound to divine identity. This was the Euro-American Israel.

Here lay the product of encoding white bodies, white selves vis-à-vis "other" peoples. The means of this encoding, the medium of this race knowledge, was the world of biblical symbols . . . of narrative meanings. To be a member of the legitimate race or folk meant being white and/or divinely affiliated. And to the end of preserving or conserving this identity, apologists from all sides rose not essentially as religious liberals or conservatives or fanatics, but fundamentally as *members of the race*, paying homage to race membership.

This page intentionally left blank

3

Ham, History, and the Problem of Illegitimacy

Introduction

One should bear in mind that American ideas about history developed under the influence of both biblical conceptions of history (i.e., *God had destined*) and European constructions of *racial* achievements (i.e., *the accomplishments of the races*). The idea that *God had destined the accomplishments of the races* is, in essence, what I have sought to communicate by suggesting, at the opening of this study, that to be American was to be destined by God. The idea was certainly not essentially American, but America, since the beginnings of colonization, *was* essentially imagined through this idea. Religious and racial reality in America could never be separated from the anxieties that attended the maintenance of racial histories.

These ideas of racial histories, more importantly, were biblical ideas, largely because race itself had been viewed through the lens of biblical narrative (e.g., Noahic ancestry). Such a racialized view of history, of the times ancient and modern, conditioned the thinking of black and white Americans. And it was the context for efforts toward uplifting the race. In American racial-religious terms, the problem of the Negro race's history inevitably comprised Hamitic enigmas because the legacy of Ham and Hamitic ancestry was the essential basis for explaining or describing the literal existence and history of Negroes.

This third chapter concerns the problem of reading history, particularly Negro history, given the prevailing dominant influence of biblical narrative. A preoccupation with biblical symbols and narratives characterized American religion. When Americans performed Israelitic identities, they were manifesting this preoccupation, which virtually demanded that folk find (read) themselves in(to) the story of the people of God, the Israelitic metanarrative examined earlier. This aspect of American religion created a two-fold problem. First was the dilemma of finding one's presence in history *qua* racialized history—for American Negroes, this meant imagining or discerning a history of the *Negro race* that stretched back into antiquity. Second was the conundrum of locating the Negro in the story of the people of God. These two problems converged, furthermore, because biblical narrative was the basis for conceptualizing antiquity.

For Negroes, the only way into this narrative was through Ham. Without Ham, there was no ancient/biblical history of the Negro race because there were no other Negroes in antiquity besides Ham's descendants. To put it differently, Ham was the portal of entry into a world in which Negroes were historical folk, able to lay claim to antiquity and having been attested in the sacred record of Christian scriptures.

The obvious difficulty, however, was that Ham represented the antithesis of being people of God. Claiming Hamitic identity meant accepting the significations of deviance and sin that were encoded upon Ham and Ham's descendants. It also meant constructing a Negro past—that is, racialized history—where there was previously none—Africans were not "Africans" or "Negroes" before the emergence of whiteness and colonization. Herein lay the crisis of history and legitimacy confronting Ham's children in America.

The "fact" of Hamitic descent, moreover, was at once a religious idea and a racial construction. Because Hamitic identity was based on the denigration of Ham, it created for blacks a fundamental problem of illegitimacy. Negro existence was one that had to be explained or accounted for because some things about it were fundamentally problematic. The conundrum of race, in other words, was largely viewed as the problem of explaining the existence of nonwhite peoples. And Negroes were regarded as the most extreme antithesis of whites. How did they come about? And why were they not Christians?

Race Histories and Historical Consciousness

Race Uplift

The period following slavery's abolishment is a prime context for understanding Hamitic rhetorics of identity and history. When the Emancipation Proclamation declared over three million of the South's slaves free in 1863, Americans felt a new era had burst upon the nation. Responses were racially divided. For whites, the Negro question more generally became the Negro *problem*. Because of burgeoning efforts to uplift the race, it is difficult to overemphasize the impact of Emancipation and Reconstruction.[1] Newly freed blacks understood events as an exercise of divine fiat. The freeing of black slaves was interpreted with reference to the Exodus story of liberation and thus became a fulfillment or replay of biblical drama. Most felt that God had at last vindicated the wrongful enslavement of blacks and had effected their freedom. Even blacks in the North and elsewhere who were not slaves were overwhelmed by the *Zeitgeist* and believed that, at long last, the time had arrived for members of the race to achieve or claim their rightful place on the stage of human history.

White backlash, white terrorism, Jim Crowism, and the legal codification of racial inequality would eventually undermine optimism over black freedom. Nevertheless, the *de juris* dismantling of American slavery launched a lasting shift in worldview and tempered the historical consciousness of blacks. A new day had dawned; times had taken a turn, and the Negro race was experiencing an era of novelty. This perception of a new era continued unabated despite the post-Emancipation nadir, and it was manifested through strategies for race uplift.

Negro Histories and Ethnology

American Negroes in the nineteenth century generated significant monographs and numerous essays in an effort to narrate a history of the race.[2] Most Americans, including many Negroes themselves, found it difficult to believe that Negroes had any pre-American history worth speaking of, aside from running around in the jungles of Africa as naked savages. Negroes, in these terms, were perceived to be an ahistorical folk. Under these circumstances, the very concept of a Negro history was amusing if not comical.

It was no mean feat, then, when George Williams in 1883 published a *History of the Negro Race in America*. This two-volume work is usually regarded as the first influential history of the Negro race. But even before Williams' lengthy work, individuals such as James W. C. Pennington and Edward Wilmot Blyden had articulated an ancient history of the Negro.[3] Blyden, in 1857, had published *A Vindication of the African Race* and *The Negro in Ancient History* in 1869. These tersely argued pamphlets, particularly the latter, demonstrated what would become the ubiquitous discursive pattern in such ethnological texts. Ethnology was the nineteenth-century science of racial history, making recourse to biblical genealogies (particularly those of Noah's sons), archaeology, classical texts and historians, and synthesizing all of these under the rubric of biblical history. The Bible was the overarching source for organizing meanings about ancient racial identity. And the Hamitic ancestry of the Negro was the unwavering ethnological assumption that governed the discourse of Negro history.

Physician and political activist Martin Robison Delany published *Principia of Ethnology* in 1880. In addition to tracing the peoples of Africa and the American Negro to the primal black man, Ham, Delany discussed at length physiological explanations of skin color and wove together an ethnological explanation of the races with biblical narrative.

Ariel's (Buckner Payne's) *The Negro, What Is His Ethnological Status?: Is He the Progeny of Ham?* represented the most extreme form of denial that Ham was the primal Negro. Blyden and other Negro writers were careful to counter such claims. As evident from previous discussion, few Americans, white or black, denied that Ham was the progenitor of the Negro race. At issue, rather, was the racial identity of ancient Ethiopians and Egyptians, particularly the latter. Many white archaeologists had begun to claim Egyptians as whites, of the Aryan race. And this very point was countered over and over again by Negro ethnologists.

In 1895, for instance, George Brent's "The Ancient Glory of the Hamitic Race" joined a growing number of essays Negroes had authored in order to counter disparaging antiblack stereotypes by emphasizing the cultural achievements and technological prowess of Ethiopia and Egypt in antiquity. Brent, like other authors, sought to instill race pride in lieu of the humiliation and shame that plagued Negro existence.

Another minister, J. L. Dart of Charleston, South Carolina, represented the attending concern of identifying Negroes in the Bible in his essay "Melchizedek a Descendant of Ham," published in 1887. This strategy addressed both the anxieties over locating the Negro race in antiquity and identifying the race in biblical narrations.

A.M.E. minister Joseph Elias Hayne was very prolific in his defense and documentation of the Negro's Hamitic descent. Hayne published *The Negro in Sacred History: Or, Ham and His Immediate Descendants* in 1887. This four-volume work traced the genealogies, settlements, and civilizations associated with each of Ham's sons in biblical narrative. Hayne, like Blyden and Williams, organized arguments from archaeological and historical scholarship in order to sustain his discussion of the biblical references to Ham. He followed this work with *The Black Man: Or, the Natural History of the Hametic* [sic] *Race*, published in 1894. *The Black Man* exemplifies Negro attempts to explain physical blackness *qua* problematic, in this respect most closely resembling the work of Martin Delany. Patent in Hayne's work is the fact that both blacks and whites considered whiteness to be normative or taken for granted and blackness as something to be accounted for. In this monograph, Hayne countered negative stereotypes of the Negro by citing craniometric studies and other authoritative medical accounts of Negro features that rendered a more positive view of the race.

Another factor common to these histories was the belief that race, the "natural divisions" of mankind, was the direct result of divine will and intervention. James Theodore Holly, an A.M.E. bishop in Haiti, gave an especially succinct explanation of this in his essay, "The Divine Plan of Human Redemption in its Ethnological Development," published in the *A.M.E. Church Review* in 1884. It was clear to Holly that God had destined the accomplishments of the races and had determined the times of their encounter with true religion (i.e., Christianity). The descendants of Shem had recorded the scriptures; the descendants of Japheth had translated and disseminated holy writ throughout the world. But, although Ham's descendants were the last people to receive the gospel, theirs was the noblest task—they would be the instruments of the millennial messianic reign.

Rufus Perry produced the next major history of the Negro race. *The Cushite, or the Descendants of Ham*, in 1893, was his contribution to the question of Negro origins and history. Despite the fact that several Negro Christians had authored works attesting to the historical existence and influence of the black race, white supremacist claims and the resilient, unabated tide of scientific racism indicated to Perry that yet another major monograph on the history of the Hamitic was needed.

Benjamin Tucker Tanner, the renowned A.M.E. bishop, published *The Negro's Origins and Is the Negro Cursed?* in 1869. Tanner's text directly addressed the two most frequent topics in Hamitic discourse. First was the originary question of the Negro race, which was the most critical, immediate stake in Hamitic discourse. Second was the proslavery argument that relied on the biblical narrative of Noah cursing Ham's descendants, Canaan and his posterity. The latter was often discussed by these authors not only because of slavery, which was increasingly regarded as a moot issue in the wake of Emancipation, but also because the Negro's dark skin was thought to be a result of the Noahic curse.

Many whites had drawn upon Ariel's interpretation of the Noahic curse to suggest that the curse effected the darkening of Canaan's skin.

It was the question of Hamitic descent, however, that Tanner would have to revisit in his 1898 publication, *The Descent of the Negro.* Tanner published this pamphlet well ahead of its scheduled time in order to respond to the three white Methodist Episcopal ministers who had questioned the "fact" that the Negro race had descended from Ham. It is patent, therefore, that even by the end of the 1890s, American Negroes were yet fighting to establish indubitably the "fact" that Ham was the primal Negro and his descendants, particularly the nations of ancient Ethiopia and Egypt, were indeed of the Negro race. Tanner's final effort toward this was yet another publication in 1900, *The Negro in Holy Writ*, which located or identified Negroes as such in biblical narratives.

Perhaps most conspicuous among Hamitic histories is the constant recourse to Psalm 68:31: "Princes shall come out of Egypt; Ethiopia shall soon stretch out her hands unto God" (KJV), which in its Authorized translation was interpreted to mean that the entire Ethiopian race (i.e., Negroes) would be quickly converted to Christianity. A historical–critical study of the psalm indicates that it refers to the Israelite deity subordinating Egypt and Ethiopia—all of Psalm 68 celebrates the idea of divine violence against the powerful nations neighboring Palestine.[4] In the hands of American Christians, however, the text was rendered as a prophecy, anticipating the conversion of the entire Negro (Ethiopian) race to Christianity. If there were such a thing as a consensus text among Christian American Negroes, this was certainly it, quoted repeatedly by any number of African American Christians of the era.

It would take some time before the ethnological debates over the origins and history of the Negro would subside. Pauline Hopkins, an African American novelist, published a *Primer of Facts Pertaining to the Early Greatness of the African Race* in 1905, in which she synthesized the dominant themes of ethnological texts written in the nineteenth century. Several others after Hopkins produced original works that responded to the common problem of locating the Negro race in antiquity and in biblical narrative.[5]

The Hamitic and the Historical

Several particulars become evident when considering Hamitic rhetorics. First of all, blacks and whites generated these rhetorics in response to a crisis of historical awareness. For instance, they were concerned with determining which racial folks were present in antiquity. Second, this stake was grounded in the claim to being among the people of God. One should keep in mind that Euro-Americans imagined themselves to be the historical Israel. In other words, it was the rule and not the exception for Euro-American religionists to identify ancient Israelites as exclusively Caucasian. What at first appears to be a far-fetched imposition of identity easily corrected by a lesson in geography and demography was considered a "matter of fact." This meant that biblical history was circumscribed in white skin. It was generally assumed that the people of God described in biblical narratives were whites. Even Adam and Eve were white. The problem was explaining where blacks came from. The ancestry of Ham, as we have seen, was the source for explaining this. Ham was the primal Negro, the original black man.

Hamitic Claims and Rhetorical Strategies

Close analysis of some major Hamitic histories of the race reveal fundamental strategies and dilemmas particular to Hamitic rhetorics. The work of the early influential Negro American historian George W. Williams is especially helpful for understanding the phenomenological problems of history bound to Hamitic identity. Williams was born in Pennsylvania in 1849. He served in the Union Army as a teenager (he lied about his age) and went on to enrol at Howard University, although he did not graduate. After completing a theological degree at Newton Theological Institute in Massachusetts, Williams began to practice law, first in New England, then in Ohio. He also worked in Ohio as a minister, government clerk, and columnist. Williams later entered politics and became Ohio's first Negro legislator. He also was named as U.S. Minister to Haiti, under a lame-duck appointment by President Chester Arthur.[6]

Despite his impressive clerical, legal, and political career, however, Williams remained haunted by the dearth of historical scholarship on the Negro race. In terms of popular thinking, there was no history of the Negro race. And certainly no trained scholar had yet written such a history. While doing research to prepare a speech on Negro achievements for an Independence Day celebration, Williams realized that the race could boast of an abundance of achievements. At that point, he decided to retire from public life and to dedicate himself to preparing a scholarly account of the Negro race's history. He was to spend 7 years carefully researching the history of the race.

Williams' connections, forged during a career that comprised a federal appointment, afforded him access to federal, public, and private archival materials, some of which he purchased himself. The result was a two-volume history of the Negro race that commanded strong reviews from black and white critics, quickly sending the work into a second edition. Williams' text, eventually entitled *History of the Negro Race in America, 1619–1880*, actually began with *ancient* history, thousands of years before American slavery, and ended with the post-Reconstruction era.

Rufus Perry's history of the race was written in the 1890s, over twenty years after Williams' landmark history. Yet, Perry was careful to point out that he was presenting a unique work, a history of the Cushite.[7] Perry and Williams certainly shared a concern for the idea of a *race* history. Both of these writers were also concerned about race pride. After decades of antiblack scholarship aimed at proving the supremacy of whites and the stark inferiority of Negroes, Perry insisted that the time had come for Negroes to "write for black men and give them proper or merited rank among the historic peoples of the earth."[8] Williams had earlier announced his own aim in similar terms. Both understood that their works should decidedly dispel the ideas of inferiority generated about Negroes. Because they were showing that Negroes had a history and a glorious one at that, no longer was there reason for whites to boast a false sense of superiority, nor was there reason for blacks to feel that they were essentially a people of inferior cultural and technical accomplishments.

Despite the ancient glory of the race, however, these authors commonly alluded to a cultural *decadence* that constituted the race's contemporary plight. This present condition of the race was due not to innate inferiority, both argued, but to harsh climate, forced displacement, and the institution of slavery. Explaining this decadence vis-à-vis the elevated ancient (Egyptian and Ethiopian) past involved accounting for the stereotypical "Guinea Negro" of West Africa, an essentialist stereotype that Perry felt comprised the most disparaging significations of Negro identity: thick lips, kinky hair, and dark skin. Perry explains, more specifically, that archaeologists and historians were frequently forced "to admit that the ancient Egyptian was sufficiently dark to be called a Cushite or an Ethiopian . . . but still denied that he was a Negro." Such racist scholarship, Perry explains, relied upon defining the American Negro or nineteenth-century African in terms definitively incompatible with ancient Egyptian identity. Whites "select the lowest and blackest type of the lowest tribe on the west coast of Africa," explained Perry, "and ask you to behold the amazing difference in physiognomy between him and the highly cultured Egyptian of antiquity, whose color, hair, and features, they say, were the same as that of the miscegenated Copt."[9]

Perry, to counter those arguments, cited Edward Wilmot Blyden's accounts of native Africans in order to suggest that "thick-lipped" Negroes had always been used as servants in Africa and Asia and did not constitute the ruling, normative class of people throughout Africa.[10] Both celebrated the assimilation of Negroes into mainstream American identity. Perry, for example, cited Crispus Attucks as exemplary of a Negro nature or essence—loyal and patriotic, despite the unrelenting evils afflicted upon blacks by Euro-Americans.[11] And Williams, writing in the wake of the Reconstruction era, was optimistic about the future of the race in America. Given the progress that blacks had made, Williams conjectured, it was only a matter of time before the very prejudice that sustained the bygone institution of slavery would itself become a relic of the past.

Joseph Elias Hayne was arguably the most successful at retrieving a dignified narrative of Hamitic history, despite the negative ideas of sinfulness and heathenism that Ham symbolized. The works of Hayne were voluminous and provided one of the most detailed histories of Ham's descendants. Hayne's most important work was a four-volume study entitled *The Negro in sacred History: Or, Ham and His Immediate Descendants.*[12] The introduction to this work, written by J. Wofford White, described Hayne's scholarship as a timely response to the dangerous possibility that Negroes might amalgamate and assimilate into white American society. White suggested that when different races encounter each other, the "stronger" race kills the weaker, the weaker are absorbed by the stronger, or the weaker emigrate.

White addressed the psychological impact of white historical constructions when he observes, "Even our own [Negro] children are . . . educated to despise themselves . . . and respect whites because all the accomplishments of [humanity] are represented to be the result of that race born white."[13] Historical work such as that by Hayne would produce a different possibility for Negroes, however, because "if it can be proved that the Negro is of noble ancestry," then the race would tackle with zeal and pride "the work of race elevation."[14] The Negro race would remain in America and would do so as a distinct race because of a burgeoning race pride grounded in a sound historical knowledge that their Hamitic ancestors were the arbiters of civilizing, technological, and cultural prowess.

Hayne, indeed, clearly articulated that his goal was to "inspire the Negro race in their march after higher civilization."[15] Hayne expressed his assurance that the work of ethnological research would produce the historical knowledge and perspectives to inspire such motivations among the race, and he outlined interpretive rules for reconstructing the history of Hamites.[16]

Most distinctive was Hayne's unmitigated praise of not only Hamites but also the figure of Ham himself. Hayne argued that Ham was Noah's youngest (pace Blyden, Williams et al.) and *favorite* son because Noah allotted to him the more beautiful lands of Africa.[17] He also found, by identifying Jupiter Ammon as an apotheosized figure of Ham, that the entire ancient world (of the Middle East) reverenced Ham and his descendants.[18] This elevated manner of representing Ham stood in sharp contrast to the more explicitly ambivalent representations by Williams and Perry.

Hayne's Christian sensibilities, to be sure, privileged the status of Israel, the explicit people of God, vis-à-vis the Hamitic races, who were on the underside of biblical narratives. Yet, Hayne's positivistic retrieval of a Hamitic past is epitomized when he smirkingly identifies Cushan-rishathaim of Judges 3:8,10 as the "powerful Black king [who] was the first great oppressor of the Israelites."[19] Hayne does not elaborate upon the theological implications of Hamites oppressing Yahweh's Israel. He emphasizes only the fact that the ruler was Hamitic (black) and powerful enough to dominate Israelites.

Hayne, finally, explicitly combated Ariel's thesis that the Negro race was pre-Adamite; he also issued invectives against the escalating influence of Darwinian evolutionary theory, which concluded that human beings were descended from animals. Hayne felt this was a subtle, pernicious manner of furthering a racist philosophy of the strong versus the weak.

Hayne was very impressed with the Negro past. By following the biblical genealogies and eponymic narratives of settlement, he located and identified a *glorious* past of the Hamitic race. Unlike George Williams, who clearly castigated the Hamites as a fallen, apostate race, Hayne did not name their religious practices as evil or apostate, although as a Christian A.M.E. minister who grounded his entire project in the "truth of Jesus Christ," he would have almost inevitably conclude the same ideas of religious ineptitude.

When Negroes argued for the Hamitic identity of the race, they employed some common strategies. Despite their different approaches, Hamitic histories and texts argued for Negro Americans' Hamitic identity as a necessary fact of existence. They all inscribed the idea that the pre-American Negro race was heathen. They all relied unquestioningly on the great story or metanarrative of Israelitic and Christian historicizing—God has chosen a people "Israel" who were in essence those belonging to Christendom. They drew upon a variety of sources, not merely the Bible but also ancient authors such as Josephus and Herodotus, classical works of Greek authors, and archaeology. The Bible, however, was far and away the most important source because its narrations of history and teleology were the basis for making "sense" of everything else. Biblical narrative was the overarching framework both chronologically and philosophically.

These black writers of Hamitic discourse, like their white counterparts, interpreted racial identities that read ancient Israelites as whites and read first peoples as white; Negroes' existence began with Ham. This did not mean that Negroes were not human, but it did mean that the origin of the Negro race was an enigma that required explanation. This was not the case for the white race. Furthermore, although the Hamitic ancestry of the Negro race linked American Negroes to all other descendants of Ham (e.g., Phoenicians and Babylonians), these writers focused exclusively on Egypt and Ethiopia as paradigmatic Negro civilizations. Also, of course, the United States is clearly the locus of their work. It is noteworthy that their stories began in Africa and the Middle East and ended up in North America because they were basing the narratives of history on the Bible.

Most important is the fact that all of these authors were beleaguered by the awkward task of mining biblical narratives and Judeo-Christian philosophies of history to represent Negroes with dignity despite the fact that these same sources compelled patent inscriptions of illegitimacy upon the bodies, selves, and identities of "the children of Ham." It is intriguing, on the one hand, that these black writers were able to produce surprisingly positive histories of the race, considering they had to redeem vilified, heathenized symbols. On the other hand, the very act of their nineteenth-century narratives of redemption recapitulated the liminality and perduring alterity to which they were responding. In other words, these were Christian authors operating under the imperatives of Christian identity, which obligated them to reinscribe the assumptions of the Christian myth, namely that there was such a thing as the heathen and that the heathen was, in Williams' terms, the very enemy of (Christianity's) God.

Williams' history exemplified a refined, comprehensive attempt to access or (re)construct a racial history, the presumption of which was a matter of course. The assumption of racial history—the accomplishments of the race(s)—is, in other words, so mundane that it goes almost unnoticed even in modern, twenty-first-century narrations of history. To appreciate the complexity of what Williams and all writers of a "people's" history must perform, demands that one bracket the ideas of race and racial history in order to problematize them as phenomenological constructions; one must recognize, for example, that the form of racial history known to Williams had been literally inconceivable a few centuries before his time. Williams, for instance, understood that "a history of the Colored people was required" because it would "give the world more correct ideas of the Colored people, and incite the latter to greater effort in the struggle of citizenship and manhood." Most compelling for him, moreover, was "the single reason that there was no [written] history of the Negro race."[20]

Phenomenology of History and Illegitimacy

The problem of having no history was, of course, produced by the construction of race identity. Until modern race identities were constituted, there was no need for their corresponding racial histories; indeed, there could have been no such thing because the identities that functioned as imperatives and subjectivities for racial histories did not exist. By Williams' time, however, white Americans were well versed in the imaginative task of reading their contemporary white identity back in time so that Adam and Eve were white, Noah was white; Greeks were white; the tribes of medieval "Europe" were white, and so on. They were adept at "locating" themselves in history through literally narrating Anglo-Saxon identity through time, across eras.

American Negroes, on the other hand, were just beginning to narrate the race through reading modern Negro identity into recent and ancient pasts. That Pennington's or Williams' performances were so novel is not easily recognized until one recalls that European and American ideas about race were a relatively new invention, as were racial histories. American Negroes, furthermore, were aware of this enigma and responded to it by an exaggerated seizure of the present (via seizing the past), a present both brimming with optimism and laden with angst.

The point here is that their task was to respond to a social world that was virtually devoid of a discourse representing Negro history. In phenomenological terms, American Negroes had no history; they were an ahistorical folk. It is fundamental to understand that, insofar as the meanings and perceptions constituted reality, it was not merely the case that no one had written the history of Negroes. *There was no history worth speaking of.* To fathom this is to perceive the category of radical absurdity, of existential angst, into which the race had been displaced. For Williams, being a member of the Negro race meant existing as an ahistorical, social self, hence Williams' determination to produce this history.

Among the most compelling assessments of this problem of history as a phenomenological one is Lewis Gordon's discussion of historical representation. Gordon explains Frantz Fanon's responses to Europeans' constitution of a historical social self that was its own center of the historical "gaze." Georg W. F. Hegel was the preeminent exponent of this notion of history—history as *Geist*. Hegel sought to explain comprehensively the historical spirit of all nations and races of the world and began by explaining why Africa was irrelevant to a discussion of history. By his understanding,

> [Africa] has no historical interest of its own, for we find its inhabitants living in barbarism and savagery in a land which has not furnished them with any integral ingredient of culture. . . . It is the land of childhood, removed from the light of self-conscious history and wrapped in the dark mantle of night . . . [21]

With the exception of Northern Africa, which Hegel designated "European Africa" in order to avoid associating civilizationist signifiers (e.g., textual traditions, mathematics, etc.) with Negroes, the very concept of African history was "out of the question" (176). Preparing to move on to those marginally historical people (Asian and Eastern nations) before culminating in the supreme form of historical humanity (Europeans), he remarked,

> We shall therefore leave Africa at this point, and it need not be mentioned again. For it is an unhistorical continent, with no movement or development of its own. And such events as have occurred in it—i.e. in its northern region—belong to the Asiatic and European worlds. Carthage, while it lasted, represented an important phase; but as a Phoenician colony, it belongs to Asia. Egypt will be considered as a stage in the movement of the human spirit from east to west, but it has no part in the spirit of Africa. What we understand as Africa proper is

that unhistorical and undeveloped land which is still enmeshed in the natural spirit, and which had to be mentioned here before we cross the threshold of world history itself.[22]

History, according to Hegel, was moving toward a telos in a dialectical progression. The events of human experience were only authentically understood in this ultimate schema of history. It was clear to Hegel, however, that Africa had no place in the scheme of things.[23]

Gordon contrasts this idea of European "History" (i.e., *Geist*) vis-à-vis "history" in the more colloquial sense of time; "History" or *Geist* is occupied by only whites. This is so because the misanthropy of colonization denied humanity and thus historical agency to Africans. In this sense, Gordon explains, " 'History' as *Geist* is where the globally dominant culture is located." More succinctly, he asks, "How can one have History when one is invisible to History?"[24]

Hegel's articulation of history as ontological and teleological both described and determined European modes of understanding (colloquial) time and events. *Geist* was the definitive happenings of the world—of all that mattered socially, intellectually, and spiritually. *Geist* was upward- and onward-bound. *Geist* was also equal and interchangeable with the constituted European locus or point of experiencing. The further away from this locus one moves, the further away from History-as-*Geist* one recedes. (*Geist*, was, for example, why European explorers could *discover* the "unknown" Americas or the "mysterious" Orient or the "dark continent" of Africa, or any other part of the world inhabited by millions of human beings but not yet settled or mapped or dominated by Europeans).

Gordon's discussion immediately centers the issues of history's constitution, location, and visibility. He recognizes that "History" itself is constituted—brought into existence, encoded, and represented—within the fabric of social reality. This process, furthermore, is neither automatic nor static. It is effected by human beings who wield the power to represent, and this activity of representing is ongoing. *Geist*, succinctly, exists because knowledge of history is associated with those who have the power to produce this knowledge. It then becomes evident, as Gordon suggests, that the site of this power and knowledge is "where the globally dominant culture is located."[25]

One should consider, furthermore, that the locus of History is not delimited by geography. American publics, with whom this study is concerned, had to contend with the weight of European constructions of *Geist* because the location of History was determined by the relationship between power and knowledge. It made no difference that they were outside of Europe, across the Atlantic, in North America. What matters, ultimately, is neither the geography nor the race—nor society—but the *culture* that is associated with this site. It has certainly been the case, however, that the culture occupying the globally dominant locus of power has been European and white. For this reason, the referents most frequently associated with mastery over fields of knowledge have been European or Euro-American.

Any assessment of this idea and force of "History" should heed the rectitude of method enjoined by Michel Foucault, who observed that "power is exercised rather than possessed."[26] Foucault brought this analysis to bear upon the history of punishment and the prison system in France. In *Discipline and Punish*, Foucault described a *knowledge* that becomes a "political technology of the body." This political technology of/over the body invests in a production of meanings; it is a strategy that is borne out in a "network of relations." In departure from the propertied notion of power endemic to the classical Marxist model, Foucault emphasized that this representational power is not "acquired or preserved" by the dominant class but derives from "the overall effects of its strategic positions." It is even "manifested and sometimes extended by" the locus of dominated persons. Foucault recognized, in other words, that the very persons who stand to lose or suffer because of representations of knowledge often themselves deploy such knowledge. For this reason, the overthrow of such power "does not, then, obey the law of all or none."[27]

He also suggested that power is necessarily linked to knowledge because "there is no power relation without the correlative constitution of a field of knowledge, nor any knowledge that does not presuppose and constitute at the same time power relations."[28] Foucault's analysis of the power–knowledge relationship is old and familiar among modern social theorists. I raise it here, however, because Foucault developed this idea through a discussion of the subjugated subject *qua* the "condemned" (prisoner). His analogy derives from the idea of the medieval political economy as the "political body" whose originary form is approximately Christological. The "person of the king" is related to the Crown through iconography, rituals, "ceremonies of submission," and political theory.[29]

The result is a surplus of power that exists on a continuum, at the opposite end of which is the body of the condemned that symbolizes "the lack of power." Just as the surplus power of the king "duplicates his body" in the (inverted, symmetrical) body of the condemned, so also does the condemned, on whose body surplus power is exercised, yield a duplicitous entity, a noncorporeal one, which Foucault calls a "soul."[30]

This "soul" (a term that includes public ideas about the identity) of the condemned person Foucault contrasted to the soul described in Christian theology that is born of sin (or chiefly represented thereby) and threatened with punishment. This soul of the condemned, in contradistinction, exists because of "methods of punishment, supervision and constraint."[31] It is a historical reality and has historical existence, furthermore, because the knowledge-as-technology over the body of the condemned is meted out against "the colonized" (*inter alios*) through *historical* agency.

Lastly, Foucault added, this soul is not merely an illusion substituted for the real person. The real condemned person, instead, is "already the effect of a subjection much more profound than himself [*sic*]." The soul actually brings into existence the condemned (or colonized, constrained subject). This soul, in effect, "is the prison of the body."[32] Criminology and the rise of criminal law introduced studies of the criminal as an ontological essence. The modern consciousness of a "criminal nature" became possible through the exercise of signifying power and performative knowledge in a particular historical context. What emerges, therefore, by virtue of this knowledge–power relation, is a production of meanings that becomes the basis for perceiving, experiencing, and existing. It is the very constitution of reality.

By way of elucidating the history of representing the condemned subject, Foucault actually provided a compelling description of how a field of knowledge encodes or determines the very existence of those who are subjugated by becoming objects of knowledge. The Hamitic, as the immediate correlative of the Foucauldian condemned, is the heathen soul produced by the elaborate meanings of the Christian myth, whose narrative knowledge locates the body of the dark race of Negroes within a prison of illegitimate existence. Foucault's "soul" as an analytic suggests that the heathen is itself what creates the respective referents.

Visibility, the third issue raised by Lewis Gordon's discussion, gives some clue about how this form of subjugation and the political body/economy of representation come to bear upon the problem of history as a phenomenological conundrum. To be "invisible to History" is to be not only ahistorical but also the negation of value.[33] The matrix of meaning, the noetic fount of narrative knowledge in the American religious schema, was the Bible. It should become clear, at this point, that biblical narration profoundly determined religious *and* scientific ideas about human origins and identity. Theophus Smith, responding to Erich Auerbach's study, notes that this comprehensive, totalizing dynamic about biblical history distinguishes it from other figural symbols.[34] Smith suggests that "biblical figuralism" is so "radical and all-encompassing" that "the Bible promises to absorb both cultural and individual histories."[35] Smith seems uninterested in examining the pitfalls of this totalizing dynamic; yet, he is clear that the historical and sense-making potency of the "biblical world" overwhelms and subordinates other histories, forcing them to find a place within the biblical schema, if at all. It noetically removed from the historical world (invisibility) those who could not find their place in biblical history.

One should understand, in other words, that the Bible was not merely a book of symbols and stories to be drawn upon for living in the world. The Bible was the story of the world. It yielded the secrets and the meaning of existence for all that was in the world. With regard to Negro origins, if not from Adam and Eve, then from where else had human beings come? (This was the question that Ariel's critics asked with a dismissive smirk upon reading his "absurd" thesis.)

The only way for American Negroes to avoid being historically invisible was to locate themselves in biblical history. Ham was the portal of entry into this world of historical visibility. The Noahic legend of generation was the code that made intelligible the experience of race identity in America. The rhetorics of Hamitic identity were the vectors in the field of knowledge that located the Negro body on the map of historical existence, among the peoples attested to in antiquity.

To be ancient was no mere luxury of legacy or racial imagining. It was an absolute necessity for racial existence. For Negroes, to identify Ham as the progenitor of the Negro race, as the original black man, literally, was to have existence as a historical referent. It meant being attested to in antiquity. To the extent that historical existence was a human quality, the Bible was the object of recourse for accessing not only divinity (i.e., knowing the divine) but also *humanity*.

These Negro Christian authors, thus, were able to articulate a history that laid claim to Negroes' humanity and that restored sense or meaning to bodies that were otherwise locked in a prison of existential absurdity. If this was so good, why the perduring angst? Why the awkward rhetorical gestures and language of signs that rendered such strained meanings? Why, for instance, would George Williams first identify Negroes with Ham and then write that Ham's descendants were "the very enemies of God"?

Recall Foucault's reminder that this technology of knowledge is not owned but exercised. *Geist*, in other words, as a site of production and power-wielding, might be inhabited by anyone who ascribes to the identity contortions of "culture" associated with the location of *Geist*. The persons authoring Hamitic texts were not only Negroes but also Christians. And the Christian self was the primary beneficiary of biblical narration. In the expressive terms of Smith and Gordon, to "conjure" history as people of God was to "signify" upon the biblical record—employing tropes to produce common meanings by referencing biblical ideas. Negro Christians were empowered, legitimized, and affirmed by occupying a locus within *Geist*, to the degree that this *Geist* was *Heilsgeschichte*—the power narrative of Israelitic election and of Christian historicizing.

Smith examines biblical figuralism and ethnogenesis (per Werner Sollors) in order to theorize biblical typology as a form of conjure. Ethnogenesis, he explains, is "self-inscription" into the world of biblical narrative. It means identifying with biblical folk (usually Israel, although Ethiopia and Hamitic folk were as commonly employed) and thereby writing/inscribing oneself into the "script" of biblical narrative as a referent.[36]

The problem for Negroes, however, was that Ham—*not* Shem nor Japheth and not Israel—was the immediate portal of entry into *Geist* and into the world of biblical narrative. This mode of biblical figuralism was fiercely differentiated from that of Puritans and of other white Christians because it encoded the ancient Negro as heathen. When Negro Christians self-inscribed the race as Hamites in the biblical record, they became "circumscribed" by the "soul" of this heathen, the public meaning of which *demeaned* its referent. To be heathen was to be spiritually backward, an unmitigated embodiment of evil, the incarnation of decadence. The heathen was, indeed, the very enemy of God.

Ham as Racial Heathen

Hamitic rhetorics as conjuration made possible the biblical ethnogenesis of black Christians. It inscribed the antiquity of the Negro in Hamitic terms and symbols. Yes, the Negro race did have an ancient past, certainly one worth speaking of. And yet, this symbolic system, so pregnant with volatile meanings of illegitimacy on the one hand and historical greatness on the other, produced a self-defeating victory at best. Black Christians were people of God. They had joined the ranks of those who worshiped the Israelitic Christian God, the God who had ordained the genocide of Ham's Canaanite descendants. By identifying with this God (divine identity), they were inevitably positioning themselves in opposition to the heathen while simultaneously depending upon the heathen to become visible agents in history.[37]

Peoplehood (as people of God) derived its very existence through identification with that God. This God, in turn, was constituted through the very acts of narration that also created (knowledge of) the heathen. To imag(in)e themselves as historical agents, as historical existents, was necessarily to imprison themselves in vilifying, dehumanizing terms of existence. The only escape from this imprisonment was recourse to divine identity—Christianization of the race. Yet, even this only further underscored the vilifying alterity (otherness) of the Hamitic race.

As a *racial* group, Negroes were heathens. As a racial group, Negroes needed to become Christian. This was the existential burden of Ham's children in America. It was the fate of the condemned soul (per Foucault), of the conjurers (per Smith) who had, in a sense, outconjured themselves. To the extent that Negro Christians were attempting to become visible to history, they were successful, employing the figuralism of biblical typology. But one should not miss the irony of their attempts to achieve legitimacy.

American publics operated within a given economy of signs, a biblical system of narratives and meanings. Shem's and Japheth's American descendants were not faced with the searing inscriptions of alterity, however, that stigmatized Negroes. White Mormons, for instance, did not experience this illegitimacy when imagining their divine identity; in fact, they viewed the Negro race as radically other. Other white Americans were merely gentiles (not the Israelitic Saints of God). But Negroes, Ham's descendants, were marked with the enmity of God and, like Augustine's Hamites, were placed in a *tertium quid* category; they were neither the people of God, nor the gentiles, but children of Ham.[38] Because they were Ham's descendants, they were not merely "gentiles"; they were something savage, something "dark" and wanton, the "blackness" of which—the illegitimacy of which—is most vividly seen in descriptions of the Canaanite or heathen.

When Ham, figuratively speaking, came to America (i.e., when Americans began to draw upon the figure of Ham), something peculiar happened. For the first time, the heathen as a production of meanings was wed to a speciously biological idea of race (or nature) and of history. This synthesis of meanings inscribed volatile signs of illegitimacy onto its referents. It became virtually impossible for Negroes to escape this signification. Racial reality was "riddled" with endless conundrums of existence and meaning, so that it became impossible merely to deconstruct ideas of racial identity or race histories—and to argue for a nonracial, nonethnic human existence.

Race and peoplehood (divine and cultural) were already established as the order of the day. It was a worldview that forced itself upon those who sought to wield it, to deploy it to their advantage. The only alternative for those (of any race) who had entered the world of Christian symbols, mediated through racial reality, was to navigate their way through it as subjugated entities, conquered, constrained, and forced to make sense of their existence amidst the alterity hardwired into the meanings of biblical narratives.

The Americanization of Ham

It was through a myriad of processes and rhetorical strategies that the figure of Ham became so central for American understanding of race, religion, and identity. America, in turn, produced irrevocable changes upon the Hamitic idea. So, what did this mean for Ham's descendants? Ham was, after all, the disobedient son. And it was his descendants whose genocide Israel's deity had commanded and sanctioned in biblical narrative. Whites imagined themselves to be essentially Christian. And because they whitened biblical history, they experienced no conflicts about salvation history. They were "in the story." American Negroes, on the other hand, found themselves hard put to explain the fact that they were without a history of Christian or Israelitic identity. It was through the American experience that they had encountered the Christian (hi)story.

The Americanization of Ham, as one might render it, produced several critical developments in the Hamitic idea. First of all, the Hamitic was unyieldingly wed to the institution of slavery because American slavery was preeminently racial. Its victims were exclusively the folk whose existence was already popularly explained in terms of Hamitic descent.

Second, Ham was decisively understood within a New World context, where America was the New World meeting place of the three great races. Blacks and whites frequently regarded America as the locus where Noahic prophecy would be fulfilled. God would "enlarge" Japheth, putatively by ensuring that whites would succeed "Shemites" and become the bearers of religious truth. And Ham was to have served them both. Repeatedly, interlocutors of the Hamitic idea indicate that the three sons of Noah had reunited in America, remaining true to their appointed roles or status.

Finally, Ham in America occupied a moral-existential *tertium quid*, a space neither Israelitic nor gentilic. In the American imagination, Ham's was a problematic existence, one whose being was marred by blackness—or more appropriately, antiblackness. Like previous proponents of anti-black sentiment, whites generated concepts and meanings that attacked the human worth of black people. Unlike before, however, white Americans based their conception on an American mytheme of Christian historicizing, a complex narration that traced the genealogy of the people of God from ancient Palestine to North America. This narration was used to make sense of American experience.

It is this last development that becomes critical for parsing the association between blackness and the heathen as constructed in the American religious experience. There emerges, in essence, a densely coded figure of Ham who was the semiotic product of both white identity and Christian identity. But this heathen is understood as Negro. Negroes, on the other hand, were obviously Christianized through the American experience. That American Negroes began to think in these terms is patent from the common concern with missions as a strategy of race uplift; by the mid-nineteenth century, one implied the other. American Christian Negroes understood themselves to be positioned to Christianize the entire race. The import of this Christianization movement is taken up in the next chapter.

This page intentionally left blank

4

Becoming the People of God

Introduction

This chapter examines black Americans' ideas about Christianizing the Negro race. No other single concern produced such broad influence over interpretations of racial histories and religious identity. Christianization, in addition to having been a major imperative of Christian identity throughout its history, became a central, urgently regarded strategy for uplifting the race in the wake of Emancipation. Inherent in the value scheme of evangelical Protestant Christianity was the belief that every individual needed to be saved, and this could occur only through noetic assent to specific creeds of the faith. Black missions, as a result, became a principal focus for black American religionists.

Prior to slavery's dissolution, few slavers were willing to allow enslaved blacks to be evangelized on their plantations. They often preferred that slaves take up nonreligious or noninstructive forms of entertainment on Sundays, if at all. At the end of the Civil War, therefore, most of the South's four million slaves stood in "need" of being evangelized. In addition to the South, with its masses of freed persons, Africa also was seen as a mission field ripe for harvest.[1]

Walter Williams has produced one of the most significant studies of this aspect of black American history. In his *Black Americans and the Evangelization of Africa, 1877–1900*, Williams argues that black American missionary developments of the late nineteenth century constituted the major impetus behind Pan-Africanism.[2] Of particular interest is Williams' recognition that black Christians of that era faced a quandary; on the one hand, they wished to speak valiantly of the black race and were drawn to the idea of being African. On the other hand, they were Christians and most frequently spoke of the "savage" African in disparaging terms. At its worst, this disparagement centered on valuations of African religion—Africans were "heathens."

Williams is careful to recognize that these forms of missionary enterprise were ultimately imperialistic and adapted the Manifest Destiny idealizations that sustained white supremacist rhetorics in the same century. That blacks were articulating the rhetorics did not change the fact. Williams identifies two factors that actively delimited the means of identification with Africans—race and culture. American Negroes and Africans were of the same racial identity, which depended upon mere physiognomic similarity—dark skin, kinky hair, and the like. American Negroes, for this reason, identified deeply with their African "sisters and brothers" across the Atlantic.

Yet, as Williams concludes, cultural identity and common interests were more important than race in determining the relationships between American Negroes and Africans.[3] The same black Christians who spoke so heartily of Africa as "the fatherland" deplored native African religious forms and sought to stamp out "idolatrous" African worship. American Negroes who were Christians also believed, as did their white counterparts, that Africa was lost in spiritual darkness and that Africans had become uncivilized and backward because they did not worship the God of Christianity.[4] Black American sentiment toward Africans, therefore, was ambivalent at best.

The most intensive pronouncements of anti-African sentiment by Americans were religious. These rhetorics were ultimate and often unmitigated, assuming that God was on the side of those Christians who were bravely venturing into a cannibalistic world of devil worshippers in order to introduce the essentials of civilization and progress. American Negroes, despite the contradictions of missionary objectives, did little to stop or challenge this imperialistic penetration into Africa.

Most frequently, they agreed to imperialistic ideals and produced a Negro version of Manifest Destiny. Because black Americans had been civilized and had encountered the "truth" of the Christian gospel, they believed they were qualified to liberate their African sisters and brothers from backwardness and spiritual blindness. By this reasoning, once Africans had embraced Christianity, God would end their sojourn of decadence and raise them to the heights of civilization and Christian progress. And although white religionists instigated the ideas of missionary conquest and Christian superiority, the rhetorics of Christianization and spiritual uplift were quickly taken over by Negro Christians themselves.

Ethiopianism

Uplifting the Race

The latter part of the nineteenth century was a pivotal era of growth and visibility for black Christianity. From the decade of the 1860s, there was a marked increase in the number of independent black churches, particularly in the North. Among the recurring themes of African American Christian theology was that of racial uplift, particularly through leading the colored race to Christ. The formal abolition of chattel slavery and concomitant movements for black advancement fueled this mission with a distinctive passion and suggested an era of newness for U.S. blacks. After years of dehumanizing oppression in the United States, black Americans were now in a position to reap the rewards of an ironic forced displacement into an America of supposed "civilization" and democratic freedom.

Ethiopianism was central to this notion of progress and uplift. Ethiopianism comprised a body of jeremiads contingent upon the conception that God, as revealed in the religion of Christianity, had effected through colonization and slavery the Christianization of black people. Persons such as Edward Blyden, Amanda Smith, and Alexander Crummell were among many who articulated the historical experience of black Americans through the language-world of this mythopoeia. Most importantly, this historicized theological vision was "authenticated" by a biblical text read as prophecy: Psalm 68:31, "Princes shall come out of Egypt; Ethiopia shall soon stretch out her hands unto God." If it can be said that there existed a broadly recognized salvation text for African American Christians, this was surely it. Ethiopia was the icon of continental Africans and Diasporan blacks. And God had orchestrated the events of history to ensure that this people would be swept by the revelation of Christianity. Here was an intense destiny encounter between history and theology.[5]

Intricate in its implications, Ethiopianism was in part a response to the dilemma of theodicy created by attempts to explain the genocide, physical brutality, and psychic atrocity wrought by enslavement and antiblack racism. Ethiopianism reincarnated white defenses of slavery as the path of salvation for the "Dark Continent." It signified the black race as a divine instrument whose constituents would demonstrate to a hypocritical world an authentic Christianity. Theodicy, however, does not delimit the concerns of Ethiopianism because it also represented a distinctive mode of existential participation in a broader, very American mytheme of divine destiny. Even before the time of the

Independence War, Americans had performed a self-understanding of being God's new Israel, chosen to be a Christian nation in order to lead the world in progressive civilization and moral example. Hence, it was not at all anomalous that U.S. blacks, grappling with the notion of a God who acted in history, should peer into the looking glass of American destiny and behold their own visage. They were the messianic people who would spread the gospel of Jesus Christ throughout their own ranks, rescuing themselves from a prior existence of spiritual darkness, thereby assuming their destined role to lead the nation and the world in social progress and spiritual excellence.

The references to Ethiopia in the Bible were understood to apply to the entire Negro race. As one black interlocutor phrased it, *no one* who had read the biblical aphorism " 'can the Ethiopian change his skin?' would doubt that these prophecies belong to the Negro."[6] If there was ever any text that approximated a sort of universally accepted scripture among American Christians, it was Psalm 68:31. American Christians regarded this as a prophecy foretelling the rise of the Negro race to greatness *once the race had become Christianized.* The history of the Negro race in these terms had been a manifestation of the divine scheme leading them to embrace Christianity.

Two years before Emancipation, Edward Wilmot Blyden, who at the time worked as the principal of the Alexander High School in Monrovia, Liberia, traveled to the United States, as he would do many times thereafter, to articulate his understanding of the missionary role American Negroes were to play in Africa. Blyden was sponsored by the white-controlled Presbyterian Mission Board. He quickly became renowned as an authoritative scholar of classical texts and civilizations. He was also very fluent in numerous languages, including Arabic, which he taught in Liberia.[7]

While in New York City in 1861, Blyden was invited to speak to members of the Presbyterian Church on Seventh Avenue. He opened his speech with the statement that Africa alone (vis-à-vis Europe and Asia) was untouched by "civilization." Quoting Psalm 68:31, he proposed that the immigration of U.S. blacks to Liberia was the overture to fulfillment of scriptural prophecy that "Ethiopia will stretch forth her hands unto God." Blyden expected a sudden conversion of Africans to the religion of Christianity, which meant it was crucial that black Americans poise themselves to help bring about this dramatic fulfillment of providential design. Singling out the black listeners of his audience, he urged,

> You were brought away [from Africa] by the permission of Providence, doubtless, that you might be prepared and fitted to return and instruct

your brethren. If you turn away from the work to which Providence evidently calls you, with the selfish hope of elevating yourselves in this country, beware lest the calamities come upon you which are threatened to those who neglect to honor their parents.[8]

Blyden believed firmly that God had purposefully allowed Africans to be enslaved by whites so that U.S. blacks might return to share the gift of civilization and human progress with that "Dark Continent." Black Americans were thus part of a divine plan in the uplift of the entire Negro race.

Blyden's theological views necessitated that he regard Africans in a disparaging light—they were heathens who needed to be delivered from the dark night of Africa's spiritual dearth. Significantly, he sought to humanize the face of Africa, usually by associating it with biblical themes. Africa, for example, was an asylum for Jesus when sought after by King Herod, he reminded his audience. And the extreme barbarism and savagery in Africa, though abundant, were due not to some innate nature of the Negro but, rather, to the continent's geography, which made Europe's civilizing penetration into Africa very difficult.[9]

But now the time of Africa's redemption had approached, and while white Christians had a general mission, as did all Christians, to spread the gospel throughout the entire world, Negroes in America had a particular mission to uplift Africa. He pointed out that, while most saw Africa merely as a source for natural resources and free labor, "only a few, very few have regarded Africa as a land inhabited by human beings," and it was these few persons who were making Africa the focus of the Christian world.[10]

The effort of publicists such as Blyden effectively set Africa on the hearts of black Americans. Thus, it was that, by the 1860s, black Americans who had traveled to Liberia had established, with the help of white philanthropy, over one hundred churches, boasted more than 15,000 converts to Christianity, had established over two hundred mission-connected schools, and were training more than 16,000 native young persons to be Christians. In addition to this, Christian missionaries in Liberia were studying over twenty dialects for the purpose of putting them into writing so that the Bible might be read and persons might benefit from a culture of literacy.[11]

There were other key propagandists who influenced American ideas about African missions. A.M.E. Bishop Henry McNeal Turner was among the foremost exponents of sending black missionaries into Africa. Turner left behind an initially promising career in politics that was eventually sabotaged by white terrorist politics and post-Reconstruction backlash. He focused on his work in the A.M.E. denomination and quickly became arguably its most influential personality of the era. Turner was visionary, tireless, and persuasive; he was to religious sentiment what W. E. B. Du Bois would later become to cultural criticism—prolific, controversial, charismatic, and a force not to be ignored.[12]

Turner believed, as did Blyden, that American Negroes were destined to uplift the race from the mire of backwardness and heathenism. For this reason, he urged emigration to Africa and missions. His position quickly put him at loggerheads with another A.M.E. bishop, Benjamin Tanner. For years, Turner and Tanner fiercely debated this issue. For Turner, there was no question that blacks had to missionize Africa and that they should settle there. Tanner, however, felt that such ranting would only play into the hands of the American Colonization Society (ACS), which was founded in 1816 in order to remove freed blacks to Africa so that Emancipation might be achieved without creating a "Negro problem" of free blacks who wanted to achieve social equality with whites. Tanner opposed missions to Africa on the basis that U.S. blacks were generally disinterested in leaving America; he petitioned the ACS to abandon their efforts to advance black emigration.[13]

Turner was not naïve about the ulterior motives of white philanthropists willing to finance black emigration to Africa; he understood that they only wished to rid the United States of a "Negro problem." But Turner reasoned that black Americans could strategically use the financial support of the ACS to further their own interests in taking the gospel to Africa. Turner believed, furthermore, that black Americans had every right to live in the United States, and he was entirely opposed to forced emigration. The subtlety of Turner's thinking is evident in a letter he penned to his son on the occasion of his son's twenty-first birthday.

> I am glad that you, like myself, believe that the time has arrived when men of this country should awaken to the moral and intellectual wants of Africa. Our people, as a race, are asleep upon that subject. I hope you will agitate that question, in common with others, till the blinded eyes of our people shall be opened to one of the gravest subjects that can possibly arrest our attention. I do not mean emigration there in mass, but the putting forth of our efforts for the moral and intellectual development of the darkened continent.[14]

Turner differentiated between mass emigration to Africa and the establishment of an Americanized, Christianized black nation in Africa. Responding to Tanner's opposition, Turner denounced the

A.M.E. denomination's lack of attention toward African missions and called for the denomination to direct resources concertedly toward African missions. He did not feign to fathom how a black person in the United States could "profess Christianity and be dead to the moral wants of his kinsmen [*sic*] in Africa." In an about face to its course then, the A.M.E. Church needed to give Americans "a knowledge of the millions who are [in Africa] in moral darkness."[15] Turner's interest in Africa was not simply for the sake of conversion, however.

> Now what is my position? Simply to found and establish a country or a government somewhere upon the continent of Africa, as I see no other place in the world to do it, where our young men and ladies can find a theatre of activity and usefulness, and commence a career for the future that will meet the wants of posterity, at the same time build up a center of Christian civilization that will help redeem the land of our ancestry.[16]

Turner identified practical and theological reasons for blacks to colonize Africa. Why wait for whites to take over the resources of the land? Blacks had a right to the inheritance of their ancestors. In a cynical attack against Tanner, Turner wrote that Tanner should

> [s]top talking about the negro doing anything by his own strength, brain and merits. Wait till the whites go over and civilize Africa, and homestead all the land and take us along to black their boots and groom their horses. Wait till the French or English find some great mines of gold, diamonds or some other precious metal or treasures, so we can raise a howl over it and charge the whites with endeavoring to take away our fathers' inheritance, and lift a wail for the sympathy of the world. So much for Dr. Tanner and his mistaken position.[17]

One should not trivialize the theological convictions Turner held concerning Africans. He understood that they were in spiritual darkness and faced spiritual jeopardy. More importantly for him, the fates of black Americans and native Africans were intertwined because they were one and the same race. Turner was persuaded, moreover, that any race that was "fossilized, oppressed, or degraded must emigrate before any material change takes place in their civil, intellectual or moral status, otherwise extinction is the sequence." With the creation of a "civil and Christian negro [*sic*] nation," Turner was certain that the Negro race could circumnavigate the bleak nightmare of their future in America by creating an idyllic refuge of a Westernized/Christianized black-controlled Africa.[18]

From throughout the North and South, black men and women traveled to Africa—usually to Liberia or Sierra Leone—specifically to spread the "light of the Gospel of Christ." The African Methodist Episcopal denomination and the National Baptist Convention were the two largest black denominations and were thus positioned to finance their own missionaries. But the National Baptist Convention lacked the cohesive structure necessary to coordinate a concerted financial effort—the individual churches were very Congregationalist in sensibility, affording greater autonomy at the cost of denominational unity. Thus, it was the A.M.E. denomination that sponsored the greatest number of black missionaries. And it was largely due to Turner that the A.M.E. Church's successful missions to Africa were realized.

Rev. Lewis G. Jordan of Meridian, Mississippi, served as the secretary to the National Baptist Convention (NBC), USA, from 1896 to 1921. The convention was formed in 1895, and Jordan was appointed head of the Foreign Mission Board. He instigated the observance of African Mission Day by black Baptist churches. Traveling throughout Africa to open mission stations, his guidance moved the NBC from having not a single foreign missionary to developing a significant force to missionize African countries such as Liberia and South Africa.[19]

In 1904, he brought back from Africa seven men who attended Morehouse College, Spelman University, and West Virginia State.[20] This represented a new strategy for evangelizing Africa—native Africans themselves were to be trained and could become more effective missionaries of the Christian gospel.

Between 1877 and 1900, at least 113 American Negroes served as Christian missionaries in Africa,[21] a large figure in light of the fact that black denominations had relatively few resources for financing missions. The majority of Negroes who wished to take Christianity into Africa usually had to work under the auspices of white denominations, which used black missionaries only as a last resort, reserving them for the harshest climatic regions of Africa.

It is well known that nineteenth-century Negro "race leaders" were, to some extent, missionaries of Europeanized culture. A number of authors, such as Anne Knupfer, Wilson Moses, and Evelyn Brooks Higginbotham, have addressed the ironic Victorian ideals of Pan-Africanists, Negro educators, and other radical Negro race leaders. What concerns us here, however, is the logic (*ratio*) of American Christianity that rendered black missions a meaningful, intelligible enterprise.

Ethiopianism was a particular example of the pervasive religious logic of divine identity that has been central to Christian tradition and the Judaic legacy of election. Walter Williams identifies this logic as the theory of providential design, which became a source for supporters of colonization seeking to justify black emigration to Africa in theological terms. Williams correctly locates therein the source of American ideas about the Negro race's destiny.

The Christian myth, in its Israelitic aspect, has especially depended upon a philosophy of history that rendered meaning to world events from the beginnings of time to the present. The myth of Ethiopianism, however, provided a means of both explaining the theodical enigma of black suffering and providing an intelligible mode of participating in Christian identity.

Why was the situation of Africa so urgent? The reason was both historical and moral. Blyden, like his contemporaries, regarded as axiomatic that "civilization is handed from one people to another, its great foundation and source being the omnipotent and all-merciful God of the universe."[22] And Africa was patently "alone among Europe and Asia as still untouched by civilization."[23] Christian religionists also believed that civilization's degeneration was due to a change in moral circumstances. Here again, Africa was believed to have forsaken fidelity to the one true God of Christianity; hence, its decline into heathen abandon and idolatry.

Most compelling about this religious logic was its narrative force. According to the Christian myth, ancient Israel had been the chosen people of (Christianity's) God, becoming a light and exemplum to "the nations"—that is, those who were not people of God. According to Christian theological tradition, Israel was in essence the Christian church, the saints of God, whose task it was to eke out a righteous existence among the nations and, ultimately, to point all other people to the revealed truth of God. The zenith of this theological style in the history of American religion is constituted by the points at which America itself is signified as God's new Israel.[24] Occurring more frequently, however, were the claims by specific (religious, ethnic, or cultural) groups that they were God's Israel or "remnant" or elect/chosen, vis-à-vis "others."

The American spin on this narrative was developed in synthesis with a racialized worldview, which in turn was conditioned by the legacy of European Christian colonization—taking the Christian truth to the far and distant lands of the heathens. The colonialist era, as Walter Williams intones, marked the beginning of global Christianity; until then, worldwide Christian expansionism had been hoped for and talked about but unrealized. By the nineteenth century, however, this was no longer the case. Christianity was a significant presence throughout the world. The major Christian denominations were developing bolder and more comprehensive strategies for converting the world to the Christian religion.

Add to this the sudden and unprecedented conundrum of racial history with which American Negroes had to contend, and one quickly realizes how difficult it would be to imagine an outcome significantly different from that which developed; Negro religionists in America during the latter part of the nineteenth century increasingly articulated their plight in terms of a divine scheme meant to effect the eventual salvation/Christianization of the Negro race.

Slavery had been a cruel, demeaning system. It occasioned, nevertheless, the sojourn of the Negro race in a New World of Christian civility. As a result, the "Ethiopian race" had taken hold of the gospel of truth. Africa's children, scattered so far from home—Diasporan orphans—were now able to return having acquired the gospel and the goods of civilizing influence. They could "return" to the heathen land of their ancestors bearing the gifts of civilization, culture, and Christian salvation.

Alexander Crummell, a freeborn Negro Episcopal priest of New York City, eventually traveled to Liberia and lived there for two decades. Crummell helped to garner support for African emigration. In an 1865 address to the Pennsylvania branch of the ACS, Crummell appealed to a Presbyterian audience for support of black American missionaries, who were best "equipped" to live in Africa because they were supposedly of indigenous constitution and thus were able to thrive in the tropical climates where whites were less willing to travel.

Crummell wanted to help Africans to develop the industrial infrastructure of Western nations. And he emphatically expressed his desire to establish "Trade, Agriculture, Commerce, Art, Letters and Government" in the "fatherland." Yet, these were "but *collateral*" to the "end, aim, and object of that divine will and providence" made possible "by the means of institutions and governments, by afflictions and sufferings, and even oppressions."[25] This end was the evangelization of Africa. By virtue of their "contact with Anglo-Saxon culture and religion," Negroes in the New World had themselves become Christians and could now plant the gospel "amid the heathen population of Africa."[26] The involvement of Christian Negroes with Africa was toward this objective first and foremost.

Crummell was so enamored of Ethiopianism's vision of Christian expansionism that he was willing to support black Americans' military aggression against native Africans, whom he regarded in their "uncivilized" state as "infuriate savages."[27] Upon welcoming newly emigrated black Americans to Liberia, he advised them that they should, on the one hand to be "tender and pitiful and earnest to the heathen" who surrounded them. On the other hand, they should make every effort to "resist . . . their vicious habits . . . and their corrupting influences."[28] Most telling was Crummell's praise for the Belgian King Leopold's seizure of the Congo, which Crummell described as essential for curtailing native violence, establishing commerce, and promoting the work of missionaries.[29]

Crummell's support for imperial control over Africa and his espousal of Christian theology that encoded native Africans as "heathens" was not exceptional but rather characterized the way both black and white Christians interpreted "the African." A clearly discernible pattern of missionary urgency took over in the decades following the Civil War. The bishops of the A.M.E. denomination expressed in their address to the 1884 General Conference that the time had come for the Church to counter the powers that prevented the Christian gospel from dispelling spiritual darkness in Africa. In a militaristic tone, they urged the denomination to make headway into the "ramparts of the forts of the [pagan] enemy" in Africa.[30]

In 1880, an Illinois black Baptist association appointed their own mission agent to evangelize the "millions" of Africans who lived "in grossest darkness of heathenism."[31] Mississippi Baptist Minister R. A. Jackson was disturbed by the black Baptist churches' relative laxity over missions to Africa and, in 1894, financed his own trip to Capetown, where he established an independent Baptist church. Jackson stirred significant support among black Baptists in the United States through his correspondence and published articles. He lamented the numbers of Africans suffering in the "abyss of heathendom" and warned his fellow black American Christians that the unsaved Africans' "blood will be upon us . . . and upon our children."[32]

Narrative Logic of the Christian Myth

Edward Wilmot Blyden worked in Africa under the auspices of the Presbyterian Mission Board. Blyden's writings about Christianity in Africa were among the most influential for American audiences. Because of his rigorous intellectualism, his command of classical and theological texts, and his unsurpassed linguistic erudition (Blyden was one of the few Western intellectuals fluent in Arabic), he commanded respect from both academic and popular audiences. Blyden is particularly useful for understanding the dominant assumptions about colonial identities because, although he was incessantly critical of the racist perceptions of whites, Blyden had assimilated the epistemologies of nineteenth-century Western Christianity. He is thus an apt source for gleaning some important characteristics of the narrative logic of the Christian myth.

Blyden was fully convinced that the solution for Africa's ills lay in introducing Christian civilization to the continent. "Paganism," the indigenous religion of native Africans, was, he believed, the most abominable vice of the continent. Considerably better than unmitigated paganism was the widespread religion of Islam or "Mohammedanism," as it was often referred to by nineteenth-century Christians. But even Mohammedanism was inadequate for one simple reason—it was not Christianity. Yet, Blyden's ideas about *Christian, Islam, and the Negro Race*, as his renowned 1887 publication was entitled, elucidate the rhetorical maneuvers and racial anxieties of American (Negro) Christians toward Africa.[33]

Since the time of the Crusades, by which Christianity sought to expel Islamic influence from what would come to be regarded as Europe, Western Christians had identified Islam as the single religion that was a serious threat to Protestant Christendom. And American Protestants such as Jonathan Edwards had regarded it as a more serious threat than the Catholic faith, partly because with the growth of European "nationalism" and subsequent European superiority, Islam represented the threat of dominance by nonwhites. Before Christianity established a foothold beyond the early Christian enclaves in Northern Africa, Islam was the only missionary religion that was widespread throughout Africa. Due to traveling merchants, military campaigns by Islamic leaders, and a thriving slave trade, Islam could be found throughout Africa, although the majority of Africans in the nineteenth century still practiced indigenous religions.[34]

Christian missionaries, in the wake of European exploration and imperial ventures, set their sights on converting Africans from their "spiritual darkness" to the Christian religion. They soon realized, however, that they were late to the draw. Because Islamic conversion was well underway, Christian missionaries viewed Muslims as their sole competition in converting Africans from "idolatrous heathenism" to monotheism.

This was the situation Blyden encountered when he began his missionary work in Africa under the auspices of the Presbyterian Mission

Board. Yet, unlike most missionaries, Blyden quickly developed admiration for Islam because it seemed far more compatible with African culture, which Blyden sought to differentiate from African indigenous religions. It was the latter (religion, not culture per se) that Blyden believed Christianity obligated him to eradicate.[35] Blyden also believed that African Muslims were more dignified and less "slavish" than American Christian Negroes. This was because American Negroes encountered Christianity as slaves subjected to the humiliating conditions of white racism; but native Africans, Blyden opined, usually encountered Islam as free persons with dignity and psychological assertiveness.[36]

Most significant for Blyden, however, was the "fact" that Islam had introduced "true religion" into Africa. *No authentic knowledge of God was indigenous to Africa*, he repeatedly stated. Blyden, in fact, contended that "it was not until the ninth century of the Christian era that any knowledge of the true God began to penetrate into Negroland," when Islam made its first appearance there.[37] This meant that Africa's prior spiritual existence had been vile and futile, an evil bastion of "paganism and Devil-worship."[38]

> It is evident that, whatever may be said of the Koran, as long as it is in advance of the Shamanism or Fetichism [*sic*] of the African tribes who accept it . . . those tribes must advance beyond their primitive condition.[39]

Despite the numerous religious systems of Africa, only Islam and Christianity were valid religions because they were monotheistic. The polytheistic religions of Africa blatantly indicated to Blyden and to other Christian missionaries that "Negroland" was a *heathen* land. In light of the fact that Christianity was still grappling for a mere foothold in Africa, Blyden advocated the spread of Islam because it was "an enormous advance not only on all idolatries, but on all systems of purely human origin."[40] Until Christianity came along, a partial truth was better than no truth—this was Blyden's message to his colleagues of the Christian missionary world.

In 1866, Blyden resigned from the Presbyterian Mission Board, because the board had become incorrigibly alienated when Blyden spoke warmly of Islam. Blyden openly urged Christian missionary societies to adopt the proselytizing methods of Islam so that Africans who converted to Christianity could remain culturally "African." Blyden, from then on, considered himself a "minister of truth," thereby espousing a progressive form of pluralism. By the time of his death in 1912, Blyden virtually embraced Islam as a desirable presence in Africa, although he himself never converted. Despite his progressive pluralism, however, Blyden never questioned his condemnation of Africans' indigenous religions. Polytheism was an unforgivable enmity against (Christianity's) God and truth.

As proof of this, Blyden reasoned, one need only look to the prolific Israelitic narrations of divine punishment meted out against the ancient nations who were not among the people of God. Two examples become appropriate for illustrating the problem of narrative knowledge at hand. First is the idea of Noah's curse. Blyden, like other American (Christians), did not question the idea that (Christianity's) God could or should curse any human beings. Blyden's self-appointed task, like that of other Negro interlocutors, was to undermine the claim that Noah's curse upon Canaan (son of Ham) proved that enslaving Negroes was justified and biblical. He did this neither by rejecting biblical slavery nor by refusing to sanction curses. Blyden, rather, displaced the fulfillment of this curse from contemporary times to an ancient past; because Canaan was to be the "slave of slaves," Blyden argued that this curse was fulfilled when Israelites, formerly slaves in Egypt, escaped to Canaan and slaughtered and enslaved the Canaanites.[41] This meant that Canaanites were slaves of slaves.

This leads to a second, related example—genocide itself. Because God had foreseen that the indigenous inhabitants of Canaan would not worship Yahweh, God had caused Noah to pronounce the curse upon Canaan, which culminated in their genocide. The Israelite destruction of the Canaanites, thus, was one more example of the fact that "the affairs of nations, as of individuals . . . are constantly beneath the immediate observation and control of Jehovah," who had no tolerance for waywardness.[42] Blyden applied the same standard to the genocide of Native Americans. He identified a clear line of reasoning to show that

> the destruction of the cities of the plain of Sodom; the extermination of the nations of Canaan; the wholesale submersion and extirpation of the Egyptians in the red sea; the dispersion and denationalization of the Israelites; the diminished and diminishing numbers of the Indians of North America; and lastly, the enslavement of Africans—all the effects of sin.[43]

Namely, one sin—lack of faithful and exclusive worship of the Christian deity. Biblical narrative was a *cultural* narrative. Its domain in the nineteenth century was not merely the American *religious* imagination; it also encoded meaning for the entire social reality. Blyden's maneuver was no theological anomaly. It was, rather, well within the bounds of conventional Christian reasoning. In his effort to divorce the plight of Africans from the legacy of Noah's curse, he nevertheless conceded that slavery as witnessed in these instances was "Jehovah's" just punishment for sin. Blyden reminded his readers, however, that slavery was not endemic to the Negro race; slavery had been a worldwide phenomenon, and one should not make it the basis for creating a system of racial caste.

A lesson in the divine scheme of history is further seen when Blyden spells out the Negro race's historiography of decline. Considering the Egyptians, who represented the greatest level of cultural and technical achievement among the ancients, Blyden explains that they, like other Africans, "evidently, at one time, possessed a knowledge of the true God; but they neglected it; and in this consists their crime." Because of this, God abandoned them to their sin.[44] But this was not to be the final word. Even while "iniquity blackened [the] moral sphere" of the descendants of Ham, God made a promise regarding "their wicked land" that "Ethiopia shall soon stretch out her hands unto God."[45] It should become clear, then, that Ethiopianism was as much a response to the problem of slavery as it was to the theologies that articulated the narrative knowledge of monotheism. Ethiopia's turn to God was to the Israelitic God of Christianity, as understood through the ideology of monotheism.

One should not miss the irony in Blyden's willingness to defend any degree of violence—slavery, curses, genocide, massive suffering—if such seemed to be grounded in the narrations of the people of God. It did not matter that the victims of these narrations patently were Negroes themselves. Given the "facts" of history and (racial) existence, no violence or suffering was too great to be accepted and explained in defense of the God who exercised such grave punishments.

In fairness to Blyden, one should be quick to recognize that few Christians of the twenty-first century would differ with his refusal to question or condemn the mandates clearly attributed to Yahweh in biblical narratives. Such becomes difficult to the degree that it becomes necessary to condemn Yahweh himself. Blyden was actually more progressive than his peers, reminding them, for instance, that Africans carried on no backward doings that could not be found in the history of the Anglo-Saxon race, who had arrived culturally and spiritually after their sojourn into decadence. Nevertheless, one is left to reckon with the power of such narrative knowledge, which seems to know no limit in defending the heathen's demise, defeat, and elimination via genocide or conversion.

The fact that most Africans were not Christians was the primary basis of what historian Wilson Moses discusses as a historiography of decline.[46] This historiography comprised popular and scholarly explanations for the perceived "backwardness" of the Negro race, specifically their pre-Christian, pre-Westernized existence. Biblical narratives repeatedly demonstrated that nations who did not worship the rightful deity (that of Israel) would likely suffer unmitigated violence at the hand of that deity. This narrative knowledge inscribed a religious logic that neither Blyden nor Alexander Crummell nor any other influential religionists, black or white, ever questioned.

Here is revealed a fundamental ambivalence toward non-Christian religious forms. Black Christians emphasized that God explicitly desired that they spread the "light" of the gospel of Jesus Christ among the "benighted communities" of heathen Africa. Black peoples' status, hence, was perceived to be a dismal one to the degree that it was pre-Christian or non-Christian, and ameliorating this status was contingent upon becoming people of God. Represented in this conception of "heathen" existence lies the ideological matrix for Christian self-understanding, one aspect of black religion that did not simply fail to appreciate black pre-Christian or non-Christian identity but, moreover, fundamentally disparaged these forms.[47]

A number of scholars have interpreted African American religious history in relation to the broader phenomenon termed "American religion." Representative are the works of Martin Marty, Harold Bloom, David Turley, Marjorie Garber, Nathan Hatch, and Baer and Singer.[48] They devote attention, to varying degrees, toward religious forms beyond the pale of Christianity among African Americans. Frequently discussed are nativism and anti-Semitism, which have overwhelmingly characterized American Christian postures toward European Catholics and European Jews. But silence prevails over the deep-seated hostility and hatred toward non-Christian black religious forms such as Voodoo, Islam, and non-Christian religious systems indigenous to the Americas and to Africa. The compulsory dynamics of Christian identity typically go unexamined with respect to these forms of black religious identity. Yet such intolerant sentiment has overwhelmingly informed the ideological stances of Christianity broadly, and black Christianity has been no exception.

A few individuals have frankly addressed the ambivalence of African American Christianity, not only questioning its assumed normative image but also critically assessing how African American Christianity has disparaged other black religious forms. Foremost is Walter Williams, whose treatment of African American evangelization reads the emergence of Black Nationalism through the history of black Christian missions to Africa. Williams concludes that black Christians both celebrated the image of Africa as a homeland and denigrated it as a heathen, ungodly continent in need of becoming Christian.[49] He indicates, furthermore, that the zealous missionary ideology concomitant to Ethiopianism contributed to the Christian assaults upon African cultures and religions. Williams, without hesitation, rightly suggests that no Christian missionary activity, however well intentioned, is devoid of imperialism. Anthony Pinn provides a reading of nineteenth-century black Christianity similar to Williams'. Pinn is critical of how the ideological assumptions so keenly exemplified by Ethiopianism depended upon demeaning perspectives of non-Christian identity.[50]

Charles H. Long has interpreted African American Christianity's emergence as problem-laden, largely because Christianity has consistently vilified non-Christian forms of religious identity.[51] Robert E. Hood and Forrest G. Wood also explored this subject, although they have been less critical of blacks than they are of whites. Hood has produced one of the best historical treatments of the semiotics of blackness in relationship to Christianity theology. Most importantly, he examines how blackness has been encoded as "heathen" and non-Christian.[52] Wood has taken this one step further to problematize Christianity itself as necessarily racially hostile to blacks.

At best, Ethiopianism and black Christians' aspirations of Christianizing the race were ambivalent forces in black Christianity, producing fortitude in blacks' struggle for human justice while vitiating against an appreciation for African pre-Christian traditions. At worst, they wreaked disparagement upon black non-Christian cultures, thus magnifying self-contempt and becoming another chapter in the hostile performance of Christian identity against non-Christian peoples. At a fundamental level, the problem has been the challenges that Christian identity induced for people who read their American history as a Christian one and who image their pre-Christian history as a heathen one. Such was the burden of the children of Ham in America.

Sandy Dwayne Martin, in his *Black Baptists and African Missions*, identifies himself as an "ardent sympathizer" of overseas missions.[53] He reviews the history of tropes that Negro missionaries used to describe the condition of African heathens. And he concludes that blacks identified racially with Africans, something that whites "could not match."[54] Because black Americans did share this racial identity, the Christian awareness that they developed was more authentic, more practical than that of white missionaries.

Martin is very clear that black American Christians viewed Africans as "the most 'lost' people in the world." And he does critique black missionaries' failure to resist colonialism (i.e., the settlement, economic manipulation, and balkanization of Africa by Europeans). With the exception of a few, they were "silent" on this issue. Yet, their Christian missionary motives are admirable, in Martin's judgment, because black missionaries believed that their efforts "would serve to enlighten the indigenous peoples [of Africa] and thus advance them spiritually and materially."[55] Although their constructions of the African heathen were identical to those of whites, such feelings among black Americans are "understandable" because of the ideological milieu of blacks; that is, these were common assumptions of the time.

There is, however, a patent irony in Martin's assessment of black Christian missions to Africa. When he responds to this dilemma, he repeatedly emphasizes the idea of a common racial identity that black Americans shared with Africans. The mere fact of this common identity is rarified in Martin's treatment; it becomes the differential that justifies or renders "understandable" the demeaning, anti-heathen theologies of black Christian missionaries. In Martin's assessment, the same maneuvers and hermeneutical productions by whites toward Africans were racist, imperialist, and disingenuous because whites were not racially identified with native Africans.

At stake is the question of whether the encoding of the heathen was inordinate or justified. Martin, writing in the wake of Walter Williams' interpretive study of black missions, discretely counters Williams' attempt to problematize Christian missionary violence. He claims, instead, that a common racial identity sufficed to justify the rhetorical maneuvers, ideological pronouncements, and performed missionizing of black American Christians.

Yet, this point of racial identity is precisely where Martin fails to respond adequately to Williams. Williams demonstrates that *both* race *and* culture are important for assessing black missionary attitudes toward African heathens. Race and culture, more precisely, are phenomenally identical to the extent to which both become a basis for imagining identity. Both, moreover, produce identity imperatives. To raise the issue of identity imperative is to recognize that imagining or comprehending a self means "understanding" a proper course of action or set of behaviors. To be a member of the Negro race, for instance, was to be compelled or obligated to sustain the best interests of that race. To be a Christian (i.e., to be among the people of God) likewise was to be compelled or obligated to sustain the interests of that people or folk. Any assessment of black American Christian awareness must regard this as a central factor.

Martin's reading of black missions conflates the peoplehood of Negro American Christians and native Africans. This becomes the basis for representing white Christians as a different folk who would not be compelled to value the best interests of Africans. The "more practical" Christianity of black missionaries, however, was ingenuous and admirable, representing a legacy of which Martin may announce himself an "ardent supporter" because they were uplifting their own.

But were they? It would be ahistorical to suppose that at least some white Christian missionaries did not value the spiritual and material interests of both native Africans and black Americans. Both black and white Christians believed that they were furthering a righteous cause by eradicating the historical religions of native Africans. This was the virtually unavoidable conclusion germane to the Christian myth of salvation and history. Most of the black missionaries who traveled to Africa in the nineteenth century, in fact, were financed and supported by whites. Williams' thesis that both culture and race were factors in determining how black Americans and native Africans related is further demonstrated by the pernicious caste system that arose in Liberia—Americo-Liberians enslaved some of the native Africans and prevented them from being educated in the Americo-Liberian institutions.[56] The forms of representing difference in these overt instances were overwhelmingly more decisive than a mere fact of shared racial identity.

Ancient Identities, New People

As far as American ideologues could tell, Africans were still far and distant from the truth of the Christian gospel. Their lack of industrial and technological prowess only underscored the ineptitude of their damning heathenism. There was little in the history and traditions of the Christian religion to mitigate the idea that the non-Christian was radically other. There existed, on the other hand, an abundance of mythic ideas, texts, symbols, and narrations to induce a shared perception of a common peoplehood that was religious and simultaneously empowering (for black American Christians) yet violent, vilifying, and demeaning for native Africans and, by association, for American Negroes. One begins to realize that American Negro religionists regarded Africans as a *different people*, a heathen people.

Historian Robert Berkhofer has described the historical fascination with America as a space of novelty—the New Land, a literal and symbolic frontier. America's newness, in his analysis, was the conceptual perversion that justified genocide, land theft, and forced displacements. There was nothing new per se about America. It was already settled by millions of Native Americans. The land, furthermore, was "developed," supporting human populations, structures, and sustaining plentiful wildlife. Despite the falsified construction of this newness, however, it was because America was the New World that white settlers could so arbitrarily define it. The New World conception, more importantly, fostered the belief that America was God's land of promise for God's new Israel.[57]

Given the increase in missionary activity and the powerful influence of the Christian myth, black Americans' motivations for embracing Christian identity were informed by a religious logic of desire to distance themselves from the condition of spiritual darkness, represented by the non-Christian. Race uplift, for this reason, was inextricably wed to Christianization. Christianization, in turn, was inevitably bound to problems of legitimacy. The emphasis here is on *becoming* people of God, striving to attain divine peoplehood *qua* Christian identity. The existential meanings borne out by becoming people of God, thus, merit careful attention.

Of particular interest is the way the Negro was perceived in moral terms, given the fact that Negroes were considered heathens, as decadent. Black Americans of the nineteenth century were distinct in that they "remembered" their American history as a Christian one and their pre-American history as a heathen one. This perception, conditioned by "biblical knowledge", constituted a complex experience of peoplehood. They related to Africans because of racial categorization. Yet, to the degree that Africans were non-Christian (or pre-Christian), black American Christians distinguished themselves from Africans. In a religious sense, because they were people of God, they were a different folk.

The overarching complex of rhetorics, narrations, and histories pertinent to race uplift were contingent upon the idea that Negroes were produced through Hamitic descent, knowledge of whom was contained in scripture. And American Christians across racial groups

Gender and Illegitimacy

Perhaps the most complicated issues of race uplift involved the racialized representations of gender. American ideas about dark-bodied folk, sexuality, and the embodied particulars of Christian virtue indicate complex attempts to account for the perception that pre-Christian Negroes were decadent heathens. This decadence was at once racial and gendered. To this extent, Christian "arrival" for American Negroes was especially salvific. It was to the race's unspeakable benefit to convert to Christianity in a total, timely manner.

It is paramount to grasp the complex associations between gender and race to apprehend adequately how meanings engineered through race discourse confounded representations of black women's humanity. Race and gender are commonly viewed as disparate or at least separate. But examining the social history of attempts to study women, on the one hand, and nonwhite races, on the other, reveals a far more intricate reality. One should consider, for instance, that eighteenth- and nineteenth-century texts (particularly scientific texts) normatively relied upon one category in order to explicate the other. To speak of mammies, Jezebels, and bucks with large penises was to evoke overwhelmingly powerful images of race and sex that thrived during the nineteenth century and that even perdure into the present era.[60]

Among the guiding assumptions of nineteenth-century science was the idea that gender was a stable, natural condition of biology that could be understood with cold confidence. Whereas men were regarded as the superior gender—stronger, more intelligent, wiser, and able to thrive amidst diverse environmental challenges—the weaker sex needed to be protected and was prone to the ramifications of lesser intellect, weaker constitution, and diminished ability to navigate the outer, socially complex world of choice and circumstance that lay beyond hearth and home. As a code of biologically grounded supremacy, the analytical category of gender seemed a "natural" choice for examining and explaining racial difference. In these terms, for instance, whiteness was the masculine form of human existence. Negroes, encoded in extreme antithesis to whites, were described as a feminine race. Analogs of gender and theoretical associations between racial constitution and gender constitution thus became standard fare in scientific theories and popular ideas of race.

A number of scholars have studied the history of Europeans and Euro-Americans making meanings about nonwhites through specific, scientific discourses of gender and race. E. Frances White has proffered a compelling analysis of the influence of British scientist Charles Robert Darwin, renowned for his *Origin of Species*, which he published in 1859. This comprehensive articulation of evolutionary theory was a watershed event that wrought a paradigm shift for not only the biological sciences but also the broader culture of racial and sexual worldview. It is in a later work, however, *The Descent of Man and Selection in Relation to Sex* (1871), that Darwin set forth a more mature understanding of how evolutionary theory applied to gender and race.[61]

White provides a careful portrait of Darwin to achieve a fair analysis commensurate with his complexity. In contrast to a number of his colleagues, Darwin believed all humans were members of a common species. As White demonstrates, however, he argued this idea through relying on racist descriptions of whites and of nonwhites. He surmised, for instance, that nonwhites inevitably declined or disappeared in the wake of contact with whites because inferior races, like women, were ill equipped to deal with sudden change or complex developments. They were naturally given to a primitive state of thinking or being.[62] This inferior capacity to adapt, Darwin claimed, was the prime cause for the "disappearance" of indigenous peoples. White identifies his narrative of "disappearance" as one strategy, unwitting or not, of rendering invisible the history of genocidal campaigns that white governments (including the American colonial and U.S. governments) waged against native nations.

More significant, however, is Darwin's participation in the ubiquitous strategy of employing ethnological (ethnographic) observations of "primitive" people as data for surmising the natural state of gender or the natural role of women.[63] Based on his study of ethnography, for example, Darwin believed that sexual hierarchy or inequality was far more developed and pronounced among civilized peoples (the white race) than among "savages." As he reasoned, the more civilized a race became, the greater the restrictions men placed upon women in that race. Written in the midst of first-wave feminism, his arguments were certainly fodder for those seeking to supplant women's liberationist movements, which if successful, according to his logic, would threaten to plunge the white race backward into the abyss of savagery.

Darwin also related these racial differences of gender to aesthetics in order to theorize sexual selection, by which he meant the "natural" process through which men chose women for sexual or domestic cohabitation. The ugliness (per Darwin's gaze) of the nonwhite races was directly related to their inferiority because of sexual selection; nonwhite men lacked the aesthetic sensibility of the white race and perpetuated ugliness by systematically choosing ugly women with whom to procreate.[64] Aesthetic sensitivity was supremely cultivated by whites and was marked by their sophisticated use of cosmetics to enhance their naturally more beautiful features. Because racial instincts guided aesthetic tastes, races gradually developed very distinctive appearances.[65]

Jennifer Morgan has specifically examined white male scientists' fascination with women's breasts, particularly those of African and Native American women, as a discursive means of making race. She draws on colonial ethnological/ethnographic observations from the sixteenth to the eighteenth centuries—mostly British—in order to assess the gendered nature of racial construction.[66] Morgan identifies some important trends in these observations, among which were identifying distended/lengthy breasts as a racial marker of typical nonwhites; African women were said to be able to suckle their children, whom they usually carried on their backs, by merely tossing a breast over the shoulder. Elongated breasts, repeatedly inscribed as a marker of African and Native American womanhood, were strategically associated with the subhuman status of animals by describing the breasts of Africans as "dugs" or like "udders." White scientists also employed the sexual availability of African women particularly as an index of backwardness or racial inferiority,[67] and they regarded painless childbirth as an animalistic feature of nonwhites.[68]

White women, in contrast to Africans and Native Americans, were more civilized and refined. They were accordingly idealized as having shorter breasts, being sexually available to no more than one male, and experiencing excruciating pain during childbirth, often to the point of death[69]; only animals and those especially proximate to the animalistic could drop newborns like hot potatoes while barely ceasing from whatever task being performed at the onset of labor. Morgan also identifies the Janus-like strategies of inscribing African women as both beautiful and monstrous but ultimately inferior to the women of white men.[70] Her larger point, however, is that gender itself was a perduring category for inculcating ideas about racial identity; the perceptive observer could judge the race by the women of that race.

Londa Schiebinger has examined the fascination with studying race through discourses of gender as a disciplinary performance. The discipline of natural history, she notes, functioned overwhelmingly as a productive means for white men to construe themselves as radically different from nonwhite races and from white women.[71] Schiebinger concludes, in concurrence with White, that ideas of gender—men are fundamentally, inherently different from the 'weaker sex'—readily served to analogically interpret racial difference.

But Schiebinger goes further to assess specific methods of studying the sexes and the races. She notes that during the 1700s, for instance, anatomists began to regard skeletal structure as an index of sexual difference, one that was more reliable than reproductive organs, which had previously commanded the attention of scientists. This shift in emphasis is attested by the sudden appearance of numerous skeletal sketches after the 1730s contrasting European men and women. The interest in skeletal structure, however, was not confined to sexual differences. It also developed around the same time as a method for studying the races. European men were consistently described as superior in intellect and moral capacity to European women and to the men and women of nonwhite races.[72]

By way of further elucidating the gendered nature of race discourse, Schiebinger notes that the beard served as a distinctive marker of supremacy (i.e., white masculinity). She cites a lecture by Carolus Linnaeus, who stated that the beard was divinely bequeathed in order to distinguish men from women. In the ideological milieu of eighteenth-century science, the beard also served to mark the supremely masculine form—European men—from the *effeminate* races of men such as Africans, Asians, and Native Americans. The men of these races were frequently described as beardless and generally hairless. The German scientist Johann Blumenbach stood out as an exception to this dominant trend by arguing that Native American men did indeed have beards but chose to pluck their facial hairs. Schiebinger identifies this obsession as another instance of natural history as performative white maleness. Would the beard, she asks, have become such an important signifier of supremacy had women been firmly entrenched as shapers of scientific discourse?[73]

On a different note, publicly displaying blacks as freaks of nature or as exotic specimen was organically tied to the very violent world of colonial meanings and cultural practices. Such exhibition ably demonstrates the noetic posture of making racing—the normative subject gazing upon the "other" and in so doing constructing that centered self through voyeurism in order to disparage the "other," to account for it, to describe it—in fact, to create the other through the discursive gaze. Mary Kelly has examined the consumption that met this display in order to highlight its popular nature and to theorize the contingent, complex nature of representation and reality. She focuses on the twentieth-century film *Zou Zou*, which featured Josephine Baker as the hypersexualized native, dressed in feathers, in a cage, waiting to be set free by a white male character.[74]

Perhaps the most enthralling instance of racial-sexual exhibition is that of Sarah Bartmann, a woman of Southern African who arranged for paid travel to Europe in return for agreeing to be exhibited by her underwriters. T. Denean Sharpley-Whiting has most recently examined the case of Bartmann through a revisionist attempt to address the invisibility of black women in the analysis of French literature.[75] Sharpley-Whiting finds it ironic that recent literary criticism has generally overlooked the historical French fascination with black female bodies and the productive posture of colonial, racist gazing that immensely shaped white imaginings of the Negro for centuries. She takes up a study of Bartmann's experience in order to parse the world of meanings that constituted Bartmann's milieu.

Sarah Bartmann was born in the Cape Colony of Southern Africa in 1788. She worked as a domestic for a white settler by the name of Peter Cezar. Around the age of twenty-two, she contracted with Hendrik Cezar, Peter's brother, for travel to London, where she was first exhibited. Later, Bartmann was exhibited in Paris, France. She was soon touted as the "Hottentot Venus." Bartmann was not caged, but she was regularly placed on display with no clothing so that spectators, for a small fee, could look upon her unusually large buttocks. By January of 1816, Bartmann had died, evidently of small pox and alcohol poisoning.[76]

It was after her death, however, that the most troublesome aspects of voyeurism emerged. A certain George Cuvier, a distinguished medical scholar, dissected her body, devoting most of his attention to her genitalia. Sharpley-Whiting notes that Cuvier was fascinated to no end with Bartmann's overgrown labia minor, which he called a "Hottentot apron." Cuvier published his study of Bartmann's genitals, comparing her pelvic structure and vagina to those of monkeys. He regarded her as the missing link between animals and humans. He made a cast of her body and preserved her genitals. To this day, almost two centuries later, Sarah Bartmann's genitals remain on display in the Musée de l'Homme (Museum of Man) in Paris.[77]

Sharpley-Whiting identifies Cuvier's ambivalent descriptions of Bartmann, depicting her as both titillatingly attractive through her sexual exoticism and monstrously repulsive because of her animalistic features (per Cuvier). Through Cuvier's inscription of Bartmann as negress-beast, Sharpley-Whiting rightly identifies a supreme form of racial violence—dehumanizing in the most literal terms the person of Bartmann and the image of an entire race.

What does it mean that for centuries European men sketched, dissected, published, exhibited, and lectured about the breasts, pelvises, buttocks, and vaginas of African women, consistently representing them as beastly savages? This question underlies the numerous studies of white men's strategies of representing black women. And no historical-empirical investigation of white identity and of race-gender construction is complete without devoting central attention to the issue. Sharpley-Whiting asserts an inquiry of the sexual-pornographic gratification that Cuvier and others achieved through their actions. Although there was some public outcry against Bartmann's display as a breach of decency, it is fundamentally important to understand why racial voyeurism and white sexual gazing perdured as such a popular, widespread, fully intelligible cultural phenomenon. Bartmann was only one of many Africans and Native Americans to become a template for scientific and popular modes of imagining race and gender.

The idea and act of exhibiting blacks, manipulating their bones and genitals—these phenomena were perfectly reasonable to scientists, religionists, writers, and the like precisely because of the identity imperatives of being a European or white male. The activity of voyeurism and display was defensible and rational for reasons similar to those justifying the numerous modern day animal zoos, safaris, and scientific observations of "the wild." It brought the strange, exotic, and unfamiliar into proximity with those who were normal and familiar. The history of attempts to explain the perceived radical difference of black men and women, both of whom were sexually exoticized, actually encoded them as wanton, dangerous, and evil. As Kelly Brown Douglas has emphasized, black sexuality emerged as the semiotic production/achievement of complex systems of white male supremacy, and it effected the erasure of black people's human status. They were like animals, sexually volatile and hyperlibidinous, and they were ripe for exploitation. Through a complex history of meanings and practices, being black and female began to mean being sexually deviant. In the language of Sharpley-Whiting, black women became trapped within "an essence of themselves created from without."[78]

The era of colonization was not the first time that men had taken up the pen to inscribe women and thereby construct them through the noetic lens of masculinity. During the early third century of the Common Era, the African bishop Tertullian, for instance, took liberty to exhort Christian virgins to veil so that men would not become susceptible to their hypnotic, entrancing gaze.[79] Ironically, however, it is women who have become victims of the semiotic masculine gaze, being constructed and refashioned from auspiciously human into crafty, sexual creature, or white hysterical case study, or evil witch, or dirty black wench. The innovation of the colonial era, in other words, was to constitute and to rarify an idea of race through complex configurations of meanings and discourse, by deploying gender as an analytical core. This production of meanings was the very making of whiteness, constituted through strategies of displacement and inscription—projecting sexuality onto nonwhites in order to inscribe whiteness as Christian, civilized, and pure, in contrast to hyperlibidinous, sexually wanton *heathens*. The "question of woman," for black women, then, was inextricably linked to the task of resisting the stereotype of being beastly and evil.

A number of black American Christian women responded to the problem of determining what it meant for a black female to be a "woman." As Mary Church Terrell, who served as the founding president of the National Association of Colored Women (NACW), asserted, "a White Woman has only one handicap to overcome—a great one, true, her sex; a colored woman faces two—her sex and her race. A colored man has only one—that of race." Although later analysis might alter Terrell's diction and proffer that sexism—not being a woman—was the handicap, Terrell was right on target when she identified black women's search for humanity as both racialized and gendered.[80]

The overriding signifier of authentic womanhood was the mantle of Christianity. Whites had fostered images of "the African" as savage and of black women as sexually promiscuous and thus immoral. This representation compelled black women to seek ideal womanhood in an unfulfilled Christian development. For example, (Victorian) Christian ideals of the moral woman most frequently defined the images to which black women appealed. This ideal of (Victorian) Christian womanhood underlay much of American Christianity. And it was necessarily the case, in light of racist representation, that the African past was devoid of a suitable model for being human/woman, not simply because of cultural differences between African and European civilizations, but also because *Christ was not in Africa.* Africa, in other words, was not Christianized. Here again, the discrete religious differences between Northern and Southern blacks were not lost on those seeking to interject an organic "civilizing" influence there. The Southern Negro, in the immediate wake of Emancipation, was understood to be base and closer to the unchristianized African savage because the previous system of plantation life had mitigated Southern blacks' assimilation into Protestant Christian Americanism.[81]

The unique psychosexual, racist representations that whites imposed onto black bodies meant that black women faced a peculiar dilemma, furthermore. The surrogacy and vulnerability of black women's bodies to white men's and white women's abuse during enslavement, their status as objects for breeding, and the asexual connotations derived from the iconic role of the black mammy ironically left them with the burden of proving their moral worth and integrity. They were compelled to negate the assumption that a black woman could not be a "lady."

Terrell's words at the NACW's first national convention indicate this very concern. She urged that "only through the home" could any social group "become really good and truly great." For this reason, the NACW aimed to influence the way black families constructed the home and familial domain "to inculcate right principles of living and correct false views of life. Homes, more homes, purer homes, better homes," was the battle cry for their campaign. Outlining a politics of respectability, Terrell echoed the common sentiment of club women when she insisted, "So long as the majority of people call that place home in which the air is foul, the manners bad and the morals worse, just so long is this so called home a menace to health, a breeder of vice, and the abode of crime." And who would bear responsibility for allowing such decadence to continue without intervention? Not only "the inmates of these hovels," but also "those who sit calmly by and make no effort to stem the tide of disease and vice."[82]

Terrell emphasized "pure" homes largely because she was responding to whites' accusation that the typical Southern, one-roomed cabin of indigent blacks resulted in immoral development among the race. The cultivation of "morality and modesty," she pontificated, stood no chance of happening so long as "families of eight or ten men, women and children are all huddled promiscuously together in a single apartment."[83] These ideas of Christian homes, moral uplift, and racial vice or racial "filth" inspired grassroots campaigns by black Christian women to institute what they perceived to be more dignified forms of living, creating greater access to education, job skills, business and domestic training, and societal knowledge. Underlying all of these forms of advancement, however, was the assumption that Christianization was the chief method and guarantor of the Negro race's "arrival."

The black church, therefore, was to be the vehicle of cultural and anthropological elevation for blacks, especially in the South. Cooper and Terrell, far from being a solitary voice crying out in the post-Emancipation wilderness, articulated a broadly held understanding of the church's function and its gendered implications. The club movements among African American women attest to this. By 1903, black women had created over 400 clubs, each with a membership ranging from 50 to 200. The work of these clubs combined a social activism with a distinctively Christianized moral vision for the future of the race and the role of women.[84]

Anna Julia Hayes Cooper is among the most provocative of writers and thinkers to consider for understanding the deeply gendered implications of the categories of the "heathen" and the "nonhistorical." Cooper was born ca. 1858 in Raleigh, North Carolina. After graduating from a substandard school for Negroes, Cooper matriculated at Oberlin, where she eventually earned an M.A. (in 1887). Education and social settlement were among the key areas of her activism. She worked as principal of the M Street High School in the Washington District of Columbia. Perhaps most noteworthy is the fact that Cooper authored the first African American feminist text—*A Voice from the South*. Cooper would, in her sixties, complete a Ph.D. at the Sorbonne in Paris, this despite considerable resistance from her Negro male colleagues in the United States.[85]

Cooper's is not the most celebrated life. In contrast to some of her contemporaries (e.g., W. E. B. Du Bois, Henry McNeal Turner, or Ida B. Wells Barnett), she is far less quoted and less studied. Yet, her strategies of uplift and her public intellectual influence patently demonstrate that she avidly interpreted the material challenges and existential conundrums that commanded the attention of American religionists. As an attentive, brilliant thinker and educator, Cooper was well attuned to the intellectual and cultural domains of her time.

Unlike Crummell and Blyden, who were trained theologians, Cooper never wrote explicitly of Hamitic descent. In fact, Cooper was not concerned with the idea of a Negro presence in antiquity, assuming rather that all the significant historical accomplishments of the Negro race lay before it—thus, the task of historical entry for Negroes. Yet, even absent an explicit regard for Hamitic narrative strategies, Cooper faced a common chore of assessing the worth and potentiality of the "heathen Negro," a category of belief with which she was intimately familiar, endowed by her (Episcopal) Christian knowledge. For this reason, she responded to what constituted the immediate implications of a Hamitic crisis: rescuing the black race from heathen existence, and exiting the platform of Negroes' historical anonymity.

Cooper believed firmly that the Negro race should convert to Christianity *en toto*. She expressed this with a sense of urgency that was not anomalous but, rather, that reflected the most common sentiment of her time. Converting blacks to Christianity meant rescuing them from a condition of godless existence and historical anonymity. Evangelical missionary programs, in these terms, were a form of historical and anthropological rescue. Christian conversion endowed blacks with (divine) humanity and created a portal of entry into *Geist*. More importantly, Cooper never separated the "question of woman" from Negroes' Christianization. It will become evident, in fact, that she understood one to concern the other. Understanding Anna Julia Cooper's response to and influence upon Christianization will elucidate the gendered problems of legitimacy whereby Hamitic anxieties shaped American religion.

In 1886, the colored clergy of the Protestant Episcopal Church convened in Washington, D.C. Cooper, then a graduate student at Oberlin, was invited to address those in attendance. Cooper seized upon the occasion to engage the pressing "question of woman"; she wanted to persuade the clergy that the full participation and agency of colored women was not merely expedient but absolutely essential to advancing the civil, cultural, and spiritual uplift of the race. Her speech, "Womanhood: A Vital Element in the Regeneration and Progress of a Race," would later appear as the opening chapter of *A Voice from the South*.[86]

Cooper began her address by identifying *feudalism* and *Christianity* as the two founts from which modern civilization had inherited its "noble ideal of woman." Through interrogating gender ideals, Cooper suggested a sensibility of history that privileged modern civilization over the primitive, which she narratized through summing up the history and the inferior development of Chinese and Arab cultures. It is because these societies fettered women with deprecating and limiting roles, she suggests, that they were "destitute . . . of the principle of progress."[87]

On the other hand, feudalism (which cultivated chivalry and thereby elevated the status of woman) and Christianity, more importantly, had injected European civilization with the progressive ideal that women were the equal of men. It was the Christian gospel that uniquely viewed "woman as an equal, as a helper, as a friend, as a sacred charge."[88]

Cooper outlines a history of the Christian church from the fall of the Roman Empire to its revival (and culmination in Roman

Catholicism). She relies upon the historical narratives of Anglo-Saxon identity, which glorified the idea of descent from Germanic barbarians who were Christianized and who thereby wed fierce, noble conquest sensibilities with the moral traditions and mythology of the Christian church. The result, according to this narrative tradition, was a European civilization that far exceeded anything existing before. This was the "bud" of civilization that Cooper believed America was to "flower" to maturity.

Cooper's philosophy of history evidences its theological trappings as she explains that "the Gospel is a germ" or seed that infiltrates civilization and grows to maturity, conquering and uplifting the total culture. The presence of the different races in America, Cooper elsewhere explains, was itself the direct result of God's intervention, destined to unfold in a Herderian production of complementary racial contributions that would foster the progress of civilization.[89]

America, as Cooper understood it, was the final frontier of civilization. It was the last stage of divine performance in which the grand finale of civilization's drama would play out. This meant that the Negro race in America was at an especially pivotal historical moment. If Negroes were to participate in this consummate drama, then it was vital for (male) race leaders to understand that "the fundamental agency under God" in the uplift of the race "must be the black woman."[90] At stake in this struggle for sexual equality was the teleological drama of Christianization and civilizing progress.

Cooper emphasized the absolute necessity of "elevated" and "trained" womanhood by reminding her listeners that women were in charge of rearing children. In practical terms, the entire race would pass through their hands and would undergo their influence. Womanhood as motherhood, for this reason, was "the most sacred and solemn trust" ever bequeathed by God to humankind (59). And given the corrupting, decadent conditions of enslavement, black womanhood had to be regenerated, restored, and its dignity protected.

An elevated black womanhood, furthermore, would mean that individual success would no longer substitute for elevating the entire race. "A race is but a total of families. The nation is the aggregate of its homes" (63). It stood to reason that when black women, the keepers of the domestic sphere, became empowered and integrated into social participation, entire Negro families would benefit.[91]

Evangelical missions were the means to this end of race elevation. Of interest on this score is Cooper's attitude toward the South. The South was home to the vast majority of American blacks; the Great

Migration to the North was still decades away. And the majority of the South's blacks had not yet been "civilized" through Christianization. The "Southern Negro," thus, was a prime "[m]ission field for the Church" (64). Cooper's Victorian ideals of culture and her Episcopalian religious background afforded her little patience with "the rank exuberance and often ludicrous demonstrativeness" of "their [the South's] people." Despite the cultural backwardness of Southern Negroes, however, Cooper clinched her appeal by assuring her audience, "the task of proselytizing the American Negro is infinitely less formidable than that which confronted the Church in the Barbarians of Europe" (65). The Negro race would need to traverse the same terrain that whites had once crossed (they too had been heathens and had emerged from a barbaric, idolatrous past).

Cooper strategically appealed to the masculinist interest of her mostly male audience. Instead of arguing for an elevated womanhood merely on the basis that it would benefit black women, she pointed to the benefits that would accrue to "the race,"—read "men." Her language, moreover, was not imbued with the more strictly theological terms of Ethiopianism and Hamitic descent. But her theology of destiny nevertheless resonated with her listeners because they shared fundamental assumptions about *history* and *race*: both were used by God to accomplish divine purpose. And converting the Negro race to Christianity was the absolutely necessary means for that purpose.

One should note that Cooper, moreover, did not articulate a fatalistic theology of destiny—if women are not elevated and trained for leadership, the race will fail. She suggested, rather, that there was a greater divine plan at work—Western civilization *qua* Christian civilization. And the race must enter that world of Christianity or remain uncivilized, backward, and morally wanton. It should become evident, also, that Cooper did not subordinate the "question of woman" to the expedience of race uplift. Rather, she understood equality of the sexes to be the prime indicator of civilization, the unique circumstance wrought by Christian domination. There was no distinction between the history of Christianity and world (i.e., secular) history. The world, specifically America, was merely the stage on which the divine drama was being performed. Again, Christianization was the portal through which woman and, thereby, the race would enter history—hence, the urgency with which Cooper stressed the evangelization of the Negro race.

Yet, this very urgency, this totalizing view of Christianity, demonstrates the problem of (il)legitimacy that plagued black

American existence. Cooper hinted toward this ambivalence when, for example, she referred to the "Southern Negro" in duplicitous terms. On the one hand, she opined that the Protestant Episcopal Church, with its elevated, refined style of worship, was uniquely suited to correcting the vulgar faults of "their people"—that is, the South's Negroes, discursively distancing herself from "those people."[92] On the other hand, she identified with Southern Negroes through circumlocution when she enjoined the denominational leaders in her audience to accept advice on missionizing Southern Negroes from "a Black woman of the South."[93]

Black Worthlessness

In addition to responding to the problem of Negro missions, Cooper also addressed the value placed on Negro humanity. In her essay, "What Are We Worth?", Cooper discussed, from a patently materialist perspective, the value of human life, of human labor, and racial contributions. After explaining, at length, that labor increases the value of all material (i.e., converting raw materials to processed goods), Cooper suggested that Negro labor must be the core of elevating the respectability of the race. She extended this reasoning to include the immaterial, moral contributions of individuals and groups.

Drawing on the familiar assumption of a racial essence, Cooper opines that Southern whites' decadent moral principles had lowered the quality of Negro constitution; to this end, she pits white Puritan idealism against Southern white culture. Christian elevation and labor—productivity—must counter this dissipatory effect in order to cultivate the highest potential of the race. For the most part, Cooper maintains that racial worth must be assessed solely on the basis of labor and productivity. What one produces is the final indicator of what one is worth. This is the cold and bitter truth of reality. And if the Negro race were to advance, it would need to heed this axiom. Embedded in her discourse, however, are pronouncements of intrinsic human worth. It is Cooper's ambivalence on this score that indicates the most daunting implication of her discussion: Negroes are worth less than whites. She alludes to intrinsic human worth in order to avoid this devastating conclusion.

One of the most compelling interpretations of Cooper is by T. Denean Sharpley-Whiting, who provides a Fanonian reading of Cooper's views on gender and racial worth. Sharpley-Whiting takes Cooper's views on culture and productivity as a cue to contemplate the *existential* worth of blacks. "To ask blacks what they are worth," says Sharpley-Whiting, "is in fact to ask them to justify their presence, their continued existence."[94] Sharpley-Whiting situates her reading of Cooper's discussion by considering Frantz Fanon's analysis of colonization's dehumanizing effect on the signified worth of nonwhites. Writing in the context of the Algerian war for independence against France, Fanon explained that "natives" (namely Algerians *qua* nonwhites) signify "not only the absence of values but also the negation of values."[95]

Sharpley-Whiting applies this to the racial conditions of Cooper's era to explicate a glaring problem: the *inevitability* of black worthlessness. Negroes *were* laborers; Cooper, in fact, states this in order to debunk the misrepresentative myth of the lazy, slothful Negro. The centuries of slavery and ruthless demand of unrequited toil in the wake of Emancipation should have made the materialist question of their worth a nonissue.

But the question of worth, for Cooper, was never merely a racial one; it was also a gendered problem. As Sharpley-Whiting phrases it,

> If one is male, one is valued; if one is female, one is less valued—if one is black and female, one has no value. . . . Trapped in a valued-less existence, what resources are open to the worth less (black males) and the worthless (black females)?[96]

Existential value, Sharpley-Whiting emphasizes, is not merely a materialist issue. "Economic worthlessness, and disease, mediated through racial difference, are experienced internally or psychologically."[97] At this level, value (existential worth) becomes a fundamental obsession of racial existence. It is inevitably tied to race narratives and semiotic constructions. White male skin becomes the signifier of value. And any retreat or distance from this sign is a descent into the dark, feminine abyss of anti-value.

One must understand racial and gendered worth(lessness) in these terms in order to grasp the dimensions of what was at stake for American Negroes of Cooper's era. They were advancing from a past void of history and beleaguered by a racial and gendered worthlessness. To become people of God ostensibly meant breaking free from the suffocating distortions of illegitimacy and worthlessness. This is why Cooper advances without reserve the process of Christianization. The deep anxieties that animated her shrewd yet vilifying discourse perdured because the racial, religious, and gendered symbols communicated basic perceptions of human status and worth. It is necessary to perceive that human status is gendered so that one might appreciate what was at stake in race uplift discourse of the nineteenth century.

Nineteenth century feminists such as Terrell and Cooper are frequently critiqued for their ambivalent feminism—they advocated the sphere of domesticity as the appropriate role of women and accepted the notion of a definitive feminine nature. They also viewed the Church and Christianity both liberatively and uncritically. On the one hand, it is true that they were responding to a reality in which their speech defied an otherwise racist portrayal of black women as sexual deviants. On the other hand, the logics embedded in the Christian myth demanded that they despise the figure of the heathen. They were agents of an antiblack, anti-African religious contempt rooted in Christian identity.

Black religionists, ultimately, sought to counter racist proscriptions that would otherwise bar them from accessing social, material, and political economies. In doing so, they participated fully in the idea of being people of God, following the concomitant narrative logic.[98] Rhetorics of race and gender uplift, for this reason, depended preeminently upon Christianizing the race. This idea, in turn, confounded black women's experience of gender in starkly sexualized and racialized terms because it assumed that non-Christian black womanhood, and thus non-Christian black women, were morally evil and sexually wanton. Ultimately, it afforded them the benefits of a power discourse—that of being people of the deity. The cost of this empowerment, however, was a virulent denigration of blackness that prompted Negroes to flee the dark symbolism of pre-Christian Negro existence in Africa and to promote a vilifying derision of Negroes in the American South.

Race and the American People(s) of God

The preceding chapters of this study have examined how American Christians responded to racial and religious existence through recourse to the Hamitic idea. More specifically, Christian identity was articulated and understood necessarily by referring to those who were not people of God, by encoding and elaborating upon the existence of those beyond the pale of Christian identity. This final chapter will demonstrate that the resulting conundrum of alterity and existential illegitimacy, as manifested in American rhetorics of Hamitic identity, is a perduring problem of anti-heathen meanings endemic to divine identity itself. The study will conclude by arguing that divine identity must be interpreted in light of the American episode of Hamitic identity, with critical attention toward the dehumanizing distortions, semiotic wrangling, and existential absurdity that such has induced.

Narrating Black Christianity's Emergence

The Hamitic idea, as represented in nineteenth-century American Christianity, emerges as the underside of the narrative knowledge that the Christian myth communicates. It is within light of this narrative knowledge that one should consider the hermeneutical postures of scholars examining the history and emergence of black American Christianity. African American religion has been the object of sustained intellectual inquiry since at least the time of W. E. B. Du Bois' sweeping Atlanta University studies of the "Negro Church."[1] Scholars usually approach African American religion, or black religion, by assessing the historical development of African American Christianity— and this in its institutional form of the black Church most frequently. Black Christianity, thus, becomes the normative lens through which is

read the religious history of African Americans. And it is this historicizing trend that rings problematic in light of the conundrums of
divine identity.[2]

This historiographical assumption, because it renders Christian
identity normative for black Americans, oversimplifies the history of
American religion and produces a narrative logic denying that non-
Christian blacks and non-Christian religious forms have been significant
to black religious history. Such historicizing assumptions semiotically
disfigure and dehumanize the non-Christian subject by devaluing that
subject. More importantly, this mode of historicizing celebrates the
erasure or decimation of non-Christian forms and non-Christian identities, through cultural genocide, as a positive development in black
religion. The Christian myth of being people of God, to this extent,
justifies the acts of domination and erasure that attended the performance of Christian identity. This violence is gilded as "Christian arrival"
through perennial acts of narration that celebrate or elevate the conquest of the Christian myth over dark peoples.

This problem in historical scholarship is evident, for example, with
the subject of Ethiopianism, which was arguably the most influential
ideological force among nineteenth-century black American Christians.
Ethiopianism as a religious ideology successfully animated the discourse of race uplift among missionaries, women's clubs, educators,
and the like because it persuasively articulated a pragmatic vision for
Negroes' participation in a broader social and spiritual arena. Most
important was its religious message of redemption for spiritual darkness: the Negro could become Christian. Dark folk could emerge from
their pre-American history of heathen existence and their American
decline into cultural depravity (because of slavery) and become whole.
Preeminently, this meant becoming Christian. And this Christian
ascent communicated that being a "member of the race" meant being
Christian, being among the people of God. It demanded a departure
from the "dark" existence of the pre-Christian past. By the noetic exigencies of this myth, the non-Christian was spiritually ugly, reprehen-
sible, a marker of hell.

Ethiopianism has been the focus of serious academic attention in
recent scholarship. Wilson Moses, for example, has produced considerable work on the subject through his interpretations of Black
Nationalism. Also of major importance is Albert Raboteau's work.
Moses emphasizes that Ethiopianism, as an understanding of destiny
and chosenness, is especially American and thus radically continuous
with dominant forms of American Christianity. Raboteau's work on

this theme has likewise helped to uncover its historical role, especially noting how responses to race and slavery have differentiated performances of being God's (American) Israel.[3]

These studies have not, however, addressed Christianity's disfigurement of the non-Christian (or, in semiotic terms, the construction of the non-Christian) as such. Classic and recent treatments of African American Christianity's emergence consistently fail to examine how Christian loathing, which has historically assumed a hostile posture toward non-Christian identities, has significantly informed the disposition of American (*including* African American) Christianity. Consistently ignored is the deep, ironic self-contempt derived from not only Westernism but also Christianity. The rise of black Christianity is instead virtually always celebrated as a grand arrival whose occurrence implies no major problems.

Carter G. Woodson's classic history of the "Negro" church, for example, did not take issue with the cultural assault exercised against blacks through missionary religion; Woodson, in fact, called for more blacks to propagate Christianity throughout the ranks of the black race. The same was true of E. Franklin Frazier. Frazier interpreted black religious history in terms that denied the very existence and significance of African-derived and otherwise non-Christian religiosity among U.S. blacks—with the exception of twentieth-century "cults"; he was also oblivious to the social import of a "remembered" non-Christian past vis-à-vis Christianity in the New World. Such omission is especially unfortunate, given his repeated insistence upon the virtually complete annihilation of blacks' Afro-religiosity and his sustained examination of missionary efforts, which he read as wholly benevolent.[4]

Nor have most recent works departed from this trend. Lawrence Mamiya and C. Eric Lincoln, for example, illustrate this disposition in their important history of African American churches. Although they consistently survey the missionary programs of black Christian denominations, the deep-seated anti-Africanness of such missionary religion is patently a nonissue for them. Even such keen revisionist scholarship as that of Evelyn Brooks Higginbotham and William Andrews, while sustaining a gender-critical historiography of excellent quality, is nevertheless unconcerned with the way Christian identity itself, which was defined in opposition to non-Christian womanhood, confounded black women's experience of gender.[5]

The most common historiographical pattern is to highlight with honor and pride the fact of African cultural presence, particularly West African religiosity, while refusing to critique the hostility of

African American Christianity toward black "heathen" existence as a problem of Christianity per se. Albert Raboteau, Mechal Sobel, Eugene Genovese, and Vincent Harding demonstrate this hermeneutical posture.[6] Raboteau's *Slave Religion*, for example, places African survivalism at the fore of discussion. He examines the complex patterns of retention that inform African American culture, arguing that African religions were indeed very much a part of black church beginnings. But Raboteau does not address the anti-African sentiment deeply embedded in black Christianity itself. He assumes, instead, that black Christian conversion was necessary and wholly auspicious.

Black Theology and the People of God

Black theology is the area of scholarship that has most extensively articulated this interpretive theme.[7] The context for black theology's emergence was both intellectual and social. Black theology was inspired by the Black Power movement, whose radical call for unmitigated black self-determination was shocking yet liberative because it was unconcerned with white Americans' response or support. The Black Power movement sought, rather, to redirect the efforts of blacks so that African Americans would embrace their blackness and would be freed to practice solidarity with themselves. The message of the movement was that blacks did not need whites. Blacks needed power.[8]

Today, a number of black theologians have taken on the task of articulating what Christian identity means in light of blackness and liberation. The earliest and most comprehensive statement of black theology, however, emerged with the work of James H. Cone. Every major work of black theology, in fact, responds to and builds upon the scholarship of Cone. In his seminal *Black Theology and Black Power*, Cone conceded that Black Power was a radical, even shocking call for blacks to seize the day and to embrace self-determination. Its basis was not friendly relations between the races. Social justice for oppressed blacks, rather, was its chief contingency, the exigencies of which subordinated amiable race relations to the need for ending racism and white rule over the lives and material reality of blacks *by any means* that blacks deemed necessary. And yet, Black Power, Cone insisted, was not unchristian, nor was it some ill-conceived message to be tolerated given the lack of alternatives for the desperate black masses. Black Power, rather, was "Christ's central message to twentieth century America."[9]

Out of this crisis arose the question: Who are the people of God? The concern comprised the ecclesiological. This necessitated, however, a further question: What did it mean to be the people of God in the world? What was the existential import of being God's people? How does being the people of God translate into practical, lived reality? Black theologians agreed that the work of God was the work of liberation, of bringing freedom to those who had been deprived of their very humanity. But where did this leave white and black Christians in relation to each other, for instance? And what role should violence play in this struggle? Finally, how should one speak about God's identifying with the oppressed?

"The Christian church is that community of people called into being by the life, death, and resurrection of Jesus."[10] Thus, any statement of ecclesiology, Cone posits, is necessarily a statement about Christology. Insofar as the church is the people of God, Cone has argued that being God's people is contingent upon participating in Christ's work of liberating the oppressed. Jesus has freed blacks because he has come into the world and taken on blackness. Because blackness is God's revelation to modern America, furthermore, only those who become black (regardless of their skin color) are the true church. Succinctly, this means that being part of the true church, for white Christians, demands treason to whiteness and lived commitment to the struggles of the poor and of peoples of color.[11]

Most important in biblical tradition, Cone identifies, is the theme that God is the God of the oppressed. God takes sides in the events of human history, instead of remaining neutral on the sidelines. The preeminent biblical instance of this was God's decision to choose Israel and to deliver them out of slavery. Modern Christians, Cone urges, should recognize that God has made the goals of black freedom God's own work. God has *chosen* blacks not to suffer but to be free because they are made to suffer against their will.[12]

Responding to the objections of whites and some blacks who felt that blackness was exclusive, Cone argued that becoming black is in fact what creates the possibility of authentic reconciliation. Cone explained authentic reconciliation by way of emphasizing that God has reconciled blacks to their blackness so that they are empowered to embrace and not loathe their identity. Reconciliation also has direct implications for whites as well. They are freed from bondage to whiteness and can experience their humanity by committing themselves to fighting against racism and white supremacy in order to advance the freedom struggles of oppressed people.[13]

In his *We Have Been Believers*, James Evans examines this same idea of being people of God in relation to African American Christians.[14] Evans notes especially that black churches were born not of heresy trials and doctrinal disputes but of black Americans' freedom struggles and resistance to social forces of exclusion and dehumanization. This development, furthermore, was not happenstance. It was, in fact, through the "timely" revelation of God, he suggests, that African Americans came to realize they were the people of God.[15] Moreover, in departure from those who would analytically deracinate the black church from any discrete cultural matrix (e.g., E. Franklin Frazier), Evans argues that the African heritage of blacks did not hinder but sustained their existence and identity, grounding their faith in a relevant form of social existence. It was the Bible, however, that communicated to African American Christians their identity as people of God. The emergence of African American Christianity, he concludes, is inseparable from the history of racial solidarity and cultural tendencies. Evans draws upon Victor Turner's notion of *communitas* and Emil Brunner's notion of the *ekklēsia* in order to articulate an understanding of ecclesiology. Preeminently, he posits, the black church is the chosen people of God and must live out that chosenness through service (*diakonia*). Most succinctly, this service means participating in God's liberation work.[16]

Among the most provocative of early black theologians was Joseph Washington. Washington's *Black Religion* identified white churches as the true locus of Christianity. Black Christians, he felt, had retained barely enough residual African culture to prevent their successfully assimilating into Christianity; ultimately, they had produced a racial religion that was something other than Christianity.[17]

Of even greater implication was Washington's argument that black Christians were chosen to suffer so that Americans, specifically white Americans, would be redeemed. Washington conceded that slavery was a cruel and vicious system. Yet, it had effectively bound together blacks and whites. God effected the enslavement of Africans in America in order to release "whites from their blasphemous bondage to whiteness and racial superiority."[18] This idea of redemptive suffering on the one hand recognized that the genocidal deaths and violations endemic to enslavement and America's racial caste system were not for naught. A purposeful God had been working a divine plan through them. And yet this very idea reduced blacks to expendable entities whose suffering and deaths were justified because it would benefit white Americans.

Albert Cleage, Jr., articulated that blacks as a racial group were the chosen people of God, not because they were Christians nor *by analogy* to the story of Israel. Blacks were God's chosen people because Israel was a racially black nation.[19] Cleage called for Americans to recognize that Jesus was not white but was a man of color; in fact, Cleage emphasized, Jesus was black. This black messiah had come to restore the black nation of Israel by restoring dignity and black rule. Cleage emphatically denied that blacks' experience of inhumane brutality, poverty, and suffering was redemptive. In the immediate wake of Martin Luther King, Jr.'s death, Cleage reminded his audience that although he had disagreed with King's belief that blacks' suffering was redemptive, Cleage "loved everything [King] did." Cleage recognized in King the ability to lead blacks to stand against whites so that they would look "each other in the face, eyeball to eyeball."[20] This was an act of courageous action that indicated black dignity. But blacks' suffering was not redemptive.

Given the imperative of responding to a history of domination, black theologians sought through dialogue to work out the most authentic understanding of the gospel and liberation. It was in this context that Charles H. Long articulated his view of American Christianity. Long, who emphasized a history of religions approach, urged black theologians to respond to the symbolic and phenomenological problems of Christianity. As a mythic structure, Long indicated, the Christian world of symbols and meanings threatened the very substance of black religious thought. Because Christianity was a language system of knowledge, it represented a colonial *reality* vis-à-vis the reality of pre-Christian blacks.[21] For this reason, he concluded, no black theology could be authentic if it was not grounded in black experience. Long also highlighted the need to articulate black religious experience through considering Africa (as a historical reality and religious symbol), the involuntary status of blacks' presence in the United States, and the experience of God.[22]

Long later recognized the work of Cone and Native American theologian Vine Deloria to represent what he termed "theologies of the opaque." By this, Long recognized that they functioned to deny whites the authority to define reality arbitrarily for the historical victims of colonization.[23] This was the point of departure for embodying through discourse a type of freedom that chooses to be, to exist, despite the strictures of constraint that would prevent its doing so.[24]

Another point of dissent was voiced by James Deotis Roberts, who argued that black Christians should opt for a more conciliatory approach to whites (pace Cone, who leveled a sharp critique of whiteness as demonic). Roberts responded specifically to the proposals of Cone and Albert Cleage in order to correct what he viewed as their unmitigated Christocentrism and nationalism, respectively.[25]

In his discussion of a "Search for Peoplehood," particularly, Roberts rejected Cleage's emphasis on the Black Messiah and the black nation as nationalism in "religious dress." This critique was ironic because Roberts referred to Israel as the original chosen people. And in no way did he regard this Israelitic claim to being the chosen nation of God as nationalism, although it is precisely such. Cleage's emphasis on being the chosen nation, in a sense, was actually most faithful to the Hebrew meaning of being Israel. Roberts' analysis seems to miss this point entirely.

Roberts defended the idea that black Christians must make meaning of their suffering because the cross, which symbolizes suffering, must never be separated from the Christian faith.[26] He ultimately proposed an idea of peoplehood based on the church as a family. Blacks had a special peoplehood, however, because their American experience of suffering had positioned them to "enter into a stewardship of suffering" so that they might save or purge the larger (white) society.[27]

Roberts drew upon the language and caveats espoused by Charles Long in order to suggest that black theology could not depend upon a Barthian Christocentrism (pace Cone) because such a framework was exclusivist and undermined recourse to the cultural resources of blacks. Roberts, in fact, faulted Cone for not drawing upon African religions in order to articulate a liberationist message of black religion.[28] In light of the fact that Roberts did not do this himself, however, his critique remains puzzling.

To his credit, Roberts was one of few black theologians who appealed *directly* to Long's arguments in order to clarify the claims of black theology. Ironically, however, Roberts himself did not utilize African or African-derived religions in order to provide a theological framework. It becomes clear from his discussion, in fact, that Roberts conflates black religion into Christianity and the church, reproducing the "invisibility" that Long critiques. He failed, moreover, to engage Long's fundamental point that the very symbolic world and religious logic of Christianity rendered problematic black existence and indigenous or pre-Christian histories. Roberts instead drew upon the Pauline language of "the household of God image" in order to argue that, through the fatherhood of God, all Christians become one family. It is through the patriarchal language of family, therefore, that the meaning of being people of God is fully realized.[29]

Womanist theologians have pointed to the sexist tendencies by black male theologians who repeatedly ignored the historical agency of black women and who failed to address directly the perduring sexism in black churches. The writings of Delores Williams, Jacqueline Grant, and Kelly Brown Douglas, for instance, have interpreted the life of Jesus and biblical traditions in light of black women's concerns. They have also foregrounded the manner whereby African American women in the past distinctively appropriated Christianity to address the problems of survival in a racist, sexist, classist society.[30]

Williams, interestingly, has responded to uses of the Exodus theme by proffering a hermeneutic of "identification ascertainment," which interrogates divine violence meted out against innocent peoples in the biblical texts (e.g., the genocide of Canaanites) by ascertaining with which characters in the text biblical authors have identified and with which characters in the text contemporary theologians identify.[31] The strength of Williams' analysis is evidenced when she clearly states that the Exodus story is merely another part of a narrative of conquest and death to those who are not among the people of God. What is more, Williams rightly notes that even Jesus is implicated in the anti-gentile ethnocentrism of Judean religion—she cites, for instance, the Matthean attribution (10:5–6) that the message of the kingdom is exclusively for Israel.[32] Black theologians and all other Christian theologians would do well to ponder this constructive critique.

Williams seems to diagnose black theologians' emphasis on the Exodus story and election as a particularly *masculinist* preoccupation. It is certainly true that black male theologians excluded black women's experiences from the discourse of liberation and did so through an imperative of male identity. The focus on the Exodus, however, derives from preoccupation with an identity compulsion that is not masculinist but *Christian*. Succinctly, this imperative is a desire to identify with the deity who wins—Yahweh—and with the people of that deity. It would be desirable if divine identity and the narrative logic of election were limited to men or to performances of masculinity. Unfortunately, any serious study of the many women (including African American evangelical women) who have participated in missionary activity and evangelical conversion reveals that this is not the case. Victory over the heathen has historically been endemic to the Christian discourse of men and women alike.

What is perplexing, given the critical hermeneutics she employs, is Williams' recourse to the character Hagar in order to secure a locus or narrative site for discussing black women's experience. Not only does she seem to assume without hesitation the historicity of the narrative, but she also suggests its efficacy in enabling "black people to see their roots in the biblical story."[33] One should ask, What biblical story? Since Williams uses the singular here, it would seem that she is referring to the Israelitic metanarrative. This desire to locate the "roots of black people" in the Bible has been a perennial difficulty because, as the immediate study has indicated, the construction of biblical racial histories is contingent upon deploying meanings of illegitimacy and rendering world history invisible. In light of her critiques, her use of the Hagar narrative urges serious attention toward this problem. One could argue, in fact, that Williams' brilliant analysis of the ideological struggle behind such texts demonstrates why blacks should desist from seeking "their roots" in the Bible.

Despite the long history of critical responses, however, the most frequent pattern among theologians is to disregard the problems of divine identity and the attempts to enter the biblical story. Even now, in the twenty-first century, it is still unusual for any Christian theologian to publicly consider that the most despised persons in biblical narrative are not Israelites nor the poor but those who are *not* God's people, most notably the Canaanite descendants of Ham.[34] As a result, seldom is a connection made between the theological roots of divine identity and the contemporary performances of divine identity that have resulted from centuries of encoding the non-Christian as evil.

Also problematic is the continuing claim that the biblical deity is on the side of the oppressed. Itumeleng Mosala has developed an elaborate analysis of this idea among black theologians in North America and in South Africa. Mosala notes, for instance, that black theologians commonly employ a category of the "Word of God" that places the Bible above critique. The very language of the Word of God animates a discourse that renders invisible the histories of struggle that underlie biblical texts.

To the claim that God is on the side of the oppressed, posits Mosala, one must ask, "Which God—Baal, or El, or Yahweh? the white God or the black God? the male God or the female God? All were Gods of the Israelites."[35] Most importantly, these Gods were associated with different class strata in Israelite society. Yahweh triumphs because the urban, ruling-class, landholding, royal stratum triumphed over landless, disinherited Israelites. It is biblical texts themselves, Mosala refrains, that indicate this history of struggle, ironically, the very texts to which Christian theologians appeal in order to make the claim that God is on the side of the oppressed. For this reason, "no theology of struggle," Mosala urges, "can any longer afford not to recognize the biblical texts' witness to the fact that there are many Gods."[36]

Yet, this is precisely what black theologians have done. Writing just a few years after Mosala's critique, Josiah Young, Jr., sought to develop a more sophisticated description of the Word of God with no hint of taking seriously the perspectives and caveats that Mosala proffered.[37] In fact, in his attempt to recover the ancestral legacies of Edward Blyden and Alexander Crummell, Young does precisely what Mosala warns against by regarding the Bible as the Word of God; the history of struggles in those texts is rendered invisible. By way of connecting black theology to African legacies, Young celebrates Crummell's and Blyden's tireless efforts to Christianize the race, which necessarily meant eradicating black heathenism. It is perhaps no accident that Young seems to miss entirely this irony.

Other works have explicitly rejected a critique of Christian identity as problem, arguing instead that only Western or Eurocentric appropriations of Christianity are at fault. This is evident in the works of Eddie Glaude, C. Eric Lincoln and Lawrence Mamiya, Dwight Hopkins and Gayraud Wilmore. In his *Introducing Black Theology of Liberation*, for example, Hopkins carefully recapitulates Charles H. Long's critique of the conquest legacy upon which Christianity has thrived—Long observes that when Christianity arrives on a continent, it vilifies and/or renders invisible non-Christian forms. Yet Hopkins seems to dismiss Long's major point when he merely repeats the claim that African American Christianity is best suited to represent all African Americans collectively, Christian and non-Christian.[38]

Eddie Glaude contends that African Americans identified with Israel because their historical struggles recalled "the pattern of salvation revealed to them in the Bible."[39] But such a claim must be qualified in light of the fact that blackness has been a very "Canaanite" experience, one quite contrary to that of Israel. The Israelitic metanarrative of salvation, moreover, is contingent upon conquest and genocide, representing a terse departure from African American historical struggles for freedom.

There is a reason for this refusal to foreground the struggles in the text and the violence of the narratives. *Ultimately, it is the God who orders the genocide of the Canaanites whom Christian theologians refuse to question.* This is perhaps the most significant reason why Cone, Young, Dwight Hopkins, and others have either ignored or explicitly contested the caveats that Mosala has sounded. They are committed not to the Gods of Israel but to Yahweh, the God who triumphs over the Gods of oppressed Israelites and Canaanites. Even Williams, who is critical of the narratives that glorify the genocide of indigenous Canaanites, is careful to avoid directly critiquing the character of Yahweh. And yet, it would appear that this level of analysis and response is precisely what is required in order to address adequately the violence of divine identity.

In these historical terms, there exists no innocent version of Christianity. Black Christianity has been no exception to this. Walter Williams, in his *Black Americans and the Evangelization of Africa*, sought to demonstrate the forms of identity violence that attended black missions.[40] Gayraud Wilmore, in a strident defense of black missionary religion, insisted that Williams' work was self-depreciating and that black missionaries were not guilty of the same "cultural imperialism and racism" that whites produced. In his effort to "set the record straight," Wilmore seems to be more committed to Christian expansionism than to the victims of Christian expansionism. He is completely unwilling to admit that colonialism and the Christian myth triumphed over dark peoples because of the vices of not only Westernism but also *Christianity*, including black Christianity.[41] Wilmore, rather, celebrates this conversion as a wholly positive development.

Christians, in the main, must address with integrity the contradiction of claiming to be for justice while deploying texts and meanings that reinscribe patterns of religious hatred by vilifying the heathen. If they wish to hold onto the narratives without openly and forthrightly critiquing the violent acts of domination and alterity that inhere to those narratives and the God of that alterity, then they should at least *qualify* their language so that it is clear that they are not committed to freedom for all peoples but only for those who are people of God. Christian theology, to this end, might do well to carry a disclaimer—a warning—so that at least those who are on the underside of such theology will not be misled into thinking they are included.

Those who would dismiss the problem of divine identity violence as trivial or inconsequential should consider that the meaning of being people of God is always historically situated and existentially charged; it has yielded tremendous material consequences in recent times. Some might proffer that the genocide of Canaanite peoples narrated in biblical texts never actually happened. This is a valid point. Yet, it fails to address the issue because the point of the narratives is not mere historicity but ideology. Robert Allen Warrior, for this reason, has proffered that "the Canaanites should be at the center of Christian theological reflection and political action. They are the last remaining ignored voice in the text, except perhaps for the land itself."[42] Warrior, along with Regina Schwartz, recognizes that biblical scholarship has almost unanimously rejected the historicity of the conquest narratives. Alternative theories of settlement, less violent, have been proffered.[43] But, again, this misses the point. Warrior notes that most people continue to read the text as it stands, not as biblical scholars might want them to read it. All that remains for us is the narratives. The most urgent problem, then, is not that of history but of ideology.

Only those who are, for instance, prepared to define the language of divine identity before occupied Palestinians, the most patent example of modern-day "Canaanites," should dare to speak further about being the Israel of God or the people of God. Modern history has witnessed the most wry, unjust turn of events in Palestine. And American Christians have been among the most unheeding in supporting an Israeli state that, through strategies of religious nationalism, continues to justify displacing, brutalizing, killing, and otherwise dehumanizing Palestinians.[44]

On the other hand, there will be those who are more committed to the language and narratives of divine identity than to the causes of historical peoples who unjustly suffer beneath the grinding wheels of a discourse and ideology that dehumanize the heathen and that justify incredible acts of domination, control, and disparagement. These theologians, in light of the critiques by Long, Mosala, Warrior, Schwartz, and Delores Williams, may respond that the narratives afford contemporary Christian peoples some hope and empowerment, without which they will suffer intolerably.

Those who take on this perspective will be quick to point out that the language of being people of God has been a steadfast source of strength and is central to the identity of Christian faith. But this only means that their faith will lose its identity if it acts upon the belief that the well-being of historical peoples is more important than the narratives of divine violence and divine identity. In other words, it is an alternative way of expressing that their very identity as people of God is made possible because they tread upon the bodies and blood—the identities and selves—of those on the underside of Christian narrative knowledge.

It would seem, however, that black theology particularly is well positioned to take on the task of articulating the interests of those who have been silenced in biblical texts and, more urgently, contemporary Hamites. As a "theology of the opaque," black theology emerged from the urgent need to articulate the implications of a subaltern, oppressed history. Its very origin was constituted through the act of speaking power to an identity-location that was represented in the most horrid, negating terms. The virulent heterosexism so rampant, for example, in American Christianity—black Christianity has been no exception to this—is a compelling opportunity to engage the relationship between the struggles of the text and the liberation of the oppressed.

Gary Comstock and Elias Farajaje-Jones have demonstrated that biblical texts demonized Hamitic peoples by attacking their sexuality. "Canaanites," "witches," and "faggots" have been on the receiving end of the same violent divine identities, which are constructed by naming the "people of God" *qua* those who are not the "other."[45] It is no coincidence that idolatry and nonreproductive or same-sex relations have been intimately linked. Narratives such as the Sodom-and-Gomorrah tale have functioned in modern contexts to demonize the identities of those who are not God's people—worthy of only the most vicious, divinely approved genocide or dehumanizing negation through denial of civil and human rights. American Christianity is in dire need of a public, critically informed discourse that begins with critiquing the ideologies of divine identity in order to address Christianity's complicity with heterosexism, American colonization, xenophobia, and the myriad of contemporary crises intersecting with divine identity.

Dark Bodies and Divine Identities

The foregoing has argued for a corrective to the discourse of divine identity by assessing its impact on non-Christians. But it is also necessary to consider what effect divine identity has upon Christians themselves. It is true that identifying with Yahweh's Israel was affirming and empowering for black Christians. I have demonstrated at length this empowerment and defense of blacks' humanity specifically through examining the Hamitic texts produced by black Christians. It is also true, however, that the narrative imposed absurdity and disparagement onto black Christians. In essence, it is necessary to ask why black Christianity is the dominant (and thus dominating) form of black American religion, a form that continues to demonize (black) non-Christian identities.

What has been the history of domination that effected the conquest of the Christian myth among "the children of Ham"? It is, in part, the history of constructing the heathen or non-Christian as illegitimate vis-à-vis the people of God. The production of meanings germane to divine identity, in essence, is borne out by inscribing the heathen character as a dark symbol whose only viable option is self-erasure through conversion to Christian identity.

The perennial African American "problem of being" fundamentally comprises the struggle to imagine and to perform a "black" (othered) self. This problem of being is by no means peculiar to blacks or to peoples of color. It is, rather, an enduring struggle for all human beings. This study has focused on its particular instance, however, *qua* Hamitic identity. The Americanized figure of Ham induced racialized contradictions of existence through defining a religious (Christian) identity. In this sense, the problem of illegitimacy has been one of religious identification.

Alternatively, one might say that the conundrum of the heathen as Hamitic was *racial*, to the degree that being (or not being) people of God constituted the phenomenal condition of belonging to a folk or people—that is, the experience of racial belonging. Through a complex configuration of social forces and historical circumstances, Western Christian identity came to define the non-Christian as heathen and to dehumanize the heathen in turn. At the same time, burgeoning ideas of Anglo-Saxon identity configured the origin of whiteness through the narrative knowledge of the biblical world. Given that the primal state of human beings was understood to be white (Adam and Eve), the foundational biblical narratives of Christian culture encoded Christian supremacy to depict the figure of Ham through "dark" hues of the racialized heathen.

America, in this schema, was experienced as the literal meeting place of the three races, the descendants of Noahic generation: Shemitic, Hamitic, and Japhetic. When biblically minded Americans interpreted nation and race in these terms, a marvelous conflation of time, space, and history occurred. In the Israelitic theater of the New World, modern peoples imaged themselves as new people by performing ancient identities. When the Israelitic/Christian myth of *divine* identity was superimposed onto the modern mythology of *racial* identity, the resulting significations were unprecedented. In essence, two different systems of peopling were operating in synthesis to create a volatile field of knowledge . . . and power. This field doubly racialized its referents.

Some peoples were identified with God; they were children of Shem and Japheth. They were white and Jewish.[46] The very success of white conquests, furthermore, made manifest the destiny of whites, specifically, to become a beacon to the rest of the world, a city on a hill, the Israel of God. Then there were the children of Ham, who were the present reminders of a divine curse, living icons of enmity with God, paragons of decadence. Their only hope was to effect the most expeditious retreat from being heathen by becoming the people of God.

To be Christian and white/"Japhetic" was, therefore, to exist under a double affirmative. This affirmative was further elevated through masculinity for white males. On the underside of this aggregate identity were the folk who lived the double negative of Hamitic/Negro and heathen, even if the latter only by historical association. And this negation was further vilified through femininity; black women were further disfigured by it. Because of this, black physical bodies signified unmitigated existential, even corporeal illegitimacy. To be white was to be a descendent of Japheth, a sublime existence. To be Negro, however, was to experience one's body, one's physicality, becoming imprisoned within the "soul" of the heathen.

Entry into the biblical world of Christian symbols created this experience. Such an entry gave sight to American eyes so that they might peer into the very beginnings of human existence and behold the origin and journey of the three great races. This noetic vision was *ultimate* knowledge and constituted the terms of ultimate existence. For Africans, passage into the New World would eventually become entry into this semiotic world of meanings and absurdities. The characterization of Ham is evident from the fact that nineteenth-century interlocutors consistently recognized that Hamitic identity was non-Christian. Ham, in other words, symbolized those who were *not* affiliated with the God of Christianity, the Israelitic deity.

The figure of Ham was not, however, entirely negating. Ham signified historical, ancient existence of the Negro race and technological, cultural, civilizationist ideals of accomplishment. It is this more positive, historicist interest in Ham that animated Negro Christians' participation in the Hamitic idea. This recourse made feasible arguments for Negroes' humanity and historical existence, and it allowed for Negroes' participation in *Geist* (i.e., in the History that mattered). Part and parcel of this historical interest was the fact that Negroes could be accounted for in the biblical record.

Robert Hood described at length the meanings that Christian tradition has assigned to blackness, and he concluded that not until the era of American slavery did there emerge significant changes to the tradition because black people themselves began to augment the tradition. For the first time, positive meanings were assigned to blackness from within the Christian theological tradition.[47] The same might be said of Ham. For centuries, in different traditions, Ham had been associated with black or dark-skinned Africans. This "body" of meanings repeatedly disfigured and disparaged the referents of such symbolism. This means that black Christians who inscribed Hamitic identity in positive terms produced something novel in the history of Christian theology. For the first time, Christians conceived of the Hamitic and the semiotics of blackness in dignified terms.

Hamitic rhetorics were thoroughly angst-ridden, however, because when Negroes signified upon the Hamitic, they inevitably reinforced the very meanings that induced them to make recourse to Ham in the first place. Biblical narratives share a common goal of identity maintenance. Such a phenomenological common denominator of biblical texts, made evident in this study, meant that deploying the narratives as resources for affirmation and freedom consistently privileged the identity of those who were people of God by *necessarily* disparaging and vilifying the identity of those who were not-people-of-God. Simply put, writers such as Benjamin Tanner and Edward Blyden had to agree that Ham, although mighty in his posterity's accomplishment, was illegitimate, ungodly, and stood condemned. Ham was evil. The figure that saved them from historical nonexistence or insignificance at the same time encoded them as heathens, racialized heathens.

There was hope, however. Negroes could become people of God. Both individually and collectively, the race could become Christianized. The escape from illegitimacy (conversion) meant agreeing with its ideological basis. It meant accepting as axiom that the legitimate people were necessarily those who were affiliated with the Judeo-Christian deity. It also meant performing yet another cycle of identity violence via Christian missions,[48] not merely against ancient narratized figures but also against contemporary heathens, be they the heathens in Africa or the heathens among Southern Negroes. Even Negro Christians who never personally pursued missionary work (most Christians did not) nevertheless participated fully in an identity contingent upon characterizing or "knowing about" the heathen "soul."

Conversion to Christianity did *not* eliminate the searing marks of illegitimacy upon the Hamitic race. The basis of their identity was at once racial (black) and religious (heathen). Once having converted to Christian identity and having joined those who were people of God, they were still bound to the figure of Ham because they remained descendants of Ham. They neither desired nor were able to cease signifying Hamitic identity because Ham made possible Negro/Hamitic history, accomplishment, and presence in antiquity while also "clinging" to Negroes as an illegitimate marker.

Finally, one should keep in mind that those authors making recourse to Hamitic identity were *Christians*. Those caught beneath the grinding wheel of Hamitic illegitimacy and racial absurdity were among the people of God. They were biblically minded folk. The conundrum induced by divine identity, thus, is *primarily* concerned with Christians and their texts, with Christians and their rhetorics, with Christians and their dilemmas when faced with a Christian problem of illegitimacy. Any doubts about this should be undone by considering that Christians produced the primary sources examined in this study.

The problem of divine identity is therefore a Christian one, first and foremost. Anyone studying Hamitic rhetorics, thus, should understand that those "burned by" the narrations of divine identity are the divinely identified themselves. The violence of identification arises primarily for those who participate in such narrative knowledge, such biblical symbols. In these terms, *Christians become the victims of their own wielding, of desperate attempts to identify in divine terms.*

This suggests that the very act of narrating divine identity is induced by anxieties over illegitimacy. Consider that Africans encountered the Christian myth en masse through contact with Europeans. Yet, these same Europeans bore memories of having once been heathens. Just as colonization was the violent context through which Christianity was made global and spread among non-European nations, so also was violence the milieu for Europeans' experience of Christianity as it spread throughout Europe. The same patterns of illegitimacy that affected colonized peoples had plagued Europeans.

By the time of the Reformation, however, Europeans thought of themselves not as heathens but as Christians, essentially. At the same time, Europeans were beginning to encounter more nonwhites as a result of colonization. And they viewed nonwhites as historically non-Christian, as unique targets for missionary activity. This explains why European settlers in America could gaze upon their ancestral lands and envisage not a land of heathen savages but one of Christians. One should consider, however, that perhaps thousands of European women (mostly) and men were killed as a result of the witch trials throughout Europe and New England by the eighteenth century.[49] This phenomenon was, in essence, concerned with eradicating the pre-Christian religions of Europeans. So, despite the fact that European or European American identity was being equated with Christian identity, the specter of the heathen did linger, to some degree, in European Christian consciousness. The cycle of perduring angst does not end there, however. Just as Africans' encounter with Christian illegitimacy might be seen as having its precedent in that of Europeans, so also might the latter be understood as recapitulating even earlier episodes of Christianity's spread.[50]

The Christian myth assumes its origins in a historically stable locus of people who were the "original" people of God—a pristine, pure, non-Canaanite Israel. The Christian claim to being true Israel is most commonly seen as appropriating the legacy of this *original* Israel. This appropriation developed, in fact, because Christians claimed an Israelitic status in direct response to anxieties over illegitimacy and impending political consequences.[51]

One should ask, then, whether anxiety over illegitimacy constitutes the origin of biblical narratives that inscribe divine identity onto some by also circumscribing "others" who are not people of God. Biblical narratives depict an original Israel that *precedes* the narratives acts of representation, a people who come into being by virtue of being chosen by their God, only later to be described in narrative recollection. This narrative depiction, however, should not be mistaken for historicity. The narrative strategy arises in order to account for the Canaanite roots of Israel by naming those roots as foreign grafts, as intrusions due to the influence of surrounding nations who are not people of God. The prevailing ideas of a monotheistic, non-Canaanite, pre-monarchical ancient Israel, after all, is a misguided, fallacious reconstruction and obfuscates an understanding of the originary struggles, conflicts, and reinterpretations of history at stake in the discourse of divine identity.[52]

The logic of the narrative traditions dictates that Israel, as the people of God, comes to exist vis-à-vis those who are not Israelite. These "others" are the Canaanites of Palestine. The most stringent imperatives of Israelitic identity arose over cultic purity. Biblical narratives of Israel assume that Hamitic peoples repeatedly effect the dissipation of Israelites' exclusive piety to Yahweh. In the sexualized invectives of Israel's prophets, Israel "whores with" the nations and falls away from the originally pure faith of early Israel. By the emplotment of biblical texts, Israel dwindles from twelve tribes to merely Judah. In the wake of Babylonian captivity, Judean religion proper emerges as the religion of those who left and returned; it is the faith of the exiles. Ironically, the Ezra–Nehemiah reformation (Ezra 9–10) is contingent upon ethnic cleansing, expunging those who never left; they are the polluting presence, the people of the land, who are anachronistically said to have mixed with the Canaanite nations.

Archaeological searches for an ancient Israel consistently turn up artifacts of Canaanite societies—implements of polytheistic worship, figurines of female and male deities, and the like. Even the biblical stories of ancient Israel depend upon the presence of Canaanite religion among Israelites; thus, the image of Asherah is at one time in the Jerusalem temple and is legitimated for a brief time by the temple institution.[53]

Yahweh religion emerges in opposition to the more widespread Canaanite religious forms present throughout Israel. In light of archaeological and textual evidence, the most compelling resolution of the historical problems of Israelite religion points to its origins in Canaanite religion. In historical, nontheological terms, Yahweh, the chief deity of ancient Israel, is a Canaanite deity. In fact, the ethnic and cultural origins of ancient Israel itself are Canaanite.[54] If this is the case, there is no mystery about the exaggerated attempts to narrate Israel as radically distinct from "the Canaanites." Claiming an Israelite origin that is not Canaanite depends upon explaining the overwhelming Canaanite presence and character of Israel. Because "being Israel" symbolizes being Yahwist and *not* Canaanite, an illegitimate category, the project of narrating Israel in essence becomes an attempt to explain away illegitimate origins.

Israelitic narration as the people of God is not a reflection after the fact upon being people of God vis-à-vis those who are not. Rather, Israelitic narration is an attempt to create knowledge about heathens, on one hand—that is, Canaanite peoples—who were the perennial threat to another people, on the other hand—the people of God. Narrating the people of God is necessarily a semiotic and noetic act committed to producing "knowledge" about those who are people of God and those who are not. In these terms, it is narrative knowledge that creates the people of God by necessarily constructing the heathen—encoding in negating terms the existence of those who are not God's people.

The important suggestion here is that narrating divine identity is a noetic practice, a rhetorical strategy that arises with illegitimate peoples. It should become evident, in other words, that the Israelitic form of divine identity that guides the Christian myth (being the people of God) originated because of a condition of illegitimacy and not because of a pristine historical reality of being a divine people.

There is one further consideration that should inform an understanding of Israelitic narration. Israelites themselves were victims of this narrative practice. Itumeleng Mosala argues this point when he emphasizes that Yahwist religion developed in opposition to the religious practices of rural Israelites. Perhaps no biblical text depicts this victimization of Israelites more sharply than does the Ezra–Nehemiah corpus, according to which women and children of Judah (those who never left) are sent away because they are defined outside of the community of exiles and threaten the cultic purity of the people of God (Ezra 9–10). One should understand, in other words, that the fascination with performing Israel or divine identity is motivated by anxieties that in turn inscribe (il)legitimacy in volatile terms.

Furthermore, the ideological engine that drives the production of meanings concomitant to divine identity ultimately has no loyalty to the divinely identified. Divine identity, in phenomenal terms, is a semiotic Frankenstein; it bears no loyalty to those who wield it. Israelites, Samaritans, Jews, and Christians have been burned by divine identity. They have also been empowered by it. Despite the empowerment and legitimacy afforded by this narrative knowledge, however, the long history of Christian anti-Semitic persecution or as shown herein, the American episode of the Hamitic idea, should make very clear that *no one has been immune to the existential violence of divine identity*. Like the deity Yahweh, as characterized in biblical texts, it gives and it takes away; it cannot be reined in or pinned down. The power of divine identity is not located or propertied with particular people but is created through a field of narrative knowledge, a web of meanings, in which differently located peoples become entangled.

Thus, tracing the history of narrating Israel leads one not to an original, authentic people of God but to a perduring problem—existential illegitimacy. For this reason, the author would suggest that the problem of divine identity and (il)legitimacy borne out in the Christian myth is preeminently phenomenological and must be interrogated as such. To say that it is phenomenological is to indicate, for instance, that the origins of narrating the Israelitic people of God do not lie with a pristine historical Israel proper. It begins, rather, with an existential condition—illegitimate existence. Alternatively, one might consider the specious task of locating "Israel" as a phenomenal onion, a product without a core because it is inherently and thoroughly constituted by layers that are positioned as if encircling a core when there are in fact only layers of "posturing." Being the people of God means assuming a phenomenological posture. And it is precisely this posture that, at the beginning of this study, I referred to as the phenomenal posture of ecclesiology.

It should become evident, therefore, that a critical study of divine identity cannot relegate the problems of illegitimacy to the realm of us-and-them (e.g., it is not a problem for "us"; it is only a problem for "them"). The people-of-God idea is loyal to none. It encodes a reality that insists upon bifurcating humankind; in this sense, it sustains the *perception* of alterity. At the same time, even those who occupy the identity locus of being people of God are victims of the "knowledge" that creates their identity because divine identity blindly imposes conundrums and absurdities. One should ask, then, whether those who are divinely identified are indeed compelled to sustain the narrative acts lest they realize that they were never the people of God.

On this score, the author would suggest, the heuristic value of the Hamitic idea in America is realized. The condition of illegitimacy that plagued African American Christians of the nineteenth century is an exaggerated instance of what is generally true with any people of God; to participate in divine identity is to be haunted by the specter of illegitimate existence. This does not mean that the people of God have not benefited from the signification. Vine Deloria and Itumeleng Mosala, for instance, have clearly shown that the stakes of historical and material existence are against "Canaanites" and in favor of people of God. Both Deloria and Mosala have argued that the Israelitic form of Christian rhetoric was complicit in the seizure of land, genocide, and the dissolution of the human rights' of Native Americans and Azanians (black South Africans), respectively. Without overshadowing the material violence that has occurred, I want to clarify the problems of existence that inhere to divine identity.

American Religion in Hamitic-Canaanite Perspective

African Americans are the only social group who came to the United States (primarily by force) eventually believing they had left a land (Africa) of heathen existence. This heathen, Hamitic "past," in all likelihood will continue to signify, in part, what it means to be black. One will search hard to find a more apt metaphor. To date, black American Christians finance missions to Africa for the express purpose of converting "the heathen." African American Christians, furthermore, like other American Christians, most frequently relegate non-Christian peoples to a category of illicit existence. The Hamitic idea in America is arguably the most intensified example of how the Christian myth in America sustained racial and religious ideas of legitimate and illegitimate existence.

Given the violent constructions of identity that derive from divine identity, the author would suggest that public ideas of the Christian myth and its referents must be viewed through a Hamitic reading. In other words, American Christianity and its religious and racial implications cannot be rightly understood without an interpretive perspective (hermeneutics) that takes seriously the *problem* of violently constructing the heathen as illegitimate. I will refer to such a perspective as a Canaanite perspective.

A Canaanite perspective recognizes, first of all, that the most victimized characters in biblical narrative are those who are not the people of God. The most despised and rejected are those who are defined in extreme opposition to the people of the deity, the divinely identified. Such a perspective begins with recognizing that the most distant, shadowy figures of alterity—those denied the basic trait of humanness—are the descendants of Ham. Their existence is encoded to signify the very opposite of what it means to be human and "of God," so much so that they *cannot* remain who they are and at the same time be human, the people of God.

Biblical narrative knowledge of Hamites reveals that they are immoral, sexually perverse, hyper-libidinous miscreants who deserve to be depopulated. Their very existence threatens social purity. Next to genocide, their sole modicum of hope is to end their own existence, to stop being who they are, and to become "people of God." This is the only escape. One witnesses this relevance of a Canaanite perspective toward explicating the conundrum of racial existence, for example, in Frantz Fanon's facetious suggestion that "for the black [person], there is only one destiny. And it is white."[55] Fanon refers to the imprisonment of the black within an absurd existence because "the black" has been defined as the very negation of value. Aside from doing away with the very idea of race (an impossible feat?), it would seem that the only escape from absurdity would be recourse to occupying the identity of "the white." Black existence, like that of the biblical Hamite, is delimited by the malevolent definitions of value and negation that move Fanon to diagnose with precision the plight of black nonexistence, that "the black is not a [person]." Of course, Fanon realized that "the black man who wants to turn his race white is as miserable as he who preaches hatred for the whites." It was also patent to him that "the white" is trapped in whiteness just as "the black" is trapped in blackness. Both categories of identity are arbitrarily defined for the purpose of constructing racial supremacy and domination over dark peoples.[56]

American Christianity has been indelibly influenced by the construction of white identity as Christian (Israelitic) and racially superior. This has meant that blacks, defined in extreme opposition to the former, were left to contend with an absurd existence. This is why James H. Cone, in *Black Theology and Black Power*, employed the Tillichian notion of being and nonbeing to describe African Americans' struggle against whiteness. Whiteness, he argued, assumes that "whiteness is 'being' and blackness is 'non-being.'" The choice to affirm one's humanity when one has been defined as "other," then, necessarily means "affirming that which the oppressor regards as degrading." This is the only way to counter the semiotic terrorism of whiteness—a head-on embrace of despised black humanity.[57]

It is the heathens, the non-Christians—those who are on the underside of divine identity, as such has been demonstrated in this study—who must be valued as legitimate existents. The author would suggest that any critical articulation of Christian theology must heed the problems of identifying as people of God. Such a response would necessarily seek to correct the history of vilifying non-Christian identities and cultures through a commitment to end Christian expansionism (i.e., Christian missions). This would be a first step in a sort of nonmaterial reparations, without which the histories of Christianity's constructing the heathen would merely pass uncorrected.

This analytical posture also recognizes the totalizing knowledge form that Christian history assumes, with its attending narratives and logic. Such is seen, for example, in Paul's message to the Galatians (4:3) that they must abandon their "elementary" religion and "elemental" spirits (*stoicheia*) so that they might get on with the business of being people of Paul's God. In other words, a primary requisite of Christian knowledge is giving up one's nonbiblical history and religion.[58]

The ultimate concern here is the legacy of American identity as a phenomenology of divine peoplehood, sustained by strategies of encoding enemies as evil. The United States, more so than any other nation, has witnessed incredibly strained attempts to imagine ancient peoples as the racial or cultural forebears of modern folk. Quite recently, rhetorics of biblical, divine identity have been openly deployed without the slightest hint of discomfiture to justify heterosexist discrimination and to encode queer-identified people as a decadent, godless minority who threaten the integrity of an otherwise godly, Judeo-Christian nation. In the twenty-first century, the Bible is *still* a weapon, and the battle of divine identity has not abated. The terms of strategic exchange have been transformed (few would invoke the legends of Ham, Shem, or Japheth today), but the lines of identity allegiance are still drawn to define the people of God in opposition to the interests of illegitimate peoples, the humanity of whom, like that of Hamites, is barely discernible beneath the semiotics that encode them as evil.

The central problem of the Hamitic idea was its tendency to compel blacks to locate themselves in a biblical record and in a framework of history that was already configured against their location of identity. Public discourse about identity, history, and religious consciousness, if informed by a "Canaanite" perspective, must interrogate any and all "master narratives." Most importantly, Christian discourse, in light of colonizing histories, should examine the *motivations* for finding one's "roots" in "the biblical story." It is not sufficient merely to indicate that such attempts are empowering; the consequences of that power have produced existential and physical violence upon the peoples who have existed both within and beyond the pale of such knowledge forms and narrative logic. It is for this reason that some postcolonial theorists of religion have pointed to the pitfalls of historically oppressed peoples using the Bible to argue for their freedom; this strategy, although well intentioned, indicates the degree to which they have been conquered.[59]

The idea of being people of God has produced modern attempts to perform ancient identities. These attempts result in recent innovations on a long-standing problem. Ultimately, the problem is not ancient texts. After all, as Wilfred Smith has rightly noted, scripture is something that people do, a phenomenon that they choose to enact.[60] And although human choices are constrained by predisposition and semiotic inheritances, the ability to choose different responses to perduring problems is perhaps more urgent now than ever before. Christian identity per se, furthermore, need not remain an expression of this problem, although the long history of Christian identity violence does suggest a grim outlook.

This is a problem that derives from the age-old desire to be what perhaps no one has ever really been—a divine race, people of God—instead of the illegitimate folk we perhaps all are, unauthorized by a dazzling deity. In metaphorical terms, could it be that we are not children of God but orphans of humanity? Ultimately, it would seem, the problem lies with the persistent refusal of modern peoples to denounce violence when it is divine. And until modern peoples—be they Christian or not—regard as intolerable the violence of biblical narratives, of demeaning "knowledge," and of contemporary claims to righteous empire and dehumanizing alterity, modern peoples will continue to produce and suffer from these conundrums of existential illegitimacy and identity violence.

This page intentionally left blank

Notes

Preface

1. The word *heathen* has a complex etymological history. *Heathen* has most frequently denoted "irreligious," "uncultured," and "uncivilized"; its meanings have not necessarily assumed a religious context. My use of the word reflects its deployment in the context of European colonization and, in light of the primary sources examined in this study, chiefly reflects its meaning "non-Christian." It is true that even during colonization (including the nineteenth century), *heathen* connoted primitivism or cultural backwardness. Its primary referent, however, was the figure of the non-Christian.

1   The People(-ing) of God

1. I use the term *Israelitic* to indicate contemporary appropriations of "Israelite"—being people of God—as represented in the Israelite narrative of election. Only the bygone, ancient society is appropriately termed "Israelite." But contemporary peoples, through participating in an idea of identity, may be "Israelitic."
2. Homi Bhabha's description of narrative knowledge has become very important for understanding how popular narratives constitute "knowledge" and organize meanings. See his "Introduction," in *Nation and Narration*, ed. Homi Bhabha (London/New York: Routledge, 1990), 3. See also Regina M. Schwartz, *The Curse of Cain: The Violent Legacy of Monotheism* (Chicago: University of Chicago Press, 1997).
3. See Conrad Cherry, ed., *God's New Israel: Religious Interpretations of American Destiny*, rev. ed. (Chapel Hill: University of North Carolina Press, 1998).
4. Schwartz, *The Curse of Cain*; Martin Marty, *Modern American Religion*, 3 vols. (Chicago: University of Chicago Press, 1986–96); Schwartz, *Righteous Empire: The Protestant Experience in America* (New York: Dial Press, 1970); Gayraud S. Wilmore, *Black Religion and Black Radicalism: An Interpretation of the Religious History of African Americans*, 3d ed. (Maryknoll, NY: Orbis Books, 1998); Sydney Mead, *The Lively Experiment: The Shaping of*

Christianity in America (New York: Harper & Row, 1963); Eddie S. Glaude, *Exodus!: Religion, Race and Nation in Early Nineteenth-Century Black America* (Chicago: University of Chicago Press, 2000); Michael Walzer, *Exodus and Revolution* (New York: Basic, 1985); Albert J. Raboteau, "African Americans, Exodus and the American Israel," in *Religion and American Culture,* ed. David Hackett (New York: Routledge, 1995); Raboteau, *A Fire in the Bones: Reflections on African-American Religious History* (Boston: Beacon Press, 1995); Cherry, ed., *God's New Israel.*

5. Perry Miller, *The New England Mind,* 2 vols. (Boston: Beacon Press, 1961); Reginald Horsman, *Race and Manifest Destiny* (Cambridge: Harvard University Press, 1981).

6. Raboteau, "African Americans, Exodus and the American Israel"; Raboteau, *A Fire in the Bones;* Glaude, *Exodus;* Forrest G. Wood, *The Arrogance of Faith: Christianity and Race in America from the Colonial Era to the Twentieth Century* (New York: Alfred A. Knopf, 1990).

7. Raboteau, *A Fire in the Bones,* 4. These writers by and large argue that African American Christianity more consistently represented the idea of manumission and social freedom associated with the Israelitic theme of Exodus because Black Christianity assumed a decidedly antislavery, antiracist stance. The same was not generally true of white religionists.

8. Delores S. Williams, *Sisters in the Wilderness: The Challenge of Womanist God-Talk* (Maryknoll, NY: Orbis Books, 1993), 143–153.

9. James H. Cone, *A Black Theology of Liberation,* rev. ed. (Maryknoll, NY: Orbis Books, 1990); James H. Evans, *We Have Been Believers: An African American Systematic Theology* (Minneapolis: Fortress Press, 1992); Dwight Hopkins, *Introducing Black Theology of Liberation* (Maryknoll: Orbis Books, 1999); Hopkins, *Down, Up, and Over: Slave Religion and Black Theology* (Minneapolis: Fortress Press, 2000); Garth Baker-Fletcher, *Xodus: An African American Male Journey* (Minneapolis: Fortress Press, 1996).

10. Glaude, 75, 76, 81.

11. Wilson Jeremiah Moses, *Black Messiahs and Uncle Toms: Social and Literary Manipulations of a Religious Myth* (University Park, PA: The Pennsylvania State University Press, 1982).

12. David Howard-Pitney, *The Afro-American Jeremiad: Appeals for Justice in America* (Philadelphia: Temple University Press, 1990); Jon Butler, *Awash in a Sea of Faith* (Cambridge: Harvard University Press, 1990); Nathan Hatch, *The Democratization of American Christianity* (New Haven: Yale University Press, 1989). Moses' studies, although erudite and complex, conspicuously ignore the insights and hermeneutics arising from many theorists in poststructuralism and cultural studies. One result of this is a minimal, underdeveloped assessment of American whiteness or whiteness as Americanness. More generally, Moses works the social histories of black Americans into a Millerian grand narrative. At no point does he identify the problems of this narrative, which stem primarily from making performative whiteness the normative category for explaining social circumstances that comprise many peoples and a variety of conflicts.

13. Among theologians, Anthony Pinn has produced a unique response to the normalization of Christian identity in *Varieties of African American*

Experience (Minneapolis, MN: Fortress Press, 1998); Charles H. Long, *Significations: Signs, Symbols, and Images in the Interpretation of Religion* (Philadelphia: Fortress Press, 1986); Theophus H. Smith, *Conjuring Culture: Biblical Formations of Black America* (New York/Oxford: Oxford University Press, 1994); Judith Weisenfeld, "Difference as Evil," in *The Courage to Hope: From Black Suffering to Human Redemption*, ed. Quinton H. Dixie and Cornel West (Boston: Beacon Press, 1999); Schwartz, *The Curse of Cain*; Vincent Wimbush, "Introduction," in *African Americans and the Bible: Sacred Texts and Social Textures*, ed. Vincent Wimbush (New York/London: Continuum, 2000); Forrest G. Wood, *The Arrogance of Faith*. Randall Bailey, "What Price Inclusivity: An Afrocentric Reading of Dangerous Bible Texts," in *Voices from the Third World* 17 (June 1994): 133–150; Randall Bailey and Jacquelyn Grant, eds., *The Recovery of Black Presence: An Interdisciplinary Exploration* (Nashville: Abingdon, 1995).

14. Vine Deloria, *Custer Died For Your Sins: An Indian Manifesto* (New York: Macmillan, 1969; reprint, Norman, OK: University of Oklahoma Press, 1988); Deloria, *God is Red: A Native View of Religion*, 2d ed. (Golden, CO: North American Press, 1992); Robert Warrior, "A Native American Perspective: Canaanites, Cowboys, and Indians," in *Voices from the Margin: Interpreting the Bible in the Third World*, ed. R. S. Sugirtharajah (New York/London: Orbis/SPCK, 1995); George Tinker, *Missionary Conquest: The Gospel and Native American Cultural Genocide* (Minneapolis: Fortress Press, 1993).

15. Elizabeth Davis, *Lifting As They Climb* (New York: G.K. Hall & Company, 1996); Evelyn Brooks Higginbotham, *Righteous Discontent: The Women's Movement in the Black Baptist Church*, 1880–1920 (Cambridge/London: Harvard University Press, 1993); Beverly Washington Jones, *Quest for Equality: The Life and Writings of Mary Eliza Church Terrell, 1863–1954* (Brooklyn: Carlson, 1990); Anne Meis Knupfer, *Toward a Tenderer and a Nobler Womanhood: African-American Women's Clubs in Turn-of-the-Century Chicago* (New York: New York University Press, 1996); Dorothy Salem, *To Better Our World: Black Women in Organized Reform, 1890–1920*, Black Women in United States History (Brooklyn, NY: Carlson Publishing Company, 1990).

16. Kelly Brown Douglas, *Sexuality and the Black Church: A Womanist Perspective* (Maryknoll: Orbis, 1999).

17. John David Smith, ed., *The Biblical and "Scientific" Defense of Slavery, Anti-Black Thought*, 1863–1925 (New York: Garland Publishing, Inc., 1993); Thomas Virgil Peterson, *Ham and Japheth: The Mythic World of Whites in the Antebellum South* (Metuchen, NJ: Scarecrow Press, 1978); Donald Matthews, *Religion in the Old South* (Chicago: University of Chicago, 1977); Samuel Hill, Jr., *On Jordan's Stormy Banks: Religion in the South: A Southern Exposure Profile* (Atlanta, GA: Mercer University Press, 1983); Charles Reagan Wilson, *Baptized in Blood: The Religion of the Lost Cause (1865–1920)* (Atlanta: Atlanta University of Georgia Press, 1980). Scholars frequently regard racism, in its vilest and most cruel forms, as a Southern phenomenon and thus as atypical of Northern religion. Paul Griffin has devoted a

full study to counter this misrepresentation in his *Seeds of Racism in the Soul of America* (Cleveland, OH: Pilgrim Press, 1999). Griffin demonstrates, for instance, that Northern religious forms, primarily through Puritan religion, were a potent ideational source of American racism.

18. Stephen Haynes, *Noah's Curse: The Biblical Justification of American Slavery* (New York: Oxford University Press, 2002). Haynes' is a cogent analysis of white religionists who argued for slavery as a divinely sanctioned institution. He devotes little attention to African Americans due to the scope of his project, but he does indicate clearly that black Americans participated in Hamitic rhetorics. See Robert Hood, *Begrimed and Black: Christian Traditions on Blacks and Blackness* (Minneapolis: Fortress Press, 1994).

19. See Peterson, *Ham and Japheth*; Mathews, *Religion in the Old South*; Hill, *On Jordan's Stormy Banks*; Wilson, *Baptized in Blood*.

20. Griffin, *Seeds of Racism* (Cleveland: Pilgrim Press, 1999).

21. George M. Fredrickson, *The Arrogance of Race: Historical Perspectives on Slavery, Racism, and Social Inequality* (Hanover, NH: Wesleyan University Press, 1988); Stephen Jay Gould, *The Mismeasure of Man* (New York/London: Norton & Company, 1981).

22. Lewis R. Gordon, *Africana Existentia: Understanding Africana Existential Thought* (New York: Routledge, 2000).

23. American Negroes did not necessarily understand Hamitic identity to mean racial inferiority. As I will discuss in this study, Negroes frequently argued for racial equality on the basis of Hamitic identity and the legacy of Ham's posterity.

24. William Haller, in his *The Elect Nation: The Meaning and Relevance of Foxe's Book of Martyrs* (New York: Harper & Row, 1963), provided a fine analysis of how white New Englanders imagined themselves to be God's Israel during the early settlement period. Claims to this identity were conditioned by persecution, particularly that directed against Protestants during the Reformation and counter-Reformation. Hall suggested, for example, that John Foxe's *Book of Martyrs*, which narrated a genealogy of the people of God culminating in the rise of (English) Protestants, was likely as common an object in New England homes as the Bible. Also helpful is Haller's *The Rise of Puritanism, Or, The Way to the New Jerusalem: As Set Forth in Pulpit and Press from Thomas Cartwright to John Lilburne and John Milton, 1570–1643* (1938; reprint, New York: Harper, 1957).

25. Wilson Jeremiah Moses, *Afrotopia: The Roots of African American Popular History* (Cambridge: Cambridge University Press, 1998), 47.

26. By "American religion," I certainly intend to comprise a concern with American Christianity, especially Protestant Christianity, which has been far and away the most influential religious force in America, for better or for worse. I do not, however, exclude from "American religion" non-Christian religions in America such as Islam, Judaism, spiritualist movements, Utopian societies, African-derived religion, and the plethora of Eastern-derived religious movements. Also, I am aware that, since Robert Bellah's seminal essay "Civil Religion in America," *Daedalus* (Winter 1967), there has been little consensus on the designation "American religion." One should certainly recognize, nevertheless, that the concern with "being American" or with

inscribing the meaning of American identity is essential to what Americanizes religious experience in the United States.

27. See John David Smith, ed., "Introduction," in *The Biblical and "Scientific" Defense of Slavery*. Ethnology was the nineteenth-century science of studying racial difference.

28. It is with good reason that Wilson Jeremiah Moses, in his *Afrotopia*, locates the origins of Afrocentrism not in twentieth-century discourse but in nineteenth-century rhetorics that were preeminently religious. His scholarship has elucidated the complex ambivalence over Americanness and pan-Africanism in African American histories. Moses' treatment of contemporary Afrocentric thinkers, however, often seems ironic and skewed. He employs terms such as "intellectual thuggery" to describe the work of black writers who rightly argue for a revisionist examination of ancient civilizations and who are responding to a long history of racist, disingenuous scholarship contingent upon denying basic human qualities (such as culture and history) to nonwhites. It is puzzling that Moses reserves such vituperative language for these theorists but does not consider white racist scholarship to be "thuggery." See his "Introduction," in *Afrotopia*.

29. This pamphlet was to be a part of a larger, two-volume work subsequently published as *The Dispensations in the History of the Church and the Interregnums* (Kansas City, MO: B.T. Tanner), 1899. Tanner, however, was compelled to release this essay early because of its perceived urgency.

30. Benjamin Tucker Tanner, *The Descent of the Negro; Reply to Rev. Drs. J.H. Vincent, J.M. Freeman and J.H. Hurlbut* (Philadelphia: A.M.E. Publishing House, 1898), 9.

31. Tanner here alludes to the work of the pseudonymous "Ariel" (Buckner Harrison Payne), who sought to show that Negroes did not descend from Adam and Eve in his *The Negro, What Is His Ethnological Status?: Is He the Progeny of Ham? Is He A Descendant of Adam and Eve? Has He A Soul? Or Is He A Beast in God's Nomenclature? What Is His Status as Fixed by God in Creation? What Is His Relation to the White Race?* 2d ed. (Cincinnati, OH: [published for the proprietor] 1867).

32. Tanner, *Descent of the Negro*, 13–14, 23.

33. Theophus Smith has developed the use of this term with specific reference to American religious forms in his *Conjuring Culture*. I discuss Smith's work in a later chapter.

34. Tanner, *Descent of the Negro*, 10–11.

35. George W. Williams, *History of the Negro Race in America, 1619–1880* (1883; reprint, New York: Arno Press and The New York Times, 1968), 1, 12. A few nineteenth-century ideologues denied that Ham was the progenitor of the Negro, namely "Ariel" (Buckner Payne) and Charles Carroll—at the turn of the century, the latter published *The Negro a Beast* (1902). Williams, familiar with the work of Ariel, refers repeatedly to his work and indicates that Ariel's was patently a minoritarian position; most Americans dismissed Ariel. I will develop this point later.

36. Rufus Perry, *The Cushite, or The Descendants of Ham as Found in the Sacred Scriptures and in the Writings of Ancient Historians and Poets from Noah to the Christian Era* (Springfield, MA: Willey & Co., 1893), 12.

37. George Williams provides an interesting response to this curse-of-Ham conundrum. He first points out that it was Canaan proper, not Ham, who was cursed. But several others make this point. His response is unique because he attacks Noah's moral reputation, arguing that Noah was not upright but was an unrighteous drunkard who evoked a curse of his own accord, in the absence of divine inspiration. By Williams' logic, not only was such a curse outside of divine will, but it also failed the test for authentic prophecy—it was not of God. See Williams, *History*, 7–8.

38. See Cherry, ed., *God's New Israel*. Numerous European settlers came to America as prisoners, of course, condemned to serve out their sentences as guinea pigs in the colonial experiment. I do not mean to reinforce the erroneous portrayal of European settlers as generally upper class, dignified, high-churched settlers of the upper class. My point here is that, because Christianity dominated the culture of Europe, the people of the culture regarded Christian identity in normative terms.

39. See Reginald Horsman, *Race and Manifest Destiny* (Cambridge: Harvard University Press, 1981).

40. Williams, *History*, 109. It is of course patent that the Canaanite and the Hamitic are not strictly identical designations. Ham was the progenitor of several peoples, among whom were the Canaanites. The significance of the associations between the Hamitic and Canaanite peoples, however, is their relationship to the people of God, the Israelitic people in contrast to whom they are repeatedly represented as other. To be either Canaanite or Hamitic, in other words, was to be heathen.

41. A number of studies have suggested such theological implications behind American ideas of race. Leading works include Wood, *The Arrogance of Faith*, and Gordon, *Existentia Africana*.

42. Eddie Glaude offers the most theoretically astute examination of the Israelitic idea as foundation for American religious consciousness that directly addresses African American Christianity's emergence in his *Exodus!* A classic comprehensive study of biblical narrative's influence upon American consciousness is Martin Marty's *Righteous Empire: The Protestant Experience in America* (New York: Dial Press, 1970).

43. Hood, *Begrimed and Black*. Especially relevant is Hood's penultimate chapter entitled "The Children of Ham in America." Hood concludes that antiblackness (a semiotic development distinct from though closely wed to antiblack racism) is a pervasive phenomenon whose roots perhaps lie deep in human psychology, unbounded by culture or time. He reckons that perennial attempts to eradicate antiblack racism, because they underestimate its magnitude, are futile at best.

44. Gay L. Byron, *Symbolic Blackness and Ethnic Difference in Early Christian Literature* (New York: Routledge, 2002). Byron is careful to avoid the anachronism of reading modern race and racism back into antiquity. In fact, she avoids using the terms. She does, however, clearly recognize the veritable semiotic antiblackness to which Hood was attentive.

45. Schwartz, *The Curse of Cain*, 5, 7, 123–124.

46. Ibid.

47. Audrey Smedley, *Race in North America: Origin and Evolution of a Worldview* (Boulder, CO: Westview, 1993), 21, 231–234.
48. Hood, *Begrimed and Black*. See Byron, *Symbolic Blackness*; David Goldenberg, *The Curse of Ham: Race and Slavery in Early Judaism, Christianity, and Islam* (Princeton/Oxford: Princeton University Press, 2003); Cottrel R. Carson, "'Do You Understand What You Are Reading?': A Reading of the Ethiopian Eunuch Story (Acts 8.26–40) from a Site of Cultural Marronage" (Ph.D. diss., Union Theological Seminary, 1999).
49. Marty, *Righteous Empire*.
50. Robert N. Bellah, "Civil Religion in America," *Daedalus* (Winter 1967): 1–10.
51. Ibid., see especially Bellah's *The Broken Covenant: American Civil Religion in Time of Trial*, 2d ed. (Chicago: University of Chicago Press, 1992).
52. Conrad Cherry, "Introduction," in his edited *God's New Israel*.
53. Albert J. Raboteau, "African Americans, Exodus, and the American Israel," in *Religion and American Culture*. See especially, Raboteau's *A Fire in the Bones*; Glaude, *Exodus!*
54. Glaude, *Exodus!*, 44–45.
55. Ibid., 75–76.
56. Ibid., 70–76.
57. Ibid., 54.
58. Charles H. Long, "Civil Rights—Civil Religion: Visible People and Invisible Religion," in *American Civil Religion*, ed. Russell E. Richey & Donald G. Jones (New York: Harper & Row, 1974).
59. Vincent Wimbush has most recently advanced a phenomenological theory of hermeneutics. See his "Introduction," in *African Americans and the Bible: Sacred Texts and Social Textures*, ed. Vincent Wimbush (New York/London: Continuum, 2000). This approach takes as primary subject not the ancient past but the present, in order to identify a phenomenal principle that subsequently elucidates problematic forms encountered in the study of texts and textualities, be they ancient or modern. Sites of contradiction or dissonance, in this schema, intensify phenomena and enhance their heuristic value. It is evident from his discussion that the "present" is not necessarily an immediate one but might be a "recent past" vis-à-vis an ancient one. The interpretive framework of this study owes much to Wimbush's hermeneutical formulation.
60. I am aware that the term *race* is notorious for evading singular usage or meaning. I use *race* here to denote specifically the signification of peoplehood, the social experience of being a people vis-à-vis other peoples; this is, in social and existential terms, the fundamental idea of racial identity.
61. Recent critical studies of race have repeatedly emphasized that race is an arbitrary construction, a convention of identity with no basis in genetics or biology. See Smedley, *Race in North America*; Etienne Balibar and Emmanuel Wallerstein, *Race, Nation, Class: Ambiguous Identities* (London: Verso, 1991); Kwame Anthony Appiah, "The Uncompleted Argument: Du Bois and the Illusion of Race," in *Overcoming Racism and Sexism*, ed. Linda A. Bell and David Blumenfeld (Boston: Rowan and Littlefield Publishers, 1995); Joan Ferrante and Prince Brown, Jr., eds., *The Social Construction of Race and Ethnicity in the United States* (New York: Longman, 1998).

62. One might consider, as a modern example of this confluence, contemporary Jewish identity, which is duplicitously understood in racial (biological) and religious terms.

63. Gould, *The Mismeasure of Man*.

64. Stow Persons, *American Minds: A History of Ideas* (New York: Henry Holt & Company, 1958).

65. Smedley, *Race in North America*, 11, 16, 17, 309.

66. Ibid., 180–181. Smedley cites, as an early example, the nineteenth-century debate over whether Native Americans could possibly have been the Mound Builders, those responsible for producing impressive dirt mounds encountered by whites in the wake of the Trail of Tears. Of course, Native Americans constructed these mounds. But whites such as Noah Webster argued that white explorers certainly must have produced them because "savages" were racially incapable of exhibiting the sufficient level of technical skill. Also relevant is Martin Bernal's *Black Athena: The Afroasiatic Roots of Classical Civilization*, 2 vols. (New Brunswick: Rutgers University Press, 1987). Bernal provides a compelling assessment that describes how Europeans laid claim to ancient civilizations by interpreting them as "white" in order to construct a narrative of white (Greek) racial accomplishments vis-à-vis the empty or irrelevant histories of other peoples in antiquity (namely, "Black Africa").

67. Several studies provide an apt overview of these racial diatribes. Among these are William Stanton, *The Leopard's Spots: Scientific Attitudes toward Race in America, 1815–59* (Chicago: University of Chicago Press, 1960); George Fredrickson, *The Black Image in The White Mind: The Debate on Afro-American Character and Destiny, 1817–1914* (New York: Harper & Row, 1971); August Meier, *Negro Thought in America, 1880–1915: Racial Ideologies in the Age of Booker T. Washington* (Ann Arbor: University of Michigan Press, 1963); and John S. Haller, *Outcasts from Evolution: Scientific Attitudes of Racial Inferiority, 1859–1900* (Urbana: University of Illinois Press, 1971).

68. In chapter 2, I will examine specific instances of scientific theories of race that depended upon religious assumptions and theological arguments. This synthesis of scientific and religious arguments in race ideas is ably demonstrated in several studies. See the references cited above.

69. Schwartz, *The curse of Cain*, 147.

70. Robert F. Berkhofer, Jr., *Beyond the Great Story: History as Text and Discourse* (Cambridge/London: Belknap Press, 1995), 39.

71. Schwartz, *The Curse of Cain*, 8.

72. See Edward W. Said, *Culture and Imperialism* (New York: Vintage, 1993); Homi Bhabha, "Introduction," in *Nation and Narration*; Joyce Appleby, Lynn Hunt, and Margaret Jacob, *Telling the Truth about History* (New York/London: W. W. Norton & Company, 1994); Schwartz, *The Curse of Cain*.

73. Appleby et al., *Telling the Truth about History*, 103.

74. Schwartz, *The Curse of Cain*, 5. See especially Keith W. Whitelam, *The Invention of Ancient Israel: The Silencing of Palestinian History* (New York: Routledge, 1996). Whitelam examines the ways the West has been imagined through

configuring ancient Hebrews, Greeks, and Romans as Western peoples—
arbiters of monotheism, white values, and high culture—vis-à-vis the decadent
contemporaries of those ancient Western peoples.

75. Schwartz, *The Curse of Cain*, 5–7.

76. Of course, many publicists such as Frederick Douglass, Henry Highland
Garnet, and David Walker took great exception to this signification. They rad-
ically disagreed with equating the views and values of white racism with
Christianity. See Frederick Douglass, *Narrative of the Life of Frederick
Douglass, An American Slave* (Boston: Anti-Slavery Office, 1845), 77–82,
118–125; David Walker, *Appeal to the Coloured Citizen's of the World*, ed.
Peter P. Hinks (Boston: D. Walker, 1829; reprint, University Park, PA:
Pennsylvania State University, 2000); Henry Highland Garnet, *The Past and
the Present Condition and the Destiny of the Colored Race; A Discourse
Delivered at the Fifteenth Anniversary of the Female Benevolent Society of
Troy, N.Y., Feb. 14, 1848* (1848; reprint, Miami: Mnemosyne, 1969).

77. Samuel Morton, *Crania Aegyptiaca; Or, Observations on Egyptian
Ethnography, Derived from Anatomy, History and the Monuments*
(Philadelphia: J. Penington, 1844).

78. George R. Gliddon and Josiah Nott, *Types of Mankind: Or, Ethnological
Researches Based Upon the Ancient Monuments, Paintings, Sculptures, and
Crania of Races, and upon Their Natural, Geographical, Philological and
Biblical History: Illustrated by Selections from the Inedited [sic] Papers of Samuel
George Morton and by Additional Contributions from L. Agassiz, W. Usher, and
H. S. Patterson* (Philadelphia: J. B. Lippincott, Grambo, & Co., 1854).

79. Arturo de Gobineau, *The Inequality of Human Races*, trans. Adrian Collins
(New York: G. P. Putnam's Sons, 1915). De Gobineau wrote that all accom-
plishments of human civilization were due to the white race, even in Africa.
See de Gobineau, 210–211.

80. See Paul Finkelman, *Dred Scott v. Sandford: A Brief History with Documents*
(Boston: Bedford Books, 1997).

81. Smedley, *Race in North America*, 262–263; John S. Haller, Jr., "Civil War
Anthropometry: The Making of a Racial Ideology," *Civil War History* 16
(1970): 309–325; Haller, *Outcasts from Evolution*.

82. John Van Evrie, *White Supremacy and Negro Subordination; Or, Negroes a
Subordinate Race, and (So-Called) Slavery Its Normal Condition, with an
Appendix, Showing the Past and Present Condition of the Countries South of
Us*, 2d ed. (New York: Van Evrie, Horton & Co., 1868).

83. Edward Wilmot Blyden, *The Negro in Ancient History* (Washington City:
McGill & Witherow, 1869).

2   Divine Identity and the Hamitic Idea in Historical Perspective

1. Among the best studies of ideas about Ham are Stephen Haynes, *Noah's
Curse: The Biblical Justification of American Slavery* (New York: Oxford,
2002); and David Goldenberg, *The Curse of Ham: Race and Slavery in Early*

Judaism, Christianity, and Islam (Princeton/Oxford: Princeton University Press, 2003). Despite his impressive efforts to avoid anachronisms and essentialism, Goldenberg relies upon the troubling concept of "black African." He uses this, for example, in order to distinguish between Egyptians and Ethiopians (he does not consider Egyptians to be "black Africans"). This concept of the "black African" was developed by racist intellectuals of the eighteenth and nineteenth centuries in order to avoid attributing examples of cultural prowess or achievement to "blacks." The concept is in every sense a product of white supremacist strategies to dehumanize Africans by inscribing them as having no history or culture. Unfortunately, Goldenberg is not alone in his use of the concept—most contemporary scholars have uncritically taken up its use. Haynes' text also provides extensive treatment of American Christian ideas about Nimrod as a villainous ancestor of Negroes. See especially chapters 3 and 6 of Haynes' study.

2. Psalms 78:51 employs the phrase "tents of Ham" (*'ohel Chām*) as a locution for Egypt. Psalms 105:23, 27 and 106:22 employ the phrase "land of Ham" (*'erets Chām*) to idealize Egypt as the conquered enemy of Yahweh's Israel.

3. Ephraim Isaac, "Ham," in *The Anchor Bible Dictionary*, ed. David Noel Freedman (New York: Doubleday, 1992), 3:31–3:32.

4. David Goldenberg provides a very helpful summary of the history of scholarly attempts to trace the etymology of Ham. The name Ham, he demonstrates, is not etymologically related to the Hebrew root for "hot." The confusion derives from the fact that *Ham* and *hot* are identical in the Hebrew script (חם). For centuries since rabbinic Judaism, "Ham" was considered to derive from the same source as "hot" or "heat." Goldenberg identifies the writing of Philo of Alexandria as the earliest extant instance (first century C.E.) of this erroneous etymology. My own research has confirmed that nineteenth-century American Christians regularly assumed this etymological relationship between "Ham" and "heat" or "dark." See Goldenberg, *The Curse of Ham*, 150–152.

5. I take up this subject of Israelites as Canaanites at length in the final chapter.

6. Ephraim Isaac, "Genesis, Judaism, and the 'Sons of Ham'", in *Islam and the Ideology of Enslavement*, vol. 1, *Slaves and Slavery in Muslim Africa*, ed. John Ralph Willis (London/Totowa, NJ: Frank Cass, 1985), 77, 78. Isaac suggests, for instance, that because Canaanites "were the traders, sailors, and businessmen of the world of the Israelite peasantry," Israelites may have labeled them as "exploitative, commanded by their forefathers to be 'robbers, adulterers, and lazy'" (78). Isaac (78) also cites a keen example of this narrative strategy of ethnic rivalry from the second century B.C.E. book of Jubilees 10:28–34, which narratizes a curse of waywardness against Canaan. In Jubilees, this curse results because the character Canaan desires to live in the land allotted to Shem. Canaan's father (Ham) and Canaan's brothers try to convince him to leave the region. When Canaan refuses to leave, Ham himself, not Noah, curses Canaan. The narrative is an obvious attempt to explain why the "promised land" was named after the Canaanites. The slurs and demeaning inscriptions against Canaanites, as Isaac rightly argues, were political, not racial. Unfortunately, Isaac risks trivializing anti-Canaanite pronouncements when he emphasizes that they were not racially motivated. Isaac's point that the biblical invectives were not racist is very significant and is well taken. But racism is only one form

of identity violence. The trajectories of meanings about Ham and Ham's descendants are not necessarily improved upon by being recognized as political rivalry, only rightly contextualized. For an opposing view that identifies Israelites enslaving Canaanites as context for this narrative, see Goldenberg, *The Curse of Ham*, 98.

7. Ephraim Isaac, "Ham," 3:31–3:32.
8. Goldenberg, *The Curse of Ham*, 102–103, 105.
9. Ibid., 105. Also, see Robert Hood, *Begrimed and Black* (Minneapolis: Fortress Press, 1994), 156. See Robert Graves and Raphael Patai, *Hebrew Myths: The Book of Genesis* (Garden City, NY: Doubleday, 1964); such etiologies of Hamites' physiognomy were clearly present in early Judaism. Louis Ginzberg provides an example:

> The descendants of Ham through Canaan therefore have red eyes, because Ham looked upon the nakedness of his father; they have misshapen lips, because Ham spoke with his lips to his brothers about the unseemly condition of his father; they have twisted curly hair, because Ham turned and twisted his head round to see the nakedness of his father; and they go about naked, because Ham did not cover the nakedness of his father. Thus he was requited, for it is the way of God to mete out punishment measure for measure.

See Ginzberg, *The Legends of the Jews*, vol. 1, trans. Henrietta Szold (Philadelphia: The Jewish Publication Society of America, 1909), 169.

10. Haynes, *Noah's Curse*, 29, 30. See Lactantius, "Divine Institutes," ch. XIV in *The Ante-Nicene Fathers* vol. 8, 140. Lactantius composed this work in the early fourth century. Haynes draws upon Clement's "Recognitions of Clement," book IV, ch. xxvii. Haynes notes that Clement's ideas greatly influenced medieval Christians. In the American Christian context, however, Nimrod would become primarily identified with "inventing" polytheism and magic. This metanarrative of Jewish or Christian monotheism as the original status quo that suffers demise due to the invention of polytheism was popular among black American Christians of the nineteenth century. See, for instance, James W. C. Pennington, *A Textbook of the Origin and History of the Colored People* (Hartford, CT: L. Skinner, 1841; reprint, Detroit, MI: Negro History Press, 1969), 22–25.
11. Augustine, *Concerning the City of God Against the Pagans*, book XVI, ch. 2, trans. Henry Bettenson (1972; reprint, London: Penguin Books, 1984), 650. Closely related to these rhetorics of Hamites as ethnic villains is the discourse of "blacks"/blackness-as-evil. Gay Byron has produced what is far and away the best study of antiblackness in early Christianity. Byron develops a taxonomy of "ethno-political rhetorics" and assesses their emergence, complex deployment, and significance in the first few centuries of Greek and Latin Christianity. She notes that semiotic (symbolic) antiblackness (e.g., Origen's description of sinfulness as Ethiopian blackness) did not always mean that literal "blacks" or Ethiopians were equated with evil. See Gay L. Byron, *Symbolic Blackness and Ethnic Difference in Early Christian Literature*

(London/New York: Routledge, 2002), 75–76. Goldenberg also observes this issue throughout his study.

12. Goldenberg, *The Curse of Ham*, 101.

13. Ibid., 101–102.

14. Hood, *Begrimed and Black*, 7–9. Also see Bernard Lewis, *Race and Color in Islam* (New York: Harper and Row, 1971).

15. "Africa in America," *Southern Literary Messenger* 22 (January 1856): 1, quoted in Thomas Virgil Peterson, *Ham and Japheth: The Mythic World of Whites in the Antebellum South* (Metuchen, NJ/London: Scarecrow Press/American Theological Library Association, 1978), 91.

16. Audrey Smedley, *Race in North America: Origins and Evolution of a Worldview* (Boulder, CO: Westview Press, 1993).

17. Ariel [Buckner Harrison Payne], *The Negro, What Is His Ethnological Status?: Is He the Progeny of Ham? Is He a Descendant of Adam and Eve? Has He a Soul? Or Is He a Beast in God's Nomenclature? What Is His Status as Fixed by God in Creation? What Is His Relation to the White Race?* 2d ed. (Cincinnati, OH: n.p., 1867), 9, 13, 15. Emphasis in the original.

18. Ibid., 14. Emphasis in the original.

19. Ibid., 18–3

20. Ibid., 36. The beastiliness of Negroes was evident in his own day, opined Ariel, by the "fact" that gorillas stole Negro women for wives, preferring their beastly sexuality to that of female gorillas (23).

21. Ibid., 41, 43.

22. Ibid., 43.

23. Lancaster Theological Seminary moved to its present location in Lancaster, Pennsylvania, in 1893, the same year in which Schaff died.

24. The Mercersburg school of thought emphasized a Romanticist notion that humankind was unified and that Christianity could effect a sublime transformation of society.

25. Philip Schaff, *Slavery and the Bible: A Tract for the Times* (Chambersburg, PA: M. Kieffer and Co.'s Caloric Printing Press, 1861); located at the Schomburg Center for Research in Black Culture, New York City. The tract contains a preface of endorsement, dated March 1861, citing its popular reception and listing as signatories twenty-three people from the Mercersburg Seminary.

26. Ibid., 5.

27. Ibid.

28. Ibid., 6. Emphasis added.

29. Ibid. Emphasis in the original.

30. Ibid., 7.

31. Ibid., 7, 14, 32.

32. Ibid., 7.

33. Samuel A. Cartwright, "Slavery in the Light of Ethnology," in *Cotton is King, and Other Pro-Slavery Arguments; Comprising the Writings of Hammond, Harper, Christy, Stringfellow, Hodge, Bledsoe, and Cartwright, on this Important Subject*, ed. E. N. Elliot (Augusta, GA: Pritchard, Abbot & Loomis, 1860), 693, 694.

34. Ibid., 295.
35. Ibid., 702.
36. Ibid., 700.
37. Ibid., 700–701.
38. Ibid., 696, 697.
39. *Prognathous* was a common ethnological term that referred to the Negro race based on the idea that the "characteristic Negro" had a *protrusive jaw*. This feature was deemed a racial marker and was understood to approximate the physiognomy of apes.
40. Cartwright, *Cotton is King*, 707.
41. Ibid., 707, 708.
42. Ibid., 711
43. Ibid.
44. Ibid.
45. Ibid., 713, 716.
46. Thornton Stringfellow, "The Bible Argument: Or, Slavery in the Light of Divine Revelation," in *Cotton is King, and Other Pro-Slavery Arguments; Comprising the Writings of Hammond, Harper, Christy, Stringfellow, Hodge, Bledsoe, and Cartwright, on this Important Subject*, ed. E. N. Elliot (Augusta, GA: Pritchard, Abbot & Loomis, 1860).
47. Ibid., 498.
48. Ibid., 491.
49. Lewis S. Gordon, *Existentia Africana: Understanding Africana Existential Thought* (New York: Routledge, 2000), 97.
50. Martin Marty, *Righteous Empire: The Protestant Experience in America* (New York: Dial Press, 1970).
51. Eddie S. Glaude, *Exodus!: Religion, Race, and Nation in Early Nineteenth-Century Black America* (Chicago/London: University of Chicago, 2000), 75.
52. Ibid., 75.
53. Ibid., 77, 78, 79. See Etienne Balibar and Immanuel Wallerstein, *Race, Nation, Class: Ambiguous Identities* (London: Verso, 1988).
54. Peterson, *Ham and Japheth.* Peterson defines myth as that which "makes everyday attitudes and motivations fit a universal context" (95). Concerning Peterson's "Southernization" of racism, I have already mentioned Paul R. Griffin's *Seeds of Racism in the Soul of America* (Cleveland, OH: Pilgrim Press, 1999). Griffin's work is a corrective to the overwhelming trend in scholarship to narrate (!) racism and malicious white identity as a Southern aberration vis-à-vis a "normative" American democratic tradition of nonracialism.
55. Reginald Horsman, *Race and Manifest Destiny: The Origins of American Racial Anglo-Saxonism* (Cambridge/London: Harvard University Press, 1981).
56. William Haller, *Foxe's Book of Martyrs and the Elect Nation* (London: Jonathan Cape, 1963), 14–18.
57. Horsman, *Race and Manifest Destiny*, 5.
58. Jonathan Edwards, *History of the Work of Redemption*, in *The Works of President Edwards* (1817; reprint, New York: Burt Franklin, 1968), 5: 246.

3   Ham, History, and the Problem of Illegitimacy

1. Of course, not all of the South's approximately four million slaves would be emancipated until the thirteenth amendment was passed in 1865. See W. E. B. Du Bois, *The Gift of Black Folk* (1924; reprint, Millwood, NY: Kraus-Thomson Organization Limited, 1975), 186.

2. As early as 1826, an essay, evidently authored by a Negro American, anticipated the full-fledged histories of the race that would proliferate decades later. The condition of the Negro race in America, the author suggests, provides "a curious commentary upon the mutability of human affairs." The irony the author portends lies in the fact that Negroes enjoyed a glorious past "as the most enlightened on the globe." The essay continues by definitively identifying American Negroes as Cushites, the Ethiopian peoples referred to in biblical narrative. By way of citing Herodotus and other classical sources, in addition to archaeological scholarship and biblical references, the author argues that the Cushites were the founders of human arts and civilization, from which all other civilizations were descended. See R. T. X., *The Ancient Glory of the Negro Race* (n.p., 1863), 5, 6; located at the Schomburg Center for Research in Black Culture, New York City. This pamphlet, as it was reprinted in 1863, was originally published as an essay in *The African Repository* (a.k.a. *The African Repository and Colonial Journal*), a serial first appearing in March 1825 and renamed in 1849 or 1850 as *Liberia*. A prefatory note in the 1863 pamphlet indicates that the writing first appeared "in the first number" of the *African Repository*, which leaves ambiguous the volume. An additional note within the pamphlet, moreover, gives the year 1826 as the date of original publication. Reconciliation of these data would indicate an original publication date of March 1826, in vol. 2, no. 1 of the serial. In line with the author's original intent, the prefatory note suggests, "At this crisis [of the Civil War] in our country's experience, he who can wisely prosecute such a study, and successfully bring out into public view the leading thought of this brief contribution, may do much towards removing prejudice against a people who, although degraded now, were once the rulers and instructors of mankind" (4).

3. Although George William's publication was by far the most influential monograph and commanded positive critical reception from multiple audiences, James W. C. Pennington much earlier had published *A Textbook of the Origin and History of the Colored People* (Hartford, CT: L. Skinner, 1841; reprint, Detroit, MI: Negro History Press, 1969).

4. Psalms 68:31 is rendered, "Let bronze be brought from Egypt; let Ethiopia hasten to stretch out its hands to God" in the NRSV. The point is that tribute would be exacted from a subordinated/conquered Egypt, and Ethiopia would figuratively extend the hands in surrender to Israel's deity. The Psalm is a form of ethnic invective and is explicitly political. Here is wishful thinking on the part of the powerless (Israelites) that their deity would break the backs of the powerful (Egypt/Ethiopia). The American uses of this text, thus, could not have been more ironic.

5. Alonzo Potter Burgess Holly, *God and the Negro, Synopsis of God and the Negro; or The Biblical Record of the Race of Ham* (Nashville, TN: National

Baptist Publishing Board, 1937); J. J. Jackson, *History of the Black Man; an Authentic Collection of Historical Information on the Early Civilization of the Descendants of Ham, the Son of Noah: History of the Black Kingdoms of Ghana, Melle, Songhay, and Hansas, and the Early American Negro* (Bellefontaine, OH: n.p., 1921); Allen Joseph, *The Hamatic [sic] Race and Civilization* (Newark, NJ: Newark Herald Print Shop, 1935).

6. George W. Williams, *History of the Negro Race in America, 1619–1880* (1883; reprint, New York: Arno Press and the New York Times, 1968), v–vi. See John Hope Franklin, *George Washington Williams: A Biography* (Durham: Duke University Press, 1998), 8–9.

7. *Cush* (or *Kush*) is the Hebrew term translated "Ethiopia."

8. Rufus Perry, *The Cushite, or The Descendants of Ham as Found in the Sacred Scriptures and in the Writings of Ancient Historians and Poets from Noah to the Christian Era* (Springfield, MA: Willey & Co., 1893), ix–x.

9. Ibid., 49.

10. Ibid., 53, 54.

11. Ibid., 170f.

12. Joseph Elias Hayne, *The Negro in Sacred History: Or, Ham and His Immediate Descendants*, 4 vols. (Charleston, SC: Walker, Evans, & Cogswell Co., 1887).

13. J. Wofford White, Introduction to *The Negro in Sacred History: Or, Ham and His Immediate Descendants*, 4 vols., by Joseph Hayne (Charleston, SC: Walker, Evans, & Cogswell Co., 1887), 7.

14. Ibid., 8.

15. Ibid., Hayne, *The Negro in Sacred History*, 10.

16. Ibid., 13–16.

17. Ibid., 64.

18. Ibid.

19. Ibid., 41.

20. Williams, *History of the Negro Race*, v–vi.

21. G. W. F. Hegel, *Lectures on the Philosophy of World History*, trans. H. B. Nisbet (London: Cambridge University Press, 1975), 174. For a compelling analysis of the colonizing fruition of this logic, see Mahmood Mamdani, *When Victims Become Killers: Colonialism, Nativism, and Genocide in Rwanda* (Princeton: Princeton University Press, 2001), 76–79. Within this white supremacist framework was born the concept of "black Africa" (vis-à-vis what was imagined as a European-derived society and people in North Africa). Hegel's point was that true Africans or black Africans could not have possibly produced the patent signifiers of civilization such as architectural prowess (witness the pyramids of Egypt), medical technology, mathematics, literacy, and the like. Thus, the need to argue that Egyptians were not black but white. Mamdani's study is particularly significant in light of the immediate discussion because he examines a parallel history of Hamitic ideas in Rwanda that depended upon defining Hamites as whites, not Negroes. In the language-world of Rwandan colonization, Tutsis were Hamites (derived from white ancestry) and Hutus were Bantus (Negroid blacks). This theme of Hamitic whiteness never dominated U.S. American discussions of race. It was, however, quite common in Africa.

22. Hegel, *Philosophy of World History*, 190.

23. Hegel, *Philosophy of Right*, trans. T. M. Knox (London: Oxford University Press, 1967).
24. Lewis Gordon, *Fanon and the Crisis of European Man: An Essay on Philosophy and the Human Sciences* (New York/London: Routledge, 1995), 28, 29.
25. Ibid., 28.
26. Michel Foucault, *Discipline and Punish: The Birth of the Prison*, trans. Alan Sheridan (New York: Vintage Books, 1977), 26–27.
27. Ibid.
28. Ibid., 27.
29. Ibid., 29.
30. Ibid.
31. Ibid.
32. Ibid., 30.
33. Gordon, *Fanon and the Crisis of European Man*, 28, 29.
34. Theophus H. Smith, *Conjuring Culture* (New York: Oxford University Press, 1994), 70; Smith's study is excellent for its interdisciplinary scope and theoretical subtlety. See Erich Auerbach, *Mimesis: The Representation of Reality in European Literature*, trans. Williard Trask (New York: Garden City: Doubleday/Anchor, 1952) and "Figura" in *Scenes from the Drama of European Literature*, ed. Wald Godzich and Jochen Schulte-Sasse (Minneapolis: University of Minnesota Press, 1984).
35. Smith, *Conjuring Culture*, 70.
36. Ibid., 62, 63. See Werner Sollors, *Beyond Ethnicity: Consent and Descent in American Culture* (New York: Oxford University Press, 1986).
37. Smith, *Conjuring Culture*, 62. Smith explains the power of this imagining in vivid terms when he suggests that "to designate a deity . . . means also to image a self."
38. This radically differential imaging of blacks persisted officially in Mormonism until the 1970s, when a new revelation affirmed their status as equals with whites; at that point, black males were allowed to become priests in the Church of Jesus Christ of Latter-Day Saints. See Lester Bush, "Writing 'Mormonism's Negro Doctrine: An Historical Overview' (1973): Contexts and Reflections, 1998," *Journal of Mormon History* 25(1) (Spring 1999): 229–271; Dennis L. Lithgoe, "Negro Slavery and Mormon Doctrine," in *Religion and Slavery*, ed. Paul Finkelman (New York: Garland, 1989), 393–404; and Newell G. Bringhurst, *Saints, Slaves, and Blacks: The Changing Place of Black People within Mormonism* (Westport, CT: Greenwood Press, 1981). Augustine, in his *City of God*, describes the Hamites as "neither hot nor cold," allegorically neither Jew nor Gentile. They come to signify the heretics in Augustine's discourse. See his *Concerning the City of God Against the Pagans*, trans. Henry Bettenson (1972; reprint, London: Penguin Books, 1984), 650.

4   Becoming the People of God

1. Contrary to popular conceptions, most enslaved blacks were not born-again, church-going Protestants who quoted scripture or read the Bible. It was not

7. Richard Brent Turner, *Islam in the African American Experience* (Bloomington, IN: Indiana University Press, 1997), 48–50. Turner's is an excellent discussion of Blyden's complicated perspectives about Islam and African traditional religion. At no point did Blyden regard native African religions to be valid or on par with monotheism.

8. Blyden, "Hope for Africa," 17.

9. Ibid., 6.

10. Ibid., 2.

11. Ibid., 14.

12. Stephen Angell, *Bishop Henry McNeal Turner and African American Religion in the South* (Knoxville: University of Tennessee Press, 1992).

13. Henry McNeal Turner, *Respect Black: The Writings and Speeches of Henry McNeal Turner*, ed. Edwin S. Redkey (New York: Arno Press, 1971), 51.

14. Henry McNeal Turner to John Payne Turner, *Respect Black*, 47. This letter to Turner's son was first published in *The Christian Recorder*, March 5, 1880.

15. Turner, *Respect Black*, 50.

16. Ibid., 58–59.

17. Ibid., 55.

18. Henry McNeal Turner, *Christian Recorder* January 4, 1883, in *Respect Black*, 53.

19. "A Compelling Force: Notes from the Ministry of Rev. Lewis G. Jordan," *Mission Herald* (November/December 1997, January/February 1998): 7–8 (combined issue). Walter Williams, 69.

20. Ibid.

21. Walter Williams, *Black Americans*, 85.

22. Blyden, "Hope for Africa," 7.

23. Ibid., 1. In this same speech, Blyden seems to contradict himself by arguing that Siberia and Lapland were places where those of Caucasian blood were still uncivilized. Caucasians in Southern Europe, he opines, were also wallowing in degeneracy.

24. Jonathan Edwards is a classic example of this. See his "History of the Work of Redemption" in *The Works of President Edwards*, vol. 5 (1817; reprint, New York: Burt Franklin, 1968). I have already explained Edwards' style of thinking in Chapter 2.

25. Alexander Crummell, "The Regeneration of Africa," in *African American Religious History: A Documentary Witness*, ed. Milton Sernett (Durham/London: Duke University Press, 1999), 288.

26. Ibid., 284.

27. Alexander Crummell, *Africa and America* (1891; reprint, Miami, FL: Mnemosyne Publishing, 1969), 129, 130.

28. Ibid., 427.

29. Ibid., 320–321; Walter Williams, *Black Americans*, 134. Leopold's colonization of the Congo was among the most violent European forays into Africa and resulted in the genocide of over twenty million Africans of this region. Crummell, who died in 1898, did not live to see most of this genocide take place, which continued into the twentieth century. (The author would suggest that, had Crummell witnessed the full extent of this genocidal violence against

Africans of the region, he would have condemned it.) My point here is that Crummell did realize that native Africans would lose autonomy and control over their lands and would suffer some measure of physical violence under a colonial regime. See Adam Hochschild, *King Leopold's Ghost: A Story of Greed, Terror, and Heroism in Colonial Africa* (Boston: Houghton Mifflin, 1998); Roger Anstey, *King Leopold's Legacy: The Congo under Belgian Rule, 1908–1960* (London: Oxford University Press, 1966).

30. See Walter Williams, *Black Americans*, 46.
31. Ibid., 65.
32. Ibid., 71.
33. Edward Wilmot Blyden, *Christianity, Islam, and the Negro Race* (1887; reprint, Edinburg: Edinburg University Press, 1967).
34. See Karen Armstrong, *Muhammad: A Biography of the Prophet* (New York: HarperSanFrancisco, 1992), 32–34; Benjamin Kedar, *Crusade and Mission: European Approaches to the Muslims* (Princeton: Princeton University Press, 1984); Jonathan Edwards, writing in the eighteenth century, employed the triad formulation of Romanism (referring to Roman Catholicism), Mohammedanism (referring to Islam), and heathenism as the three great enemies of the (Protestant) Church. See Edwards, "History of the Work of Redemption," vol. 5 of *The Works of President Edwards*, 5: 236.
35. This is a misleading dichotomy. Religion is a form culture, a cultural aspect. It becomes, ultimately, impossible to separate the two. Blyden sought to justify the Arab-Islamic slave trade, which had developed over the centuries a veritable ideology of antiblackness derived from an Arab ethnocentrism. Among the best treatments of this aspect of Islam in Africa is Richard Turner's *Islam in the African American Experience* (Bloomington, IN: Indiana University, 1997). Turner critiques, for instance, the misleading trend of representing Islam as race-neutral before its manifestation in the United States. See also Bernard Lewis, *Race and Slavery in the Middle East: An Historical Enquiry* (New York/Oxford: Oxford University Press, 1990); John Ralph Willis, ed., *Slaves and Slavery in Muslim Africa*, vol. 1, *Islam and the Ideology of Enslavement* (London/Totowa, NJ: Frank Cass, 1985).
36. Blyden, "Mohammedanism and the Negro Race," *Methodist Quarterly Review* (January 1877): 106, 111 and *Christianity, Islam, and the Negro Race*, 11, 12.
37. Blyden, "Mohammedanism and the Negro Race," *Methodist Quarterly Review* (January 1877): 105. Blyden often referred to Africa as "Negroland," a term that emphasized that the Negro race did indeed have land or a place to claim as their own.
38. Blyden, *Christianity, Islam, and the Negro Race*, 21.
39. Ibid., 6.
40. Ibid.
41. Edward Wilmot Blyden, *A Vindication of the African Race, Being a Brief Examination of the Arguments in Favor of African Inferiority* (Monrovia: Gaston Killian, 1857), 16–17.
42. Ibid., 18.
43. Ibid., 19.
44. Ibid.

45. Ibid., 19–20.

46. Wilson Jeremiah Moses, *Afrotopia: The Roots of African American Popular History* (Cambridge: Cambridge University Press, 1998), 47.

47. What Blyden describes as a black Christian destiny to dispel black heathenism was fundamentally characteristic of black Christianity. Amanda Smith, Henry McNeil Turner, Maria Stewart, Anna Julia Cooper, and Alexander Crummell likewise espoused such a vision among both American and African blacks.

48. Martin Marty, *Modern American Religion*, 3 vols. (Chicago: Chicago University Press, 1986–96); David Turley, *American Religion: Literary Sources and Documents*, The Banks, Mountfield: Helm Information, 1998); Harold Bloom, *The American Religion: The Emergence of the Post-Christian Nation*, (New York: Simon & Schuster, 1992); Marjorie Garber and Rebecca L. Walkowitz, eds., *One Nation Under God?: Religion and American Culture* (New York: Routledge, 1999); Nathan Hatch, *The Democratization of American Christianity* (New Haven: Yale University Press, 1989); and Hans A. Baer and Merrill Singer, *African-American Religion in the Twentieth Century: Varieties of Protest and Accommodation* (Knoxville: University of Tennessee Press, 1992).

49. Williams notes, for example, that the theology of Henry McNeal Turner and Alexander Crummell was by no means anomalous but, rather, representative. They both viewed Africans as "heathens" whose only viable future lay in becoming people of Christianity's God. See Walter L. Williams, *Black Americans*, 174.

50. Anthony Pinn, " 'Double Consciousness' in Nineteenth-Century Black Nationalism: Reflections on the Teachings of Bishop Henry McNeal Turner," *The Journal of Religious Thought* 52 (Summer/Fall 1995): 15–26.

51. Charles S. Long, *Significations: Signs, Symbols, and Images in the Interpretation of Religion* (Aurora, CO: The Davies Group, 1995); and "Civil Rights—Civil Religion: Visible People and Invisible Religion," in *American Civil Religion*, ed. Russell E. Richey and Donald G. Jones (New York: Harper & Row, 1971).

52. Robert E. Hood, *Begrimed and Black: Christian Traditions on Blacks and Blackness* (Philadelphia: Fortress Press, 1994); Forrest G. Wood, *The Arrogance of Faith: Christianity and Race in America from the Colonial Era to the Twentieth Century* (New York: Alfred A. Knopf, 1990).

53. Sandy D. Martin, *Black Baptists and African Missions: The Origins of a Movement* (Macon: Mercer University Press, 1989), 189.

54. Ibid., 190.

55. Ibid., 189.

56. "Slavery and Forced Labour in Liberia," *International Labour Review* (September 1932): 417–422.

57. Conrad Cherry, *God's New Israel: Religious Interpretations of American Destiny* (Chapel Hill: University of North Carolina Press, 1998).

58. Anna Julia Cooper, "Womanhood: A Vital Element in the Regeneration and Progress of a Race," in *The Voice of Anna Julia Cooper: Including* A Voice from the South *and Other Important Essays, Papers and Letters*, ed. Charles Lemert and Esme Bahn (Lanham, MD: Rowman & Littlefield Publishers, 1998), 54.

59. William Montgomery, *Under Their Own Vine and Fig Tree: The African-American Church in the South, 1865–1900* (Baton Rouge: Louisiana State University Press, 1993).

60. This confluence of white scholarship and white theology was deeply racist, and it greatly influenced how blacks religiously assessed African history and spirituality. See Stephen J. Gould, *The Mismeasure of Man* (New York: W. W. Norton & Company, 1981); John David Smith, ed., *The Biblical and "Scientific" Defense of Slavery, Anti-Black Thought, 1863–1925* (New York: Garland Publishing, Inc., 1993); and Sylvia Jacobs, ed., *Black Americans and the Missionary Movement in Africa* (Westport, CT: Greenwood Press, 1982).

61. E. Frances White, *Dark Continent of Our Bodies: Black Feminism and the Politics of Respectability* (Philadelphia: Temple University Press, 2001); Charles Darwin, *The Origin of Species: By Means of Natural Selection; The Descent of Man: And Selection in Relation to Sex* (Chicago: Encyclopaedia Britannica, 1952).

62. White, *Dark Continent*, 93.

63. Ibid.

64. Ibid., 95.

65. Ibid.

66. Jennifer L. Morgan, " 'Some Could Suckle over their Shoulder': Male Travelers, Female Bodies, and the Gendering of Racial Ideology, 1500–1770," *The William and Mary Quarterly* 54 (January 1997): 167–192.

67. Some social customs of African societies expressed a patriarchal assumption of provision for women by requiring men to provide support—food, shelter, family, etc.—to widowed women if the deceased husband were a relative of the recent provider or husband. Whites were no less patriarchal than Africans; the distinction was the manifestation of this orientation. This practice of provision—often taken up by a relative or a wealthy local male—was read as nothing more than sexual opportunism. Meanwhile, these reports are curiously silent on the especially widespread phenomenon of prostitution among whites and the sexual prerogative that white men carried over (enslaved) women whom they purchased as property.

68. Morgan, "Some Could Suckle over their Shoulder," 171, 184.

69. Ibid., 169, 171, 176.

70. Ibid., 169–170.

71. Londa Schiebinger, "The Anatomy of Difference: Race and Sex in Eighteenth-Century Science," *Eighteenth-Century Studies* 23(4) (1990): 387–405. Schiebinger describes one German town where a colony of Africans was kept in order to satisfy the duke's interest in collecting exotica—"along with apes, camels, leopards, and elephants" (388). By "productive" I refer to what Edward Said emphasized concerning socially constructed categories of analysis or interpretive lenses—they do not impede the observer's perspective but, rather, generate that perspective and the yield of meanings. See his *Orientalism*, rev. ed. (New York: Vintage, 1979), 14.

72. Ibid., 396.

73. Ibid., 391. Schiebinger ultimately suggests in her study that the most intensive competition for status and social mobility was between European women and

African men in Europe, the latter of whom were occasionally permitted to pursue public careers as men of letters, whereas as European women who had been allowed into the universities were strictly forbidden to make practical, professional use of their education. She does not conclude some simplistic axiom such as sexism was worse than racism. Rather, she relates this competition to the investment in meanings about gender difference in symbiosis with racial difference (399–404).

74. Mary Kate Kelly, "Performing the Other: A Consideration of Two cages," *College Literature* 26 (Winter 1999): 113–136. Kelly notes both Baker's agency as a professional performer/actor who willingly took up this role and the racist, sexist structures of power and semiotics that made intelligible the violent, exploitative representations on which the film's plot thrived.

75. T. Denean Sharpley-Whiting, *Black Venus: Sexualized Savages, Primal Fears, and Primitive Narratives in French* (Durham: Duke University Press, 1999).

76. Ibid., 18, 19, 27. This was a facetious label; *Hottentot* was the term commonly employed to designate sub-Saharan Negroes, whereas *Venus* referred to the Roman Goddess of beauty and of prostitution.

77. Ibid., 28–30.

78. Kelly Brown Douglas, *Sexuality and the Black Church* (Maryknoll, NY: Orbis, 1999), 31–33; Douglas examines the experience of Bartmann and reaches similar conclusions. See Sharpley-Whiting, *Black Venus*, 10.

79. Tertullian made this argument in a tract entitled *De Virginibus Velandis*, written ca. 211 "C.E." Mary Rose D'Angelo has examined this text in comparison with Paul's Corinthian correspondence (1 Corinthians 11) reflecting a similar concern. See her "Veils, Virgins, and the Tongues of Men and Angels: Women's Heads in Early Christianity," in *Women, Gender, Religion: A Reader*, ed. Elizabeth Castelli and Rosamond Rodman (New York: Palgrave, 2001). There are innumerable instances of the masculinist production of "woman"; one could cite examples from diverse eras within a variety of religious or otherwise cultural contexts.

80. Mary Church Terrell, *Quest for Equality: The Life and Writings of Mary Eliza Church Terrell, 1863–1954*, ed. Beverly Washington Jones (Brooklyn: Carlson Publishing Company, 1990), 3.

81. For example, both black and white northern missionaries to the South interpreted the more expressive, spiritualist worship culture of Southern blacks as an index of barbarity and uncultured sensibilities.

82. Terrell, *Quest for Equality*, 135.

83. Ibid., 152.

84. W. H. Crogman and J. W. Gibson, *The Colored American: From Slavery to Honorable Citizenship* (Atlanta: J. L. Nichols & Co., 1903), 210.

85. Charles Lemert and Esme Bhan, eds., *The Voice of Anna Julia Cooper* (Lanham/Boulder/New York/Oxford: Rowman & Littlefield, 1998), 4–6, 345, 346.

86. Anna Julia Cooper, *A Voice from the South* (Xenia, OH: Aldine Printing House, 1892). Cooper's was the first African American feminist text.

87. Cooper, "Womanhood," 59.

88. Ibid., 57.

89. Anna Julia Cooper, "Has America a Race Problem? If So, How Can It Best Be Solved?" in *The Voice of Anna Julia Cooper*, ed. Charles Lemert and Esme Bhan (1892; reprint, Lanham: Rowman & Littlefield, 1998), 129–130.

90. Cooper, "Womanhood," 62.

91. On this score, see Paula Giddings, *When and Where I Enter: The Impact of Black Women on Race and Sex in America* (New York: William Morrow, 1984).

92. Ibid., 65.

93. Ibid., 66.

94. T. Denean Sharpley-Whiting, *Frantz Fanon: Conflicts and Feminisms* (Lanham, MD: Rowman & Littlefield, 1998), 32.

95. Frantz Fanon, *The Wretched of the Earth*, trans. Constance Farrington (New York: Grove Press, 1963), 41; quoted in Sharpley-Whiting, *Frantz Fanon*, 32.

96. Sharpley-Whiting, *Frantz Fanon*, 33.

97. Ibid.

98. Carol Haynes, *Divine Destiny: Gender and Race in Nineteenth-Century Protestantism* (Jackson, MS: University Press of Mississippi, 1984).

5   Race and the American People(s) of God

1. W. E. B. Du Bois, ironically, expressed that the black "church" was not originally Christian but only later became so. "The first Negro church was not at first by any means Christian nor definitely organized; rather it was an adaptation and mingling of heathen rites among the members of each plantation, and roughly designated as Voodooism . . . . After the lapse of many generations the Negro church became Christian." See his classic *The Souls of Black Folk* (1903; reprint, with an introduction by Randall Kenan, New York: Penguin Books, 1995), 216.

2. Carter G. Woodson, *The History of the Negro Church*, 3d ed. (1921; reprint, Washington, DC: Associated Publishers, 1972); E. Franklin Frazier and C. Eric Lincoln, *The Negro Church in America/The Black Church Since Frazier* (New York: Schocken Books, 1974); C. Eric Lincoln and Lawrence Mamiya, *The Black Church in the African American Experience* (Durham, NC: Duke University Press, 1991).

3. Wilson Jeremiah Moses, *Black Messiahs and Uncle Toms: Social and Literary Manipulations of a Religious Myth* (University Park, PA: The Pennsylvania State University Press, 1982); *Afrotopia: The Roots of African American Popular History* (Cambridge: Cambridge University Press, 1998); *The Wings of Ethiopia: Studies in African-American Life and Letters* (Ames, IA: Iowa State University Press, 1990); Albert J. Raboteau, *A Fire in the Bones: Reflections on African-American Religious History* (Boston: Beacon Press, 1995).

4. Woodson, *The History of the Negro Church*; Frazier and Lincoln, *The Negro Church in America*.

5. Lincoln and Mamiya, *The Black Church*; Evelyn Brooks Higginbotham, *Righteous Discontent: The Women's Movement in the Black Baptist Church, 1880–1920* (Cambridge/London: Harvard University Press, 1993);

William L. Andrews, ed., *Sisters of the Spirit: Three Black Women's Autobiographies of the Nineteenth-Century* (Bloomington: Indiana University Press, 1986).

6. Albert J. Raboteau, *Slave Religion: The Invisible Institution in the Antebellum South* (New York: Oxford University Press, 1978); and "African Americans, Exodus and the American Israel," in *Religion and American Culture*, ed. David Hackett (New York: Routledge, 1995), 75–86; Raboteau, *A Fire in the Bones*; Mechal Sobel, *Trabelin' on: The Slave Journey to an Afro-Baptist Faith* (Westport, CT: Greenwood Press, 1979; reprint, Princeton: Princeton University Press, 1988); Eugene D. Genovese, *Roll, Jordan, Roll: The World the Slaves Made* (New York: Vintage Books, 1972); Vincent Harding, *There Is a River: The Black Struggle for Freedom in America* (San Diego/New York/London: Harcourt, Brace & Company, 1981).

7. James H. Cone, *Black Theology and Black Power*, rev. ed. (Maryknoll, NY: Orbis, 1997); *A Black Theology of Liberation*, rev. ed. (Maryknoll, NY: Orbis Books, 1990); James H. Evans, *We Have Been Believers: An African American Systematic Theology* (Minneapolis: Fortress Press, 1992); Kelly Brown Douglas, *The Black Christ* (Maryknoll, NY: Orbis, 1994); Jacquelyn Grant, *White Women's Christ and Black Women's Jesus: Feminist Christology and Womanist Response* (Atlanta, GA: Scholars Press, 1989).

8. Gayraud S. Wilmore, "Introduction," in *Black Theology: A Documentary History, 1966–1979*, ed. Gayraud S. Wilmore and James H. Cone (Maryknoll: Orbis, 1979), 15–22.

9. Cone, *Black Theology and Black Power*, 1.

10. James H. Cone, *Speaking the Truth* (Grand Rapids, MI: William B. Eerdmans Publishing Co., 1986; reprint, Maryknoll: Orbis, 1999), 115.

11. Cone, *Black Theology and Black Power*, 149, 151–152; *God of the Oppressed*, rev. ed. (Mary Knoll: Orbis, 1997), 217, 218.

12. Cone, *A Black Theology of Liberation*, 54, 56, 64, 65, 66.

13. Cone, *Black Theology and Black Power*, 151–152.

14. Evans, *We Have Been Believers*.

15. Ibid., 120, 121.

16. Ibid., 128.

17. Joseph R. Washington, *Black Religion: The Negro and Christianity in the United States* (Boston: Beacon Press, 1968).

18. Joseph R. Washington, *The Politics of God* (Boston: Beacon Press, 1967), 157.

19. Albert Cleage, Jr., *The Black Messiah* (Kansas City, KS: Sheed Andrews and McNeel, Inc., 1968), 52, 54.

20. Ibid., 207–208.

21. Charles H. Long, "Perspectives for a Study of Afro-American Religion in the United States," *History of Religions* 11, no. 1 (August 1971): 54–66; *Significations: Signs, Symbols, and Images in the Interpretation of Religion* (Philadelphia: Fortress Press, 1986; reprint, Aurora, CO: The Davies Group, 1995), 31–34, 65–68, 107, 108.

22. Long, *Significations*, 188, 190, 193.

23. Ibid., 207.

24. Ibid., 209.

25. James Deotis Roberts, *Liberation and Reconciliation: A Black Theology* (Maryknoll: Orbis, 1994), 22–26; *The Roots of a Black Future: Family and Church* (Philadelphia: Westminster Press, 1980).

26. Roberts, *Liberation and Reconciliation*, 22.

27. Ibid., 26–27.

28. Roberts, *Roots*.

29. Ibid., 90, 93, 97.

30. Delores S. Williams, *Sisters in the Wilderness: The Challenge of Womanist God-Talk* (Maryknoll, NY: Orbis, 1993); Douglas, *Black Christ*; Jacquelyn Grant, *White Women's Christ and Black Women's Jesus*.

31. Williams, *Sisters in the Wilderness*, 149–151.

32. Ibid., 147.

33. Ibid., 153. On this score, Williams cites the work of Cain Hope Felder, who has sought to locate blacks in the Bible. See Felder's *Troubling Biblical Waters: Race, Class, and Family* (Maryknoll: Orbis, 1989).

34. As already evidenced, Delores Williams' was among the earliest, clearest studies to argue that the oppressed of the oppressed were not Israelites but those who were victims of the violence meted out by the Israelite deity. See Williams, *Sisters in the Wilderness*, 151. More recent studies in this vein include the work of Musa W. Dube, *Postcolonial Feminist Interpretation of the Bible* (St. Louis: Chalice Press, 2000).

35. Itumeleng Mosala, *Biblical Hermeneutics and Black Theology in South Africa* (Grand Rapids, MI: William B. Eerdmans Publishing Co., 1989), 28.

36. Ibid.

37. Josiah U. Young, *A Pan-African Theology: Providence and the Legacies of the Ancestors* (Trenton, NJ: Africa World Press, 1992).

38. Eddie S. Glaude, *Exodus!: Religion, Race and Nation in Early Nineteenth-Century Black America* (Chicago: University of Chicago Press, 2000); Lincoln and Mamiya, *Black Church*; Dwight Hopkins, *Introducing Black Theology of Liberation* (Maryknoll: Orbis, 1999), 81, 83, 85–86; Gayraud Wilmore, *Black Religion and Black Radicalism: An Interpretation of the Religious History of African Americans*, 3d ed. (Maryknoll, NY: Orbis Books, 1998).

39. Glaude, *Exodus!*, 80, 81.

40. Walter Williams, *Black Americans and the Evangelization of Africa, 1877–1900* (Madison: University of Wisconsin Press, 1982).

41. Gayraud Wilmore, "Setting the Record Straight," in *Native American Religion and Black Protestantism*, ed. Martin Marty (Munich: K.G. Saur, 1993), 82, 86, 88, 91 n. 5.

42. Robert Allen Warrior, "A Native American Perspective: Canaanites, Cowboys, and Indians," in *Voices from the Margin: Interpreting the Bible in the Third World*, ed. R. S. Sugirtharajah (New York/London: Orbis/SPCK, 1995), 280–282, 283.

43. See for instance, Norman K. Gottwald, *The Hebrew Bible: A Socio-Literary Introduction* (Philadelphia: Fortress Press, 1985), 261–284.

44. Edward Said, *The Question of Palestine* (London: Vintage Press, 1992); Rosemary Ruether and Herman Ruether, *The Wrath of Jonah: The Crisis of Religious Nationalism in the Israeli-Palestinian Conflict* (San Francisco: Harper & Row, 1989).

45. Gary Comstock, *Gay Theology Without Apology* (Cleveland, OH: Pilgrim Press, 1993), 36–41; Elias Farajaje-Jones, "Breaking Silence: Toward an In-the-Life Theology," in *Black Theology: A Documentary History, Volume Two: 1980–1992*, ed. James H. Cone and Gayraud S. Wilmore (Maryknoll: Orbis, 1993).

46. Given Christianity's uniquely anti-Semitic history, it is patent that nineteenth-century white American Christians did not regard Jews as co-religionists or co-believers but as blasphemers. White American Christian identity was defined in opposition to Jewish identity. It is also important to note the shifts that occurred after World War II, when European Jews became "white" in America (ethnic whiteness). More recently, in the twenty-first century, white American Christians have developed a perplexing public understanding of Jewish identity that embraces Jewishness *qua* pro-Israeli in order to sustain an American disposition of anti-Arabism while simultaneously continuing to encode religious Jewishness as apostasy. For an interesting exchange on the irony of this novel turn on an old theme of anti-Semitism, see "Zion's Christian Soldiers: Fundamental Christian Evangelicals Believe the Jewish State Should Control All of the Biblical Jewish Homeland," *60 Minutes*, CBS broadcast (June 8, 2003). Transcript available from Lexis-Nexis. Also, see Bashir Najim, ed., *American Church Politics and the Middle East* (Belmont, MA: Association of American-Arab University Graduates, 1982); Robert L. Brashear, "Corner-Stone, Stumbling Stone: Christian Problems in Viewing Israel," *Union Seminary Quarterly Review* 38, no. 2 (1983): 203–224. For a recent comprehensive study of this phenomenon, see Gershom Gorenberg, *The End of Days: Fundamentalism and the Struggle for the Temple Mount* (New York: Free Press, 2000).

47. Robert Hood, *Begrimed and Black: Christian Traditions on Blackness* (Philadelphia: Fortress Press, 1994).

48. By "Christian missions," I specifically refer to the programmatic campaigns by Christian missionaries to convert "others" to Christianity. Some persons might object that such is a partial or distorted characterization of Christian missions, and would prefer to associate Christian missions with humanitarian aid (e.g., providing food, clothing, shelter, education). It is patent, however, that the historical accounts (and contemporary practices) of Christian missions consistently point to *conversion to Christian identity* as the supreme and originary objective of missions. To suggest that humanitarian aid is the defining aspect of missions, therefore, becomes misrepresentative at best and dishonest or disingenuous at worst.

49. Brian Levack, ed., *Witch-Hunting in Continental Europe: Local and Regional Studies* (New York: Garland, 1992). Mary Daly has emphasized this history of witch-hunting as by and large a gendered, anti-woman phenomenon, given the fact that most of the victims were women. See her *Beyond God the Father: Towards a Philosophy of Women's Liberation* (Boston: Beacon, 1973), 62–64. There is, of course, much uncertainty regarding the definitive number of people killed—some estimates are in the tens of thousands, other estimates exceed 200 000. The anti-witchcraft movement itself, however, is *not* debatable. That many human beings died as a result of identifying Europe's pre-Christian

religion as evil is an empirical fact that should inform any serious reflection upon the history of Christian identity.

50. The author is of course aware that Christianity was present in Africa by the late-first or early-second century of the Common Era. One could also argue that Palestine, where Christianity originates, is indeed part of Africa. My discussion here concerns the Christianization of Africa during the colonial era. Colonization effected the *globalization* of Christianity. Christianity during the colonial era, for the *first* time, began to pose a widespread threat to the very existence of indigenous religions of Africa, which were essentially polytheistic. Early Christianity's presence in Africa was never able to achieve such a level of dominance and was largely confined to northern and northeastern portions of Africa.

51. Early Christianity was illegal in the Greco-Roman empire because it was (rightly) viewed as atheism in the Roman sense (i.e., monotheism), meaning that early Christians rejected belief in the Gods of Rome (the official pantheon). Since the Roman emperor was a God, this atheism directly implied treason. Imperial laws did not force Judaic religionists to worship the pantheon, however, because imperial officials were familiar with the peculiar concept of monotheism among Judeans. By worshipping only one God, Judeans were merely practicing an age-old tradition, thus no association was made between their atheism/monotheism and treason. New religious movements, however, were suspect and were closely scrutinized to enforce loyalty to the divine emperor and the pantheon. It is when the Jesus movement began to define itself as something other than Judaism (as Christianity, instead) that the movement found itself at protracted odds with the empire. If it was not Judaism, then what was it, and where did it stand on the question of imperial loyalty? This question lay at the root of the creative strategies of Christians seeking to represent their religion as an ancient tradition and not a recent invention. Marcel Simon rightly suggested that Christians read Jesus into the Old Testament in order to antiquate the Church's existence. This allowed the Church to argue that Christianity was not an upstart religion of the first century but, rather, an ancient one that was as old as Judaism or older. Simon also assessed that Paul's exegesis of the Abraham narratives served to antiquate Jesusine religion. First-century Jewish Gnosticism, moreover, contributed to making "Israel" a more fluid concept by subordinating Torah observance to knowledge (*gnosis*) of the divine. See Marcel Simon, *Verus Israel: A Study of the Relations Between Christians and Jews in the Roman Empire (135–425)*, trans. H. McKeating (Oxford University Press, 1986), xii–xvi, 71–80, 92–97; Robert L. Fox, *Pagans and Christians* (New York: Alfred A. Knopf, 1987), 318–319, 479–482. Among the clearest examples of this attempt to antiquate Christianity while defining it in contrast to Judaism is Ignatius of Antioch, *Epistle to the Magnesians 5*, in *The Ante-Nicene Fathers: Translations of the Writings of the Fathers Down to A.D. 325*, vol. 1, trans. Alexander Roberts and James Donaldson (Grand Rapids, MI: Wm. B. Eerdmans Publishing Company, 1950), 59–65.

52. I am referring to the moribund attempts to reconstruct an ancient, pre-monarchic Israel, a problem that has been the subject of several recent studies. At issue specifically is whether an ethnically or culturally distinct people called "Israel" existed during the Late Bronze Age (e.g., an era of the patriarchs, an era of

conquest over Canaanites, the period of the judges). The most intensive biblical narratives seeking to differentiate Israelites from their heathen neighbors are based on this time period. Early twentieth-century attempts to reconstruct this period of Israelite history projected ideas of a modern Western national existence onto ancient Israel and were fundamentally influenced by the modern political interests of Zionism. It is evident, at this point, that the biblical narratives describing the patriarchs and depicting ancient Israelites moving from Egypt to Palestine via conquest (or some other means of massive settlement) are ahistorical and are ideological, religious productions of a later period (perhaps post-exilic?). The theologically and ideologically driven attempts to construct a monarchic Israel as radically different from its Canaanite neighbors, moreover, have had to yield to a far more complex view of Israelites, who were, in ethnic and cultural terms, Canaanites. Niels Peter Lemche examines these problems and the nature of ancient Palestinian society in his "Israel, History of (Premonarchic Period)," in *The Anchor Bible Dictionary*, ed. David Noel Freedman (New York: Doubleday, 1992), 3: 526–545. Also, see Keith Whitelam, *The Invention of Ancient Israel: The Silencing of Palestinian History* (New York: Routledge, 1996); Niels Peter Lemche, *Ancient Israel: A New History of Israelite Society* (Sheffield: Sheffield Academic Press, 1995); Marc Brettler, *The Creation of History in Ancient Israel* (New York: Routledge, 1995). For an opposing view, see William G. Dever, *What Did the Biblical Writers Know, and When Did They Know It?: What Archaeology Can Tell Us About the Reality of Ancient Israel* (Grand Rapids: Wm. B. Eerdmans, 2001).

53. 2 Kings 21. Itumeleng Mosala, for instance, demonstrates that the Jerusalem temple institution was initially an urban, minoritarian establishment and was opposed to the "Canaanite" religions (i.e., fertility and Goddess religions) practiced by Israelite peasants. What are inscribed as foreign and polluting practices are actually the historical religions of (rural) Israelites, who were never monotheists. Even the Yahwist cult was at most henotheistic. See his *Biblical Hermeneutics*, 16–17. The most important study of ancient Israelite religion is perhaps that by Ziony Zevit, *The Religions of Ancient Israel: A Synthesis of Parallactic Approaches* (New York: Continuum, 2001). As the title implies, Zevit demonstrates at length that many Gods were widely venerated in Israelite religion and that there existed no single religion proper.

54. Concerning Canaanite religion as the basis for Israelite religion, see Judith Hadley, *The Cult of Asherah in Ancient Israel and Judah: The Evidence for a Hebrew Goddess* (Cambridge: Cambridge University Press, 2000); Susan Niditch, *Ancient Israelite Religion* (New York/Oxford: Oxford University Press, 1997); David Noel Freedman, "Yahweh of Samaria and His Asherah," in *Biblical Archaeologist 50* (December 1987): 241–249; see especially Hershel Shanks et al., *The Rise of Ancient Israel* (Washington, DC: Biblical Archaeology Society, 1992); Lemche, *Ancient Israel*; and Ephraim Isaac, "Genesis, Judaism, and the 'Sons of Ham'," in *Islam and the Ideology of Enslavement*, vol. 1 of *Slaves and Slavery in Muslim Africa*, ed. John Ralph Willis (London/Totowa, NJ: Frank Cass, 1985), 75–89.

55. Frantz Fanon, *Black Skin, White Masks*, trans. Charles Lam Markmann (New York: Grove Press, 1967), 10.

56. Ibid., 8.

57. Cone, *Black Theology and Black Power*, 8–12.

58. Musa Dube has most recently examined the strategies of encoding "others" as heathens needing to be missionized or enlightened by Christian knowledge/ gospel as a colonizing (and postcolonial) strategy of inscribing difference as ignorance. See her *Postcolonial Feminist Interpretation of the Bible* (St. Louis: Chalice, 2000); and "Go Therefore and Make Disciples of All Nations: A Postcolonial Perspective on Biblical Criticism and Pedagogy," in *Teaching the Bible: The Discourses and Politics of Biblical Pedagogy*, ed. Fernando Segovia and Mary Ann Tolbert (Maryknoll, NY: Orbis, 1998).

59. See Dube, above.

60. Wilfred Cantwell Smith, *What is Scripture?: A Comparative Approach* (Minneapolis: Fortress, 1993).

This page intentionally left blank

Bibliography

Primary Sources

Ariel (Buckner Harrison Payne). *The Negro, What Is His Ethnological Status?: Is He the Progeny of Ham? Is He A Descendant of Adam and Eve? Has He A Soul? Or Is He A Beast in God's Nomenclature? What Is His Status as Fixed by God in Creation? What Is His Relation to the White Race?* 2nd ed. Cincinnati, OH: n.p., 1867.

Blyden, Edward W. *Christianity, Islam, and the Negro Race.* 1887. Reprint, Edinburgh: University of Edinburgh, 1967.

——. "Hope for Africa." *Colonization Journal* Tract no. 8 (August 1861): 17.

——. "Mohammedanism and the Negro Race." *Methodist Quarterly Review* 59 (January 1877): 100–127.

——. *The Negro in Ancient History.* Washington City: McGill & Witherow, 1869.

——. "The Negro in the United States." *A.M.E. Church Review* 16 (January 1900): 309.

——. *Philip and the Eunuch: Or, the Instruments and Methods of Africa's Evangelization.* Cambridge: John Wilson & Son/University Press, 1883.

——. *A Vindication of the African Race; Being a Brief Examination of the Arguments in Favor of African Inferiority.* Monrovia: G. Killian, 1857.

Bowen, J. W. E., ed. *Africa and the American Negro.* 1895. Reprint, Miami: Mnemosyne Publishing, Inc., 1969.

——, ed. *What Shall the Harvest Be? A National Sermon; Or, a Series of Plain Talks to the Colored People of America, on Their Problems.* Washington, DC: Howard University Print, 1892.

Brawley, E. M., ed. *The Negro Baptist Pulpit: A Collection of Sermons and Papers on Baptist Doctrine and Missionary and Educational Work.* Philadelphia: American Baptist Publication Society, 1890.

Brent, George W. "The Ancient Glory of the Hamitic Race." *A.M.E. Church Review* 12 (October 1895): 272–275.

Cartwright, Samuel A. "Slavery in the Light of Ethnology." In *Cotton is King, and Other Pro-Slavery Arguments; Comprising the Writings of Hammond, Harper, Christy, Stringfellow, Hodge, Bledsoe, and Cartwright, on This Important Subject,* edited by E. N. Elliot. Augusta, GA: Pritchard, Abbot & Loomis, 1860.

Cole, Augustus. "The Negro at Home and Abroad: Their Origin, Progress and Destiny." *A.M.E. Church Review* 4 (April 1888): 401.

Cooper, Anna Julia. *A Voice from the South.* Ohio: Aldine Publishing House, 1892. Reprint, New York: Negro Universities Press, 1969.

Crogman, W. H. and J. W. Gibson. *The Colored American: From Slavery to Honorable Citizenship.* Atlanta: J. L. Nichols & Co., 1903.

Crummell, Alexander. *Africa and America.* 1891. Reprint, Miami, FL: Mnemosyne Publishing, 1969.

——. "The Regeneration of Africa." *In African American Religious History: A Documentary Witness,* edited by Milton Sernett. Durham: Duke University Press, 1999.

Cuvier, Charles. *Les Camites Traditionnels Et Les Peuples De Race Noire. Esquisses D'histoire Générale.* Paris, Sandoz & Fischbacher; Neuchatel, Librairie générale J. Sandoz, 1873.

Dart, J. L. "Melchizedek a Descendant of Ham." *A.M.E. Church Review* 2 (January 1887): 398–401.

Darwin, Charles. *The Origin of Species: By Means of Natural Selection; The Descent of Man: And Selection in Relation to Sex.* Chicago: Encyclopaedia Britannica, 1952.

Delany, Martin Robison. *Principia of Ethnology: The Origin of Races and Color: With an Archaeological Compendium of Ethiopian and Egyptian Civilization from Years of Careful Examination and Inquiry.* 2nd ed. Philadelphia, PA: Harper, 1880.

Douglass, Frederick. *Narrative of the Life of Frederick Douglass, An American Slave.* Boston: Anti-Slavery Office, 1845.

Foucault, Michel. *Discipline and Punish: The Birth of the Prison.* Translated by Alan Sheridan. New York: Vintage Books, 1977.

Garnet, Henry Highland. *The Past and the Present Condition and the Destiny of the Colored Race; a Discourse Delivered at the Fifteenth Anniversary of the Female Benevolent Society of Troy, N.Y., Feb. 14, 1848.* 1848. Reprint, Miami: Mnemosyne, 1969.

Ginzberg, Louis. *The Legends of the Jews.* Translated by Henrietta Szold. 7 vols. Philadelphia: The Jewish Publication Society of America, 1909–38.

Gliddon, George R. and Josiah Nott. *Types of Mankind: Or, Ethnological Researches Based Upon the Ancient Monuments, Paintings, Sculptures, and Crania of Races, and Upon Their Natural, Geographical, Philological and Biblical History: Illustrated by Selections from the Inedited [sic] Papers of Samuel George Morton and by Additional Contributions from L. Agassiz, W. Usher, and H. S. Patterson.* Philadelphia: J. B. Lippincott, Grambo, & Co., 1854.

Gobineau, Arthur de. *Gobineau: Selected Political Writings.* Compiled by Michael D. Biddiss. New York: Harper & Row, 1970.

——. *The Inequality of the Human Races.* Translated by Adrian Collins. New York: G.P. Putnam's Sons, 1915.

Gorju, Julien Louis. *Face Au Royaume Hamite Du Ruanda, Le Royaume Frère De L'Urundi: Essai De Reconstitution Historique; Moeurs Pastorale; Folklore/Par Mgr. Gorju Et Ses Missionnaires.* Bruxelles: Vromant & Co., 1938.

Grau, Rudolf Freidrich. *The Goal of the Human Race; Or, The Development of Civilisation; Its Origin and Issue.* Translated by J. G. Deimler and W. St. Clair Tisdall. London: Simpkin, Marshall, Hamilton, Kent & Co., Ltd., 1892.

Harris, Samuel. *The Kingdom of Christ on Earth.* Andover, MA: W. F. Draper, 1874.

Hayne, Joseph Elias. *The Amonian or Hamitic Origin of the Ancient Greeks, Cretans, and All the Celtic Races: A Reply to the New York Sun.* Brooklyn: Guide Printing and Publishing Company, 1905.

——. *The Black Man: Or, the Natural History of The Hametic Race.* Raleigh, NC: Edwards & Broughton, 1894.

——. *Ham and His Immediate Descendants, and Their Wonderful Achievements.* New York: Welte Press, ca. 1909.

——. *The Negro in Sacred History: Or, Ham and His Immediate Descendants.* 4 vols. Charleston, SC: Walker, Evans, & Cogswell Co., 1887.

Hegel, Georg W. F. *Lectures on the Philosophy of World History, Introduction: Reason in History.* Translated by H. B. Nisbet. London: Cambridge University Press, 1975.

——. *Lectures on the Philosophy of History.* Translated by J. Sibree. London: George Bell & Sons, 1905.

——. *Philosophy of Right.* Translated by T. M. Knox. London: Oxford University Press, 1967.

Holly, Alonzo Potter Burgess. *God and the Negro, Synopsis of God and the Negro; or The Biblical Record of the Race of Ham.* Nashville, TN: National Baptist Publishing Board, 1937.

Holly, Ambroise Theodose. *Vraies Origines Historiques des Races Humaines.* Cap-Haitien, Impr. La Conscience, 1916.

Holly, James Theodore. "The Divine Plan of Human Redemption in Its Ethnological Development." *A.M.E. Church Review* 1 (October 1884): 79–85.

——. "Sacred Chronology and the Inspired Arithmetic of Divine Revelation." *A.M.E. Church Review* 2 (July 1885): 9–13.

Honea, Kenneth Howard. *A Contribution to the History of the Hamitic Peoples of Africa.* Horn-Wien, F. Berger, 1958.

Hopkins, Pauline E. *A Primer of Facts Pertaining to the Early Greatness of the African Race and the Possibility of Restoration by Its Descendants—with Epilogue. Compiled and Arranged from the Works of the Best Known Ethnologists and Historians.* Cambridge: P. E. Hopkins, 1905.

Ignatius. "Epistle to the Magnesians." In *The Ante-Nicene Fathers: Translations of the Writings of the Fathers Down to A.D. 325.* Vol. 1. Translated by Alexander Roberts and James Donaldson. Grand Rapids, MI: Wm. B. Eerdmans Publishing Company, 1950.

Jackson, Joseph Julius. *History of the Black Man; An Authentic Collection of Historical Information on the Early Civilization of the Descendants of Ham, the Son of Noah: History of the Black Kingdoms of Ghana, Melle, Songhay, and Hansas, and the Early American Negro.* Bellefontaine, OH: n.p., 1921.

Johnson, Harvey. *The Nations from a New Point of View.* Nashville, TN: National Baptist Publishing Board, 1903.

Joseph, Allen. *The Hamatic [sic] Race and Civilization*. Newark, NJ: Newark Herald Print Shop, 1935.

M'Causland, Dominick. *The Builders of Babel*. London: R. Bentley & Son, 1874.

Minton, Theophilus. "Is Intermarriage Between the Races to Be Encouraged?" *A.M.E. Church Review* 2 (January 1887): 286.

Morrisey, Richard Alburtus. *Bible History of the Negro*. Nashville, TN: National Baptist Publishing Board, 1915.

——. *Colored People in Bible History*. Hammond, IN: W. B. Conkey, 1925.

Morton, Samuel. *Crania Aegyptiaca; Or, Observations on Egyptian Ethnography, Derived from Anatomy, History and the Monuments*. Philadelphia: J. Penington, 1844.

Norris, John William. *The Ethiopian's Place in History and His Contribution to the World's Civilization: The Negro-the Hamite. The Stock, the Stems and the Branches of the Hamitic People*. London: African Publication Society, 1981.

Optician. *Speculum for Looking into the Pamphlet Entitled, "The Negro: What is His Ethnological Status? Is He the Progeny of Ham? Is He a Descendant of Adam and Eve? Has He a Soul? Or Is He a Beast in God's Nomenclature? What Is His Status as Fixed by God in Creation? What Is His Relation to the White Race? By Ariel."* Charleston, SC: Joseph Walker, 1867.

Parker, George Wells. *The Children of The Sun*. Omaha: Hamitic League of the World, 1918.

Parker, Nathaniel. *Negro History; Ancient Life, Africa, at Home and Abroad*. Philadelphia, PA: St. Clair Spencer Printing Co., 1926.

Peabody, George B. "The Hope of Africa." *A.M.E. Church Review* 7 (July 1890): 59.

Pennington, James W. C. *A Textbook of the Origin and History of the Colored People*. Hartford, CT: L. Skinner, 1841. Reprint, Detroit, MI: Negro History Press, 1969.

Perry, Rufus. *The Cushite, or the Descendants of Ham*. Springfield, MA: Willey, 1893.

Priest, Josiah. *Slavery, As It Relates to the Negro, or African Race, Examined in the Light of Circumstances, History, and the Holy Scriptures; with an Account of the Origin of the Black Man's Color, Causes of His State of Servitude and Traces of His Character as Well in Ancient and in Modern Times*. Albany: C. Van Benthuysen & Co., 1843.

Schaff, Philip. *Slavery and the Bible: A Tract for the Times*. Chambersburg, PA: M. Kieffer and Co.'s Caloric Printing Press, 1861.

Simons, R. E. *The Three Day Negro; Yesterday, Today, Tomorrow*. n.p., n.d.

Smith, John David, ed. *The Biblical and "Scientific" Defense of Slavery*. New York: Garland Publishers, 1993.

Steward, Theophilus Gould. *The End of the World; or, Clearing the Way for the Fullness of the Gentiles*. Philadelphia: A.M.E. Church Book Rooms, 1888.

Straker, D. Augustus. "The Congo Valley: Its Redemption." *A.M.E. Church Review* 2 (January 1896): 146–157.

Stringfellow, Thornton. "The Bible Argument: Or, Slavery in the Light of Divine Revelation." In *Cotton is King, and Other Pro-Slavery Arguments; Comprising the Writings of Hammond, Harper, Christy, Stringfellow, Hodge, Bledsoe, and*

Cartwright, on This Important Subject, edited by E. N. Elliot. Augusta, GA: Pritchard, Abbot & Loomis, 1860.

(Symposium). "What Should be the Policy of the Colored American Toward Africa?" *A.M.E. Church Review* 2 (July 1885): 69.

Tanner, Benjamin Tucker. *The Descent of the Negro; Reply to Rev. Drs. J.H. Vincent, J.M. Freeman and J.H. Hurlbut*. Philadelphia, PA: A.M.E. Publishing House, 1898.

———. *The Dispensations in the History of the Church and the Interregnums*. Kansas City, MO: B.T. Tanner, 1899.

———. *The Negro in Holy Writ*. Philadelphia: n.p., 1900.

———. *The Negro's Origin, and Is The Negro Cursed?* Philadelphia: A.M.E. Book Depository, 1869.

Thomson, Patrick H. *The History of Negro Baptists in Mississippi*. Jackson: n.p., 1898.

Turner, Henry McNeal. *Respect Black: The Writings and Speeches of Henry McNeal Turner*, edited by Edwin S. Redkey. New York: Arno Press, 1971.

Van Evrie, John. *White Supremacy and Negro Subordination; Or, Negroes a Subordinate Race, and (So-Called) Slavery Its Normal Condition, with an Appendix, Showing the Past and Present Condition of the Countries South of Us*. 2d ed. New York: Van Evrie, Horton & Co., 1868.

Vibert, Theodore. *La Race Chamitique*. Paris: E. Leroux, 1916.

Walker, David. *Appeal to the Coloured Citizen's of the World*. Edited by Peter P. Hinks. Boston: D. Walker, 1829. Reprint, University Park, PA: Pennsylvania State University, 2000.

Webb, James Morris. *The Black Man: The Father of Civilization, Proven by Biblical History*. Seattle, WA: Acme Press, 1910.

Williams, George W. *History of the Negro Race in America, 1619–1880*. 1883. Reprint, New York: Arno Press and The New York Times, 1968.

Worrell, William Hoyt. *A Study of Races in the Ancient Near East*. Cambridge, England: W. Heffer & Sons, Ltd., 1927.

X., R. T. *The Ancient Glory of the Negro Race*, n.p., 1863.

Young, Robert Anderson. *The Negro: A Reply to Ariel. The Negro Belongs to the Genus Homo. He Is A Descendant of Adam and Eve. He Is the Offspring of Ham. He Is Not a Beast, But a Human Being. He Has an Immortal Soul. He May Be Civilized, Enlightened, and Converted To Christianity*. Nashville, TN: W. M'Ferrin, 1867.

Secondary Sources

Aaron, David. "Early Rabbinic Exegesis on Noah's Son Ham and the So-Called Hamitic Myth." *Journal of the American Academy of Religion* 63, no. 4 (1995): 721–759.

Adeleke, Tunde. *UnAfrican Americans: Nineteenth-Century Black Nationalists and the Civilizing Mission*. Lexington: The University of Kentucky Press, 1998.

Ahlstrom, Sydney E. *A Religious History of the American People*. New Haven: Yale University Press, 1972.

Alter, Robert. *The Art of Biblical Narrative*. New York: Basic Books, 1981.

Anderson, Benedict. *Imagined Communities: Reflections on the Origin and Spread of Nationalism*. 2nd ed. New York: Verso, 1991.

Andrews, William L., ed. *Sisters of the Spirit: Three Black Women's Autobiographies of the Nineteenth Century*. Bloomington: Indiana University Press, 1986.

Angell, Stephen. *Bishop Henry McNeal Turner and African American Religion in the South*. Knoxville: University of Tennessee Press, 1992.

Anstey, Roger. *King Leopold's Legacy: The Congo under Belgian Rule, 1908–1960*. London: Oxford University Press, 1966.

Appiah, Kwame Anthony. "The Uncompleted Argument: Du Bois and the Illusion of Race." In *Overcoming Racism and Sexism*, edited by Linda A. Bell and David Blumenfeld. Boston: Rowan & Littlefield Publishers, 1995.

Appleby, Joyce, Lynn Hunt, and Margaret Jacob. *Telling the Truth about History*. New York: W. W. Norton & Company, 1994.

Armstrong, Karen. *Muhammad: A Biography of the Prophet*. New York: HarperSanFrancisco, 1992.

Athearn, Robert G. *In Search of Canaan: Black Migration to Kansas, 1879–80*. Lawrence, KS: Regents Press of Kansas, 1978.

Auerbach, Erich. "Figura." In *Scenes from the Drama of European Literature*, edited by Wald Godzich and Jochen Schulte-Sasse. Minneapolis: University of Minnesota Press, 1984.

———. *Mimesis: The Representation of Reality in European Literature*. Translated by Williard Trask. New York: Garden City, 1952.

Augustine, Aurelius. *City of God*. Translated by Henry Bettenson. New York: Pelican Books, 1972. Reprint, New York: Penguin Books, 1984.

———. *The Correction of the Donatists*. In *The Nicene and Post-Nicene Fathers*. Vol. 4. *St. Augustine: The Writings Against the Manichaeans and Against the Donatists*. Translated by J. R. King and Chester D. Hartranft. Grand Rapids, MI: William B. Eerdmans, 1976.

Baer, Hans A. and Merrill Singer. *African-American Religion in the Twentieth Century: Varieties of Protest and Accommodation*. Knoxville: University of Tennessee Press, 1992.

Bailey, Randall C. "What Price Inclusivity: An Afrocentric Reading of Dangerous Bible Texts." *Voices from the Third World* 17 (June 1994): 133–150.

——— and Jacquelyn Grant, eds. *The Recovery of Black Presence: An Interdisciplinary Exploration*. Nashville: Abingdon, 1995.

Bailey, Raymond H. *Destiny and Disappointment. Faith of Our Fathers*. New York: McGrath Publishing Company, 1977.

Baker-Fletcher, Garth Kasimu. *Xodus: An African American Male Journey*. Minneapolis: Fortress, 1996.

Balibar, Etienne and Emmanuel Wallerstein. *Race, Nation, Class: Ambiguous Identities*. London: Verso, 1991.

Barber, Jesee B. *Climbing Jacob's Ladder: The Story of the Work of the Presbyterian Church U.S.A. Among the Negroes*. New York, 1952.

Barth, Karl. *The Doctrine of God*. Vol. II/2 of *Church Dogmatics*. 2nd. ed. Translated by G. W. Bromiley. Edinburgh: T. & T. Clark, 1936–69.

Barth, Markus. *The People of God*. Sheffield: JSOT Press, 1983.

Barton, George Aaron. *Semitic and Hamitic Origins, Social and Religious*. Philadelphia: University of Pennsylvania Press, 1934.

Baylor, Michael G., ed. *Revelation and Revolution: Basic Writings of Thomas Müntzer*. Bethlehem: Lehigh University Press, 1993.

Bederman, Gail. *Manliness and Civilization: A Cultural History of Gender and Race in the United States, 1880–1917*. Chicago: University of Chicago Press, 1995.

Bellah, Robert N. *The Broken Covenant: American Civil Religion in Time of Trial*. 2d ed. Chicago: The University of Chicago Press, 1992.

———. "Civil Religion in America." *Daedalus* (Winter 1967): 1–10.

Bercovitch, Sacvan. *Rites of Assent: Transformations in the Symbolic Construction of America*. New York: Routledge, 1993.

———. *The American Jeremiad*. Madison: University of Wisconsin, 1978.

———. *The Puritan Origins of the American Self*. Madison, WI: The University of Wisconsin Press, 1975.

Berkhofer, Robert, Jr. *Beyond the Great Story: History as Text and Discourse*. Cambridge: Belknap Press of Harvard University Press, 1995.

Bernal, Martin. *Black Athena: The Afroasiatic Roots of Classical Civilization*. 2 vols. New Brunswick: Rutgers University Press, 1987.

Beynon, Erdmann D. "The Voodoo Cult Among Negro Migrants in Detroit." *American Journal of Sociology* 43 (July 1937–May 138): 894–907.

Bhabha, Homi. *The Location of Culture*. New York: Routledge, 1994.

———, ed. *Nation and Narration*. New York: Routledge, 1990.

Bibb, Len Douglas. "A Note on the Black Muslims: They Preach Black to Be Ideal." *Negro Historical Bulletin* 28 (1965): 132–133.

Biddiss, Michael. *Father of Racist Ideology: The Social and Political Thought of Count Gobineau*. New York: Weybright and Talley, 1970.

Birnbaum, Michelle. "Racial Hysteria: Female Pathology and Race Politics in Frances Harper's *Iola Leroy* and W. D. Howells's *An Imperative Duty*." *African American Review* 33, no. 1 (1999): 7–23.

Bloom, Harold. *The American Religion: The Emergence of the Post-Christian Nation*. New York: Simon & Schuster, 1992.

Bordo, Susan. *Unbearable Weight: Feminism, Western Culture, and the Body*. Berkeley: University of California Press, 1993.

Botume, Elizabeth Hyde. *First Days Amongst the Contrabands*. Boston: Lee and Shepard, 1893.

Bozeman, Theodore Dwight. *To Live Ancient Lives: The Primitivist Dimension in Puritanism*. Chapel Hill: The University of North Carolina Press, 1988.

Bradley, David H. *A History of the A.M.E. Zion Church*. 2 vols. Nashville: Parthenon Press, 1956–70.

Bragg, George F. *History of the Afro-American Group of the Episcopal Church*. Baltimore: Church Advocate Press, 1922.

Brashear, Robert L. "Corner-Stone, Stumbling Stone: Christian Problems in Viewing Israel." *Union Seminary Quarterly Review* 38, no. 2 (1983): 203–224.

Brettler, Marc. *The Creation of History in Ancient Israel*. New York: Routledge, 1995.

Bringhurst, Newell G. *Saints, Slaves, and Blacks: The Changing Place of Black People within Mormonism.* Westport, CT: Greenwood Press, 1981.

Brown, Kathleen. *Good Wives, Nasty Wenches, and Anxious Patriarchs: Gender, Race, and Power in Colonial Virginia.* Chapel Hill: University of North Carolina Press, 1996.

Bryant, Joan. "Race Debates Among Nineteenth-Century Colored Reformers and Churchmen." Ph.D. diss., Yale University, 1996.

Burkett, Randall. *Garveyism as a Religious Movement: The Institutionalization of a Black Civil Religion.* Metuchen, NJ: Scarecrow Press, 1978.

Bush, Lester. "Writing 'Mormonism's Negro Doctrine: An Historical Overview' (1973): Contexts and Reflections, 1998." *Journal of Mormon History* 25, no. 1 (Spring 1999): 229–271.

Butler, Jon. *Awash in a Sea of Faith.* Cambridge: Harvard University Press, 1990.

Butt, Israel L. *History of African Methodism in Virginia; Or, Four Decades in the Old Dominion.* Hampton, VA: Hampton Institute Press, 1908.

Byron, Gay L. *Symbolic Blackness and Ethnic Difference in Early Christian Literature.* New York: Routledge, 2002.

Cannon, Katie. *Katie's Canon: Womanism and the Soul of the Black Community.* New York: Continuum Books, 1995.

Carby, Hazel. *Reconstructing Womanhood: The Emergence of the Afro-American Woman Novelist.* New York: Oxford University Press, 1987.

Carson, Cottrel R. " 'Do You Understand What You Are Reading?': A Reading of the Ethiopian Eunuch Story (Acts 8.26–40) from a Site of Cultural Marronage." Ph.D. diss., Union Theological Seminary, 1999.

Cherry, Conrad. *God's New Israel: Religious Interpretations of American Destiny.* Chapel Hill: University Press of North Carolina Press, 1998.

Cleage, Albert. *The Black Messiah.* Kansas City, KS: Sheed Andrews and McMeel, Inc., 1968.

Coleman, Will. *Tribal Talk: Black Theology, Hermeneutics, and African/American Ways of "Telling the Story."* University Park, PA: Pennsylvania State University Press, 2000.

"A Compelling Force: Notes from the Ministry of Rev. Lewis G. Jordan." *Mission Herald* (November/December 1997, January/February 1998): 7–8.

Comstock, Gary. *Gay Theology Without Apology.* Cleveland, OH: Pilgrim Press, 1993.

Cone, James H. *Black Theology and Black Power.* Rev. ed. Maryknoll: Orbis, 1997.

——. *A Black Theology of Liberation.* Rev. ed. Maryknoll, NY: Orbis, 1990.

——. *God of the Oppressed.* Rev. ed. Maryknoll: Orbis, 1997.

——. *Speaking the Truth.* Grand Rapids, MI: William B. Eerdmans Publishing Co., 1986. Reprint, Maryknoll, NY: Orbis, 1999.

Connerton, Paul. *How Societies Remember.* Cambridge: Cambridge University Press, 1989.

Cooey, Paula M. *Religious Imagination and the Body: A Feminist Analysis.* New York: Oxford University Press, 1994.

Copher, Charles. *Black Biblical Studies: An Anthology of Charles B. Copher: Biblical and Theological Issues on the Black Presence in the Bible.* Chicago, IL: Black Light Fellowship, 1993.

Custance, Arthur C. *Noah's Three Sons: Human History in Three Dimensions.* Grand Rapids, MI: Zondervan Publishing House, 1975.

D'Angelo, Mary Rose. "Veils, Virgins, and the Tongues of Men and Angels: Women's Heads in Early Christianity." In *Women, Gender, Religion: A Reader,* edited by Elizabeth Castelli and Rosamond Rodman. New York: Palgrave, 2001.

Davies, W. D. *The Territorial Dimension of Judaism.* Berkeley: University of California Press, 1982.

Davis, Elizabeth Lindsey. *Lifting As They Climb.* New York: G. K. Hall & Company, 1996.

Day, John. *Yahweh and the Gods and Goddesses of Canaan.* Sheffield Academic Press, 2000.

De Gobineau, Arturo. *The Inequality of Human Races.* Translated by Adrian Collins. New York: G. P. Putnam's Sons, 1915.

De Landa. *Yucatan Before and After the Conquest.* Baltimore: Maya Society, 1937.

Deloria, Vine. *Custer Died For Your Sins: An Indian Manifesto.* New York: Macmillan, 1969. Reprint, Norman, OK: University of Oklahoma Press, 1988.

———. *For This Land: Writings on Religion in America.* Edited by James Treat. New York: Routledge, 1999.

———. *God Is Red: A Native View of Religion.* 2nd. ed. Golden, CO: North American Press, 1992.

———. "A Native American Perspective on Liberation." *Voices from the Third World* 10 (December 1987): 90–98.

Dever, William G. *What did the Biblical Writers Know, and When Did They Know It?: What Archaeology Can Tell Us About the Reality of Ancient Israel.* Grand Rapids, MI: Eerdmans, 2001.

Douglas, Kelly Brown. *The Black Christ.* Maryknoll, NY: Orbis, 1994.

———. *Sexuality and the Black Church: A Womanist Perspective.* Maryknoll: Orbis, 1999.

Drake, St. Clair. *Black Folk Here and There: An Essay in History and Anthropology.* 2 vols. Los Angeles: Center for Afro-American Studies, University of California, 1987–90.

———. *The Redemption of Africa and Black Religion.* Chicago: Third World Press, 1970.

Du Bois, W. E. B. *The Gift of Black Folk.* 1924. Reprint, Millwood, NY: Kraus-Thomson Organization Limited, 1975.

———. ed. *The Negro Church.* With an introduction by Phil Zuckerman, Sandra Barnes, and Daniel Cady. 1903. Reprint, Walnut Creek, CA: AltaMira Press, 2003.

———. *The Souls of Black Folk.* 1903. Reprint, with an introduction by Randall Kenan, New York: Penguin Books, 1995.

Dube, Musa W. "Go Therefore and Make Disciples of All Nations: A Postcolonial Perspective on Biblical Criticism and Pedagogy." In *Teaching the Bible: The Discourses and Politics of Biblical Pedagogy,* edited by Fernando Segovia and Mary Ann Tolbert. Maryknoll, NY: Orbis, 1998.

———. *Postcolonial Feminist Interpretation of the Bible.* St. Louis: Chalice Press, 2000.

———. "Toward a Postcolonial Feminist Interpretation of the Bible." *Semeia,* no. 78 (1997): 11–26.

duCille, Anne. "The Occult of True Black Womanhood: Critical Demeanor and Black Feminist Studies." *Signs* 19, no. 3 (1994): 591–629.

Edwards, Jonathan. *History of the Work of Redemption*. In *The Works of Jonathan Edwards*. Vol. 5, 1817. Reprint, New York: Burt Franklin, 1968.

Evans, James H. *We Have Been Believers: An African American Systematic Theology*. Minneapolis: Fortress Press, 1992.

———. *We Shall All Be Changed: Social Problems and Theological Renewal*. Maryknoll: Orbis Books, 1999.

Fanon, Frantz. *Black Skin, White Masks*. Translated by Charles Lam Markmann. New York: Grove Press, 1967.

———. *The Wretched of the Earth*. Translated by Constance Farrington. New York: Grove Press, 1963.

Farajaje-Jones, Elias. "Breaking the Silence: Toward an In-the-Life Theology." In *Black Theology: A Documentary History, Volume Two: 1980–1992*, edited by James H. Cone and Gayraud S. Wilmore. Maryknoll, NY: Orbis, 1993.

Felder, Cain Hope. "Cultural Ideology, Afrocentrism and Biblical Interpretation." In *Black Theology: A Documentary History, Volume Two: 1980–1992*, edited by James H. Cone and Gayraud S. Wilmore, 184–195. Maryknoll, NY: Orbis Books, 1993.

Ferrante, Joan and Prince Brown, Jr., eds. *The Social Construction of Race and Ethnicity in the United States*. New York: Longman, 1998.

Ferris, William H. *The African Abroad, or His Evolution in Western Civilization*. 2 vols. New Haven, CT: Tuttle, Morehouse & Taylor, 1913.

Finkelman, Paul. *Dred Scott v. Sandford: A Brief History with Documents*. Boston: Bedford Books, 1997.

Fox, Robert L. *Pagans and Christians*. New York: Alfred A. Knopf, 1987.

Fox-Genovese, Elizabeth. *Within the Plantation Household: Black and White Women of the Old South*. Chapel Hill, 1988.

Frankenberg, Ruth. "Whiteness and Americanness: Examining Constructions of Race, Culture, and Nation in White Women's Life Narratives." In *Race*, edited by Steven Gregory and Roger Sanjek. New Brunswick: Rutgers University Press, 1994.

Franklin, John Hope. *George Washington Williams: A Biography*. Durham: Duke University Press, 1998.

Frazier, E. Franklin and C. Eric Lincoln. *The Negro Church in America/The Black Church Since Frazier*. New York: Schocken Books, 1974.

Fredrickson, George M. *The Arrogance of Race: Historical Perspectives on Slavery, Racism, and Social Inequality*. Hanover, NH: Wesleyan University Press, 1988.

———. *The Black Image in The White Mind: The Debate on Afro-American Character and Destiny, 1817–1914*. New York: Harper & Row, 1971.

Freedman, David Noel. "Yahweh of Samaria and His Asherah." *Biblical Archaeologist* 50 (December 1987): 241–249.

Frei, Hans. *The Eclipse of Biblical Narrative: A Study in Eighteenth and Nineteenth Century Hermeneutics*. New Haven: Yale University Press, 1988.

Fulkerson, Mary McClintock. "Gender—Being It or Doing It? The Church, Homosexuality, and The Politics of Identity." In *Que(e)rying Religion: A Critical*

Anthology, edited by Gary David Comstock and Susan E. Henking. New York: Continuum, 1997.

Gadsden, James, ed. *Experiences, Struggles and Hopes of the Black Church.* Nashville: Tidings, 1975.

———. *The Negro and the White Man.* Philadelphia: A.M.E. Publishing House, 1897.

Garber, Marjorie and Rebecca L. Walkowitz, eds. *One Nation Under God?: Religion and American Culture.* New York: Routledge, 1999.

Gaustad, Edwin. *A Documentary History of Religion in America*, 2nd ed., 2 vols. Grand Rapids: Eerdmans, 1993.

Gebara, Ivone. "The Face of Transcendence as a Challenge to the Reading of the Bible in Latin America." In *Searching the Scriptures: A Feminist Introduction*, edited by Elizabeth Schüssler Fiorenza. New York: Crossroad, 1993.

Genovese, Eugene D. *Roll, Jordan, Roll: The World the Slaves Made.* New York: Vintage Books, 1972.

Giddings, Paula. *When and Where I Enter: The Impact of Black Women on Race and Sex in America.* New York: William Morrow, 1984.

Gilman, Sander L. "Black Bodies, White Bodies: Toward an Iconography of Female Sexuality in Late Nineteenth-Century Art, Medicine, and Literature." In *Race, Writing, and Difference*, edited by Henry Louis Gates, Jr. Chicago: University of Chicago Press, 1985.

———. *On Blackness Without Blacks: Essays on the Image of the Black in Germany.* Boston: G.K. Hall, 1982.

Girard, Rene. *Violence and the Sacred.* Baltimore: Johns Hopkins Press, 1977.

Glaude, Eddie S. *Exodus!: Religion, Race and Nation in Early Nineteenth-Century Black America.* Chicago: University of Chicago Press, 2000.

Goldenberg, David. *The Curse of Ham: Race and Slavery in Early Judaism, Christianity, and Islam.* Princeton: Princeton University Press, 2003.

Gordon, Lewis R. *Existentia Africana: Understanding Africana Existential Thought.* New York: Routledge, 2000.

———. "Existential Dynamics of Theorizing Black Invisibility." In *Existence in Black: An Anthology of Black Existential Philosophy*, edited by Lewis R. Gordon, 69–79. New York: Routledge, 1997.

———. *Fanon and the Crisis of the European Man: An Essay on Philosophy and the Human Sciences.* New York: Routledge, 1995.

Gorenberg, Gershom. *The End of Days: Fundamentalism and the Struggle for the Temple Mount.* New York: Free Press, 2000.

Gosset, Thomas F. *Race: The History of an Idea in America.* Dallas: Southern Methodist University Press, 1963.

Gottwald, Norman K. *The Hebrew Bible: A Socio-Literary Introduction.* Philadelphia: Fortress Press, 1985.

Gould, Stephen Jay. *The Mismeasure of Man.* New York: W. W. Norton & Company, 1981.

Grant, Jacquelyn. *White Women's Christ and Black Women's Jesus: Feminist Christology and Womanist Response.* Atlanta, GA: Scholars Press, 1989.

Gravely, Will. "The Rise of African Churches in America (1786–1822): Reexamining the Contexts." In *African-American Religion: Interpretive Essays in History and Culture*, edited by Timothy E. Fulop and Albert J. Raboteau. New York: Routledge, 1997.

Griffin, Paul R. *Seeds of Racism in the Soul of America*. Cleveland, OH: Pilgrim Press, 1999.

Gustavo Gutiérrez. *A Theology of Liberation: History, Politics, and Salvation*. Rev. ed. Translated by Caridad Inda and John Eagleson. New York: Maryknoll, 1988.

Hadley, Judith. *The Cult of Asherah in Ancient Israel and Judah: The Evidence for a Hebrew Goddess*. Cambridge: Cambridge University Press, 2000.

Haller, John S., Jr. "Civil War Anthropometry: The Making of a Racial Ideology." *Civil War History* 16 (1970): 309–325.

——. *Outcasts from Evolution: Scientific Attitudes of Racial Inferiority, 1859–1900*. Urbana: University of Illinois Press, 1971.

Haller, William. *The Elect Nation: The Meaning and Relevance of Foxe's Book of Martyrs*. New York: Harper & Row, 1963.

——. *The Rise of Puritanism, Or, The Way to the New Jerusalem: As Set Forth in Pulpit and Press from Thomas Cartwright to John Lilburne and John Milton, 1570–1643, 1938*. Reprint, New York: Harper, 1957.

Handy, Robert T. *A Christian America: Protestant Hopes and Historical Realities*. 2nd ed. New York: Oxford University Press, 1984.

Harding, Vincent. *There Is a River: The Black Struggle for Freedom in America*. San Diego: Harcourt, Brace & Company, 1981.

Hardy, III, Clarence E. *James Baldwin's God: Sex, Hope, and Crisis in Black Holiness Culture*. University of Tennessee Press, 2003.

Hatch, Nathan. *The Democratization of American Christianity*. New Haven: Yale University Press, 1989.

Haynes, Carol. *Divine Destiny: Gender and Race in Nineteenth-Century Protestantism*. Jackson, MS: University Press of Mississippi, 1998.

Haynes, Stephen. *Noah's Curse: The Biblical Justification of American Slavery*. New York: Oxford University Press, 2002.

Higginbotham, Evelyn Brooks. *Righteous Discontent: The Women's Movement in the Black Baptist Church, 1880–1920*. Cambridge: Harvard University Press, 1993.

Hill, Renée Leslie. "Which Me Will Survive All These Liberations?: U.S. Third World Feminist Theories of Identities and Difference as Resources for U.S. Liberation Theologies." Ph.D. diss., Union Theological Seminary, 1996.

Hill, Samuel S., Jr., ed. *On Jordan's Stormy Banks: Religion in the South: A Southern Exposure Profile*. Atlanta, GA: Mercer University Press, 1983.

Hillers, Delbert R. *Covenant: The History of a Biblical Idea*. Baltimore: Johns Hopkins University Press, 1969.

Hobsbawn, Eric and Terence Ranger, eds. *The Invention of Tradition*. Cambridge: Cambridge University Press, 1973.

Hochschild, Adam. *King Leopold's Ghost: A Story of Greed, Terror, and Heroism in Colonial Africa*. Boston: Houghton Mifflin, 1998.

Hood, Robert E. *Begrimed and Black: Christian Traditions on Blacks and Blackness*. Philadelphia: Fortress Press, 1994.

Hopkins, Dwight. *Down, Up, and Over: Slave Religion and Black Theology*. Minneapolis: Fortress Press, 2000.

——. *Introducing Black Theology of Liberation.* Maryknoll: Orbis Books, 1999.

——. *Shoes That Fit Our Feet.* Maryknoll, NY: Orbis Books, 1993.

Horsman, Reginald. *Race and Manifest Destiny.* Cambridge: Harvard University Press, 1981.

Howard-Pitney, David. *The Afro-American Jeremiad: Appeals for Justice in America.* Philadelphia: Temple University Press, 1990.

Hunwick, John Owen. *West Africa and the Arab World.* Tema: Ghana Academy of the Arts and Sciences, 1991.

Hutchinson, William R. *Errand to the World: American Protestant Thought and Foreign Missions.* Chicago: University of Chicago Press, 1987.

Isaac, Ephraim. "Genesis, Judaism, and the 'Sons of Ham.' " In *Islam and the Ideology of Enslavement. Vol. 1 of Slaves and Slavery in Muslim Africa*, edited by John Ralph Willis, 75–89. London, NJ: Frank Cass, 1985.

——. "Ham." In *The Anchor Bible Dictionary*, edited by David Noel Freedman, 3:31–32, New York: Doubleday, 1992.

Jacobs, Sylvia, ed. *Black Americans and the Missionary Movement in Africa.* Westport, CT: Greenwood Press, 1982.

James, Larry M. "Biracial Fellowship in Antebellum Baptist Churches." In *Masters and Slaves in the House of the Lord: Race and Religion in the American South, 1740–1870*, edited by John B. Boles. Lexington, KY: University Press of Kentucky, 1988.

Jernigan, Marcus W. "Slavery and Conversion in the American Colonies." *American Historical Review* 21 (1916): 504–511.

Jewett, Robert and John Shelton Lawrence. *Captain America and the Crusade against Evil: The Dilemma of Zealous Nationalism.* Grand Rapids, MI: William B. Eerdmans, 2003.

Jones, Beverly Washington. *Quest for Equality: The Life and Writings of Mary Eliza Church Terrell, 1863–1954.* Brooklyn: Carlson, 1990.

Jordan, Lewis G. *Negro Baptist History, U.S.A., 1750–1930.* Nashville: The Sunday School Publishing Board, N. B. C., 1930.

——. *Up the Ladder in Foreign Missions.* 1901. Reprint, New York: Arno Press, 1980.

Joyner, Charles. *Down by the Riverside: A South Carolina Slave Community.* Urbana: University of Illinois, 1984.

Kedar, Benjamin. *Crusade and Mission: European Approaches to the Muslims.* Princeton: Princeton University Press, 1984.

Kelly, Mary Kate. "Performing the Other: A Consideration of Two Cages." *College Literature* 26, no. 1 (Winter 1999): 113–136.

Knapp, Steven. "Collective Memory and the Actual Past." *Representations* 26 (Spring 1989): 123–149.

Knupfer, Anne Meis. *Toward a Tenderer and a Nobler Womanhood: African-American Women's Clubs in Turn-of-the-Century Chicago.* New York: New York University Press, 1996.

Kwok Pui-Lan. *Discovering the Bible in the Non-Biblical World.* New York: Orbis Books, 1995.

——. "Racism and Ethnocentrism in Feminist Biblical Interpretation." In *Searching the Scriptures: A Feminist Introduction*, edited by Elizabeth Schüssler Fiorenza. New York: Crossroads, 1993.

Lemche, Niels Peter. *Ancient Israel: A New History of Israelite Society*. Sheffield, England: Sheffield Academic Press, 1995.

———. *The Canaanites and Their Land: The Tradition of the Canaanites*. Sheffield, England: JSOT Press, 1990.

———. "Israel, History of (Premonarchic Period)." In *The Anchor Bible Dictionary*, edited by David Noel Freedman, 3: 526–545. New York: Doubleday, 1992.

Lemert, Charles and Esme Bahn, eds. *The Voice of Anna Julia Cooper: Including* A Voice from the South *and Other Important Essays, Papers and Letters*. Lanham, MD: Rowman & Littlefield Publishers, 1998.

Levack, Brian, ed., *Witch-Hunting in Continental Europe: Local and Regional Studies*. New York: Garland, 1992.

Levine, Lawrence. *Black Culture and Black Consciousness: Afro-American Folk Thought from Slavery to Freedom*. New York: Oxford University Press, 1977.

Lewis, Bernard. *Race and Slavery in the Middle East: An Historical Enquiry*. New York: Oxford University Press, 1990.

Lincoln, C. Eric. *The Black Muslims in America*. 3d. ed. Trenton, NJ: Africa World Press, 1994.

———. *Race, Religion and the Continuing American Dilemma*. New York: Hill & Wang, 1984.

——— and Lawrence Mamiya. *The Black Church in the African American Experience*. Durham, NC: Duke University Press, 1991.

Linden, Robert O. and Richard V. Pierard. *Twilight of the Saints: Biblical Christianity and Civil Religion in America*. Downers Grove, IL: InterVarsity Press, 1978.

Lithgoe, Dennis L. "Negro Slavery and Mormon Doctrine." In *Religion and Slavery*, edited by Paul Finkelman, 393–404. New York: Garland, 1989.

Long, Charles H. *Significations: Signs, Symbols, and Images in the Interpretation of Religion*. Aurora, CO: The Davies Group, 1995.

———. "Civil Rights—Civil Religion: Visible People and Invisible Religion." In *American Civil Religion*, edited by Russell E. Richey and Donald G. Jones. New York: Harper & Row, 1971.

———. "Perspectives for a Study of Afro-American Religion in the United States." *History of Religions* 11, no. 1 (August 1971): 54–66.

Mamdani, Mahmood. *When Victims Become Killers: Colonialism, Nativism, and Genocide in Rwanda*. Princeton: Princeton University Press, 2001.

Mananzan, Mary John. "Five Hundred Years of Colonial History: A Theological Reflection on the Philippine Experience." *Voices from the Third World* 21 (June 1998): 229–246.

Martin, Sandy Dwayne. *Black Baptists and African Missions: The Origins of a Movement, 1880–1915*. Macon, GA: Mercer University Press, 1989.

Marty, Martin E. *Modern American Religion*. 3 vols. Chicago: University of Chicago Press, 1986–96.

———. *Righteous Empire: The Protestant Experience in America*. New York: Dial Press, 1970.

Mathews, Donald G. *Religion in the Old South*. Chicago: University of Chicago Press, 1977.

Mays, Benjamin E. *The Negro's God as Reflected in His Literature*. 1938. Reprint, New York: Atheneum, 1968.

Mead, Sidney. *The Lively Experiment: The Shaping of Christianity in America*. New York: Harper & Row, 1963.

Meier, August. *Negro Thought in America, 1880–1915: Racial Ideologies in the Age of Booker T. Washington*. Ann Arbor: University of Michigan Press, 1963.

Miller, Perry. *The New England Mind*. 2 vols. Boston: Beacon Press, 1961.

Montgomery, William. *Under Their Own Vine and Fig Tree: The African-American Church in the South, 1865–1900*. Baton Rouge: Louisiana State University Press, 1993.

Morgan, Jennifer L. " 'Some Could Suckle over Their Shoulder': Male Travelers, Female Bodies, and the Gendering of Racial Ideology, 1500–1770." *The William and Mary Quarterly* 54, no. 1 (January 1997): 167–192.

Morrison, Roy D., II. "Self-Transformation in American Blacks: The Harlem Renaissance and Black Theology." In *Existence in Black: An Anthology of Black Existential Philosophy*, edited by Lewis Gordon, 37–47. New York: Routledge, 1997.

Mosala, Itumeleng. *Biblical Hermeneutics and Black Theology in South Africa*. Grand Rapids, MI: William B. Eerdmans, 1989.

——. "Why Apartheid was Right about the Unliberated Bible: Race, Class and Gender as Hermeneutical Factors in the Appropriation of Scripture." *Voices from the Third World* 17 (June 1994): 151–159.

Moses, Wilson Jeremiah. *Afrotopia: The Roots of African American Popular History*. Cambridge: Cambridge University Press, 1998.

——. *Black Messiahs and Uncle Toms: Social and Literary Manipulations of a Religious Myth*. University Park, PA: The Pennsylvania State University Press, 1982.

——, ed. *Liberian Dreams: Back-to-Africa Narratives from the 1850s*. University Park, PA: Pennsylvania State University Press, 1998.

——. *The Wings of Ethiopia: Studies in African-American Life and Letters*. Ames, IA: Iowa State University Press, 1990.

Najim, Bashir, ed. *American Church Politics and the Middle East*. Belmont, MA: Association of American-Arab University Graduates, 1982.

Nelson, Hart M., ed. *The Black Church in America*. New York: Basic Books, 1971.

Neverdon-Morton, Cynthia. *Afro-American Women of the South and the Advancement of the Race, 1895–1925*. Knoxville: University Press, 1989.

Newby, I. A. *Jim Crow's Defense: Anti-Negro Thought in America, 1900–1930*. Baton Rouge: Louisiana State University Press, 1965.

Niditch, Susan. *Ancient Israelite Religion*. New York: Oxford University Press, 1997.

Niebuhr, H. Richard. *Christ and Culture*. New York: Harper & Row, 1975.

——. *The Kingdom of God in America*. New York: Harper & Brothers, 1937. Reprint, Hamden, CT: Shoestring Press, 1956.

——. *The Social Sources of Denominationalism*. New York: World Publishing, 1972.

Novak, David. *The Election of Israel: The Idea of the Chosen People*. New York: Cambridge University Press, 1995.

Payton, Lew. *Did Adam Sin? And Other Stories of Negro Life in Comedy-Drama and Sketches.* Los Angeles: Payton, 1937.

Persons, Persons. *American Minds: A History of Ideas.* New York: Henry Holt & Company, 1958.

Peterson, Thomas Virgil. *Ham and Japheth: The Mythic World of Whites in the Antebellum South.* Metuchen, NJ: Scarecrow Press, 1978.

Pieris, Aloysius. *An Asian Theology of Liberation.* Edinburgh: T. & T. Clark, 1988.

Pinn, Anthony. " 'Double Consciousness' in Nineteenth-Century Black Nationalism: Reflections on the Teachings of Bishop Henry McNeal Turner." *The Journal of Religious Thought* 52 (Summer/Fall 1995): 15–26.

Pinn, Anthony. *Varieties of African American Religious Experience.* Minneapolis: Fortress Press, 1998.

——. *Why, Lord? Suffering and Evil in Black Theology.* New York: Continuum, 1995.

Raboteau, Albert J. "African Americans, Exodus and the American Israel." In *Religion and American Culture,* edited by David Hackett, 75–86. New York: Routledge, 1995.

——. *A Fire in the Bones: Reflections on African-American Religious History.* Boston: Beacon Press, 1995.

——. *Slave Religion: The Invisible Institution in the Antebellum South.* New York: Oxford University Press, 1978.

——. *The Roots of a Black Future: Family and Church.* Philadelphia: Westminster Press, 1980.

Redkey, Edwin S., ed. *Respect Black: The Writings and Speeches of Henry McNeal Turner.* New York: Arno Press, 1971.

Richardson, Joe M. *Christian Reconstruction: The American Missionary Association and Southern Blacks, 1861–1890.* Athens, GA: University of Georgia Press, 1986.

Roberts, James Deotis. *Liberation and Reconciliation: A Black Theology.* Maryknoll, NY: Orbis, 1994.

Rogin, Michael. " 'The Sword Became a Flashing Vision': D. W. Griffith's *The Birth of a Nation.*" *Representations,* no. 9, Special Issue: American Culture Between the Civil War and World War I (Winter 1985): 150–195.

Ruether, Rosemary Radford and Herman J. Ruether. *The Wrath of Jonah: The Crisis of Religious Nationalism in the Israeli-Palestinian Conflict.* San Francisco: Harper & Row, 1989.

Said, Edward. *Beginnings: Intention and Method.* New York: Basic Books, 1975.

——. *Culture and Imperialism.* New York: Knopf, 1993. Reprint, New York: Vintage, 1994.

——. *Orientalism.* Rev. ed. New York: Vintage, 1979.

——. *The Question of Palestine.* London: Vintage Press, 1992.

Salem, Dorothy. *To Better Our World: Black Women in Organized Reform, 1890–1920.* Black Women in United States History. Brooklyn, NY: Carlson Publishing Company, 1990.

Schiebinger, Londa. "The Anatomy of Difference: Race and Sex in Eighteenth-Century Science." *Eighteenth-Century Studies* 23, no. 4 (Summer 1990): 387–405.

Schueller, Malini Johar. *U.S. Orientalisms: Race, Nation, and Gender in Literature, 1790–1890.* Ann Arbor: University of Michigan Press, 1998.

Schwartz, Regina M. *The Curse of Cain: The Violent Legacy of Monotheism.* Chicago: University of Chicago Press, 1997.

Segal, Charles M. and David C. Stineback. *Puritans, Indians and Manifest Destiny.* NY: G. P. Putnam's Sons, 1977.

Sernett, Milton, ed. *Afro-American Religious History: A Documentary Witness.* 2nd ed. Durham: Duke University Press, 1999.

Shanks, Hershel et al. *The Rise of Ancient Israel.* Washington, DC: Biblical Archaeology Society, 1992.

Sharpley-Whiting, T. Denean. *Black Venus: Sexualized Savages, Primal Fears, and Primitive Narratives in French.* Durham: Duke University Press, 1999.

——. *Frantz Fanon: Conflicts and Feminisms.* Lanham: Rowman & Littlefield, 1998.

——. "(White) Ladyhood and (Black) Womanhood Revisited: Legitimacy, Violence and Black Women." *The Black Scholar* 25, no. 4 (Fall 1995): 42.

Shavit, Yaacov. *History in Black: African-Americans in Search of an Ancient Past.* London: Frank Cass, 2001.

Shick, Tom W. *Behold the Promised Land: A History of Afro-American Settler Society in Nineteenth Century Liberia.* Baltimore: Johns Hopkins University Press, 1977.

Silberman, Neil Asher and Israel Finkelstein. *The Bible Unearthed.* New York: Free Press, 2001.

Simon, Marcel. *Verus Israel: A Study of the Relations Between Christians and Jews in the Roman Empire (135–425).* Translated by H. McKeating. New York: Oxford University Press, 1986.

Singleton, George A. *The Romance of African Methodism: A Study of the African Methodist Episcopal Church.* New York: Exposition Press, 1952.

Smedley, Audrey. *Race in North America: Origin and Evolution of a Worldview.* Boulder, CO: Westview Press, 1993.

Smith, H. Shelton. *In His Image, But . . . ; Racism in Southern Religion, 1780–1910.* Durham, NC, 1972.

Smith, Hilrie Shelton, Robert T. Handy, and Lefferts A. Loetscher. *American Christianity: An Historical Interpretation with Representative Documents.* 2 vols. New York: Charles Scribner's Sons, 1960–63.

Smith, John David, ed. *The Biblical and "Scientific" Defense of Slavery. Anti-Black Thought, 1863–1925.* New York: Garland, 1993.

Smith, Theophus H. *Conjuring Culture: Biblical Formations of Black America.* New York: Oxford University Press, 1994.

Smith, Timothy. "Slavery and Theology: The Emergence of Black Christian Consciousness in Nineteenth-Century America." *Church History* 41 (1972): 497–512.

Smith, Wilfred Cantwell. *What is Scripture?: A Comparative Approach.* Minneapolis: Fortress, 1993.

Sobel, Mechal. *Trabelin' On: The Slave Journey to an Afro-Baptist Faith.* Westport, CT: Greenwood Press, 1979. Reprint, Princeton: Princeton University Press, 1988.

Sollors, Werner. *Beyond Ethnicity: Consent and Descent in American Culture.* New York: Oxford University Press, 1986.

Stanton, William. *The Leopard's Spots: Scientific Attitudes Toward Race in America, 1815–59.* Chicago: University of Chicago Press, 1960.

Stuckey, Sterling. *Slave Culture: Nationalist Theory and the Foundations of Black America.* New York: Oxford University Press, 1987.

Sweet, Leonard. "Millennialism in America: Recent Studies." *Theological Studies* 40, no. 3 (1979): 510–531.

Taylor, Mark C. *Alterity.* Chicago: University of Chicago Press, 1987.

Thomas, Linda. *Living Stones in the Household of God: The Legacy and Future of Black Theology.* Minneapolis: Fortress Press, 2004.

Thompson, Mildred I. *Ida B. Wells-Barnett: An Exploratory Study of an American Black Woman, 1893–1930.* Black Women in United States History. Brooklyn, NY: Carlson Publishing Company, 1990.

Tindall, George B. "The Liberian Exodus of 1878." *South Carolina Historical Magazine* 53 (1952): 133–139.

Tinker, George. "American Indians and Jesus: Reflections Toward an EATWOT Christology." *Voices from the Third World* 18 (December 1995): 115–134.

——. *Missionary Conquest: The Gospel and Native American Cultural Genocide.* Minneapolis: Fortress Press, 1993.

——, Clara Sue Kidwell, and Homer Noley. *A Native American Theology.* Maryknoll, NY: Orbis, 2001.

Townes, Emilie. *In a Blaze of Glory: Womanist Spirituality as Social Witness.* Nashville: Abingdon Press, 1995.

Turley, David. *American Religion: Literary Sources and Documents.* The Banks, Mountfield, UK: Helm Information, 1998.

Turner, Richard Brent. *Islam in the African American Experience.* Bloomington: Indiana University Press, 1997.

Tuveson, Ernest Lee. *Millennium and Utopia: A Study in The Background of The Idea of Progress.* Los Angeles: University of California Press, 1949.

——. *Redeemer Nation: the Idea of America's Millennial Role.* Chicago: Chicago University Press, 1968.

Walker, Clarence E. *A Rock in a Weary Land: The African Methodist Episcopal Church During the Civil War and Reconstruction.* Baton Rouge, LA: Louisiana State University Press, 1982.

Walker, Williston, Richard A. Norris, David W. Lotz, and Robert T. Handy. *A History of the Christian Church.* 4th ed. New York: Charles Scribner's Sons, 1985.

Walzer, Michael. *Exodus and Revolution.* New York: Basic, 1985.

——. *Interpretation and Social Criticism.* Cambridge: Harvard University Press, 1987.

Warrior, Robert Allen. "A Native American Perspective: Canaanites, Cowboys, and Indians." In *Voices from the Margin: Interpreting the Bible in the Third World*, edited by R. S. Sugirtharajah. New York: Orbis, 1995.

Washington, Joseph R., Jr. "Are American Negro Churches Christian?" In *Black Theology: A Documentary History. Vol. 1, 1966–1979.* 2nd ed., edited by James H. Cone and Gayraud Wilmore, 92–100. Maryknoll, NY: Orbis, 1993.

——. *Black Religion: The Negro and Christianity in the United States.* Boston: Beacon Press, 1968.

——. *The Politics of God.* Boston: Beacon Press, 1967.

Watley, William D. *Singing the Lord's Song in a Strange Land: The African American Churches and Ecumenism.* Grand Rapids, MI: William B. Eerdmans, 1993.

Weems, Renita J. "Womanist Reflections on Biblical Hermeneutics." In *Black Theology: A Documentary History, Volume Two: 1980–1992,* edited by James H. Cone and Gayraud S. Wilmore. Maryknoll, NY: Orbis Books, 1993.

Weisenfeld, Judith. "Difference as Evil." In *The Courage to Hope: From Black Suffering to Human Redemption,* edited by Quinton Hosford Dixie and Cornel West. Boston: Beacon Press, 1999.

Welter, Barbara. *Dimity Convictions: The American Woman in the Nineteenth Century.* Athens: Ohio University Press, 1976.

West, Cornel. *Prophesy Deliverance: An Afro-American Revolutionary Christianity.* Philadelphia: Westminster, 1982.

Wheeler, Edward L. *Uplifting the Race: The Black Minister in the New South, 1865–1902.* Lanham, MD: University Press of America, 1986.

White, E. Frances. *Dark Continent of Our Bodies: Black Feminism and the Politics of Respectability.* Philadelphia: Temple University Press, 2001.

White, Ronald C. *Liberty and Justice for All: Racial Reform and the Social Gospel, 1877–1925.* San Francisco: Harper & Row, 1990.

Whitelam, Keith. *The Invention of Ancient Israel: The Silencing of Palestinian History.* New York: Routledge, 1996.

Whitted, J. A. *A History of the Negro Baptists of North Carolina.* Raleigh: Edwards & Broughton Print. Co., 1908.

Wiggins, William H., Jr. *O Freedom! Afro-American Emancipation Celebrations.* Knoxville: University of Tennessee Press, 1989.

Williams, Delores S. *Sisters in the Wilderness: The Challenge of Womanist God-Talk.* Maryknoll, NY: Orbis Books, 1993.

Williams, James G. *The Bible, Violence, and the Sacred: Liberation from the Myth of Sanctioned Violence.* Valley Forge, PA: Trinity Press, 1995.

Williams, Walter. *Black Americans and the Evangelization of Africa, 1877–1900.* Madison: University of Wisconsin Press, 1982.

Williamson, Joel. *New People: Miscegenation and Mulattoes in the United States.* New York, 1980.

Willis, John Ralph, ed. *Slaves and Slavery in Muslim Africa.* Vol. 1. *Islam and the Ideology of Enslavement.* London, NJ: Frank Cass, 1985.

Wilmore, Gayraud S. "Black Americans in Mission: Setting the Record Straight." In *Native American Religion and Black Protestantism,* edited by Martin E. Marty. Modern American Protestantism and Its World. Munich: K.G. Saur, 1993.

——. *Black and Presbyterian: The Heritage and Hope.* Philadelphia, 1983.

——. *Black Religion and Black Radicalism: An Interpretation of the Religious History of African Americans.* 3rd ed. Maryknoll, NY: Orbis Books, 1998.

——. Review of *Black Americans and the Evangelization of Africa, 1877–1900,* by Walter Williams. *International Bulletin of Missionary Research* 9, no. 3 (July 1985): 138–139.

Wilson, Charles Reagan. *Baptized in Blood: The Religion of the Lost Cause, 1865–1920.* Atlanta: University of Georgia Press, 1980.5t.

Wimbush, Vincent L., ed. *African Americans and the Bible: Sacred Texts and Social Textures*. New York: Continuum, 2000.

———. " '. . . Not of This World . . .': Early Christianities." In *Reimagining Christian Origins: A Colloquium Honoring Burton L. Mack*, edited by Elizabeth Castelli and Hal Taussig. Valley Forge: Trinity Press International, 1996.

———. " 'Rescue the Perishing': The Importance of Biblical Scholarship in Black Christianity." In *Black Theology: A Documentary History, Volume Two: 1980–1992*, edited by James H. Cone and Gayraud S. Wilmore, 210–215. Maryknoll, NY: Orbis Books, 1993.

Wittenberg, Gunther. "Let Canaan Be His Slave (Genesis 9:26). Is Ham Also Cursed?" *Journal of Theology for Southern Africa* 74 (March 1991): 46–56.

Wood, Forrest G. *The Arrogance of Faith: Christianity and Race in America from the Colonial Era to the Twentieth Century*. New York: Alfred A. Knopf, 1990.

Woodson, Carter G. *The History of the Negro Church*. 3rd ed. 1921. Reprint, Washington, DC: Associated Publishers, 1972.

Wright, N. T. *The New Testament and the People of God*. Minneapolis: Fortress Press, 1992.

Wright, William D. *Black History and Black Identity: A Call for a New Historiography*. Westport, CT: Praeger, 2002.

Young, Henry. *Major Black Religious Leaders Since 1940*. Nashville: Abingdon, 1979.

Young, Josiah. *A Pan-African Theology: Providence and The Legacies of the Ancestors*. Trenton, NJ: Africa World Press, 1992.

Zack, Naomi. *Mixed Race*. Philadelphia: Temple University Press, 1993.

Zevit, Ziony. *The Religions of Ancient Israel: A Synthesis of Parallactic Approaches*. New York: Continuum, 2001.

"Zion's Christian Soldiers: Fundamental Christian Evangelicals Believe the Jewish State Should Control All of the Biblical Jewish Homeland." *60 Minutes*, CBS broadcast. June 8, 2003. Transcript available from Lexis-Nexis.

Index